Adam Smith's Lost Legacy

Adam Smith's Lost Legacy

By Gavin Kennedy

To Sally
with thanks for everything

Gav
23/2/05

palgrave
macmillan

First published 2005 by
PALGRAVE MACMILLAN
Houndmills, Basingstoke, Hampshire RG21 6XS and
175 Fifth Avenue, New York, N. Y. 10010
Companies and representatives throughout the world

PALGRAVE MACMILLAN is the global academic imprint of the Palgrave
Macmillan division of St. Martin's Press, LLC and of Palgrave Macmillan Ltd.
Macmillan® is a registered trademark in the United States, United Kingdom
and other countries. Palgrave is a registered trademark in the European Union
and other countries.

ISBN 1–4039–4789–9

This book is printed on paper suitable for recycling and made from fully
managed and sustained forest sources.

A catalogue record for this book is available from the British Library.

Library of Congress Cataloging-in-Publication Data
Kennedy, Gavin.
    Adam Smith's lost legacy/ by Gavin Kennedy.
        p. cm.
    Includes bibliographical references and index.
    ISBN 1–4039–4789–9 (cloth)
        1. Smith, Adam, 1723–1790. 2. Economists–Great Britain–Biography.
3. Economics. I. Title.

HB103.S6K46 2005
330.15'3'092–dc22
[B]   2004056898

10   9   8   7   6   5   4   3   2   1
14   13   12   11   10   09   08   07   06   05

Printed and bound in Great Britain by
Antony Rowe Ltd, Chippenham and Eastbourne

For Ron
1936–1990

Contents

Part IV   Impartial Competition

Preface

This essay is about what Adam Smith (1723–1790) wrote or spoke about, and it criticises misleading ideas attributed to him, some of which were total inventions. By making the man and his work accessible to intelligent readers, I hope and intend that his legacy in some measure will be restored to him.

I approach Smith from a different perspective to his early biographers,[1] who left out important aspects of his life. Circumstantial evidence shows that, circumspect to a fault, he hid important sides of himself. He left Oxford in 1746 and accepted powerful political patronage to assure his election to a professorship in 1751. He deliberately failed to produce his history of jurisprudence despite keeping the pretence going that it neared completion until a few months before his death.

Because philosophy and economics could easily become a 'lifeless' story of disembodied ideas, I follow Smith's habit of introducing little diversions. His university audiences, mainly of young boys (14 to 17), had short attention spans and he believed his diversions helped their recollection of his serious points. One former student, James Boswell, reported Smith mentioning that Milton did not wear buckles but tied his shoes with string. Many years later Boswell still remembered Milton's aversion to buckles, though whether Smith's other students remembered anything else about Milton is not known.[2]

The main thrust of my argument is that Smith wrote for his times, not ours, and he wrote too when religious superstition dominated the beliefs and attitudes of men and women to a degree not easily appreciated by some scholars[3] living in secular democracies today. The rabid hostility to dissenters in this life, and warnings of hell and damnation in the next, were very real personal threats, which emotionally and physically cowed Smith and his contemporaries (but not David Hume) into circumspection. He remained determined never to cause offence to the Church, not least to protect the sensibilities of his religious mother, but also to avoid persecution by zealots, of which Scotland had plenty at the time.

Unlike Karl Marx, Smith did not see philosophers having a self-appointed mandate to change the world; he showed why it should be changed, gradually, by persuasion. Smith felt that the scope for perfection in the human condition was limited. To anybody who listened to his lectures or read his books, he shed a healthy dose of realism about human nature, when he showed how the 'great orders', or classes, of society managed their relations. What *could* be changed by deliberate human intention he felt fell far short of what *should* be changed, and what was changed in practice would always disappoint those who wanted everything to change in a hurry.

Perhaps by the third centennial anniversary of *Wealth of Nations* in 2076, the distinguished participants will convene to celebrate what Adam Smith actually intended and not merely to recount the fables created by those who misappropriated his legacy. That is my motive for writing *Adam Smith's Lost Legacy*.

Acknowledgements

No book is an author's sole creation. Ideas, notions, feelings, themes and approaches mesh around in the background of the mind and memory, sometimes for many years, more than half forgotten, occasionally rising to the surface of the author's attention, only to be drawn back down from whence they came and to where they rest again until recalled for their next moments of attention.

My interest in Adam Smith began while an undergraduate student of economics in the 1960s under Professor (later Sir) 'Ken' (Kenneth) Alexander. Those were the high tide days of 'Keynesian Public Finance, and the 'enemies', much mocked, were the 'Classical' economists, a vague term of scholarly abuse that brooked no doubts about their errors, if not moral sins. Nobody required us to read anything written by this discredited school; we were only required to know their errors. To my lasting regret, I only found out later what Smith and others wrote by studying their original works for myself, years after graduation. No classes were offered in the history of economic ideas in any university I have studied in or taught at, though I have benefited from correspondence and the exchange of published and unpublished papers with several colleagues in a 'quasi-underground' of individuals interested in the ideas and interpretations of the past giants in our profession.

In prime position among colleagues who have contributed to the germination of my ideas into *Adam Smith's Lost Legacy*, and to whom my debts can only be acknowledged inadequately, is Professor Sir Alan Peacock, a scholar interested in ideas for their own sake and not for personal adornment. His books on public finance and classical economic theory were great sources of enlightenment over the years that I taught economics and on many occasions since we became colleagues at Heriot-Watt University, including from his selfless loan of books from his library on Smith. He read and commented on most chapters and corrected them by his questioning of those ideas that lacked the necessary strength to go out into the world on their own. He is, of course, absolved from my disregarding his advice on some few occasions – a dangerous hubris in any author – but he can claim credit for any merits you may find in this book.

I have also been appreciative of the stoical patience of Professor Alan Thompson, for allowing our discussions to be hijacked for three years by 'das Adam Smith subject', for his comments on various themes, and for his corrective suggestions about what Smith would have called the proprieties of leaving statements as I originally wrote them. Dr. Hamish Thompson (University of Western Kentucky), provided a philosopher's slant on Smith's essay on astronomy and pointed out where David Hume took a critical stance on Smith's theme of the 'connecting chain of events'.[4]

Charles Ritchie read early drafts of the book. His frank comments on my grammar and style would have pleased Adam Smith, the rhetorician. Professor Keith Lumsden, Director of Edinburgh Business School, was indulgent of my wandering attention to my School duties for three years. His encouragement of the project from its start is most appreciated.

Sally MacLeod, PA to the Executive Board, managed to keep my day job on an even keel while I juggled many demands on my time associated with the final stages of preparing the manuscript. I am also grateful for the assistance of Connie Anderson at EBS who piloted the manuscript, kept it in order and delivered it to the Publisher with her usual professional coolness. Thanks must go to Amanda Hamilton, the commissioning editor from Palgrave who said 'yes' to the concept of the Lost Legacy and encouraged me throughout its transformation into a publishable project, and also to Dr Stephen Lloyd, Senior Curator at the Scottish National Portrait Gallery, who introduced me the gallery's collection of prints and Tasse medallions of Adam Smith, almost bringing him to life with his obvious enthusiasm.

Professors Brian Main, David Simpson, Patrick O'Farrell, and Alexander Scott read versions of the book during its genesis and I have incorporated many of their suggestions.

An anonymous referee made many helpful and positive suggestions (some of them in the form of imperatives!) and I am extremely grateful for all of them. The referee is of course absolved from any remaining errors or misjudgements and for my wilful disregard for his or her authoritative advice on a couple of occasions.

I should add that though some of my criticisms of some of the ideas of a few distinguished academics remains a bit robust at times despite the advice of the above mentioned colleagues nothing detracts from my overall respect for the distinguished persons upon whom I have occasionally 'turned the mouth of the cannon' (to use a phrase from one of Smith's colleagues at Glasgow when criticising his approach to Frances Hutcheson).[5] Academic debates can get a trifle tetchy at times, but only when we forget that we are criticising ideas and not the people who hold them.

Many authors of books on Adam Smith also contributed to the project, not the least, Professor Andrew Skinner, whose reputation in Smith scholarship is second to none. His editorial association with the Glasgow Edition of Smith's Works, and his own works on Smith, demonstrate the debts of all Smith scholars to his influence. I could not have gone far without access to his works, as my quotations from, and many references to, them show.

All quotations from the Glasgow Edition of the 'Works and Correspondence of Adam Smith' are by permission of Oxford University Press.

Gavin Kennedy
(gk@ebs.hw.ac.uk)
Edinburgh

Bibliographical Note

Throughout the text I refer to Adam Smith's Works by reference to their abbreviated initials and short titles as published by Oxford University Press as the 'Glasgow Edition of the Works and Correspondence of Adam Smith'.

His Works are:

[TMS and *Moral Sentiments*] *The Theory of Moral Sentiments*, 1759, edited by D. D. Raphael and A. L. Macfie, 1976, Oxford University Press; Liberty Fund, edition, 1982.

[WN and *Wealth of Nations*] *An Inquiry into the Nature and Causes of the Wealth of Nations*, 1776, 2 vols., edited by R. H. Campbell and A. S. Skinner, Textual editor, W. B. Todd, 1976, Oxford University Press; Liberty Fund, edition, 1979.

[LJ and *Jurisprudence*] *Lectures on Jurisprudence*, 1762–3 and '1766', edited by R. L. Meek, D. D. Raphael, and P. G. Stein, 1978, Oxford University Press, Liberty Fund edition, 1982

[EPS and *Philosophical Enquiries*] 'The Principles which lead and Direct Philosophical Enquiries: illustrated by the History of Astronomy', *Essays on Philosophical Subjects*, edited by W. P. D. Wightman and J. C. Bryce, and *Dugald Stewart's Account of Adam Smith*, edited by I. S. Ross, General Editors, D. D. Raphael and A. S. Skinner, 1980, Oxford University Press; Liberty Fund edition, 1982

[Corr.] *Correspondence*, edited by E. C. Mossner and I. S. Ross, 1977, revised 1987, Oxford University Press; Liberty Fund edition, 1987

[LRBL and *Lectures on Rhetoric*] *Lectures on Rhetoric and Belles Lettres*, edited by J. C. Bryce, General Editor, A. S. Skinner, 1983, Oxford University Press; Liberty Fund edition, 1985

I gratefully acknowledge the contribution of the editors and publishers for making Adam Smith's Works available in these magnificent editions and for their standardised reference system, as commissioned by the University of Glasgow to celebrate the bicentenary of the Wealth of Nations.

General Introduction

Adam Smith (1723–90), a famous contributor to the 18th-century Scottish Enlightenment, is well known for a relatively small part of his life's work and is often misunderstood for the little most people know about him. Many believe that he thought 'selfishness' was the most important motive of human economic behaviour, that he advocated laissez faire and that he favoured a minimalist 'night watchman' role for the State. However, these notions played no part in his intended legacy.

That misleading ideas about him are purveyed is reason enough to correct them. There are other reasons. Adam Smith showed that stable societies could prosper if they enjoyed liberty, justice and the rule of law and were free from the depredations of 'barbaric' neighbours, among which, incidentally, he included a minority of his fellow Scots – those 'naked and unarmed Highlanders' who 'alarmed the whole nation' in 1745.[1]

Adam Smith did not foresee an 'industrial revolution' nor did he anticipate 'capitalist' societies, neither knowing the words nor the phenomena. He did not consider it appropriate for society to be run by or for 'merchants and manufacturers' – 'perhaps, the worst of all governments for any country whatever'[2] – and nor did he accept that the rich and powerful, including kings, had the right to oppress a populace with punitive laws (hence his sympathy for the American colonists). He certainly did not encourage laissez faire (two words he never used) because he was aware of the limitations of markets and of the usefulness of the State (as well as the State's limitations), and nor did he support leaving the poor without realistic opportunities of sharing in their country's wealth. In short, Smith's ideas did not qualify him to become the 'High Priest of Capitalism' (and neither was he a sort of 'socialist'). He was, however, a firm believer in the positive influence of commerce on society.

Different approaches

Smith was not aligned to any political faction, though some authors today extol his virtues from the 'left', and others laud his commercialism from the 'right'. He tried to influence Statesmen of high rank. Such advice as he gave was mostly private; he left his public advice to his books and lectures. He believed that the natural forces present in human nature and society, if allowed to operate without the interference of those desiring rapid change, and without the resistance of those as determined to prevent it, would make society more wealthy, more secure and, crucially, more harmonious.

Smith was no utopian 'man of system'. Fanatics were out of touch with 'how the world works' and usually demanded, unrealistically, that everything be changed at once. This was not his way. He saw clearly the failings of such people and mocked their arrogance. A revolutionary reformer, he wrote:

> seems to imagine that he can arrange the different members of a great society with as much ease as the hand arranges the different pieces on a chess-board. He does not consider that the pieces upon the chess-board have no other principle of motion besides which the hand impresses upon them; but that, in the great chess-board of human society, every single piece has a principle of motion of its own, altogether different from that which the legislature might choose to impress upon it. If these two principles coincide and act in the same direction, the game of human society will go on easily and harmoniously, and is very likely to be happy and successful. If they are opposite or different, the game will go on miserably, and the society must be at all times in the highest degree of disorder.[3]

How much misery might be avoided if people desisted from 'the madness of fanaticism' and refrained from becoming 'intoxicated with the imaginary beauty of [their] ideal system[s].'[4]

Smith did not conceive of society as a grand chessboard, its players reading scripts pre-written by fantasists and fanatics. He believed in working through the governing arrangements of society. In a passage remarkably relevant for today, he called on those 'prompted by humanity and benevolence' to 'respect the established powers and privileges even of individuals, and still more those of great orders and societies, into which the state is divided' and suggested that a reformer be contented 'with moderating, what he often cannot annihilate without great violence', and above all to remember that '[w]hen he cannot conquer the rooted prejudices of the people by reason and persuasion, he [must] not attempt to subdue them by force ...'.[5]

Smithian impartiality

Smith's ideas of society had three strands to them: the '*impartial* spectator', or how people exercised their moral sentiments and treated others humanely; '*impartial justice*', or how justice accrued through time into impartial regimes of jurors and judges, obeying the rule of law, not the rule of men; and '*impartial competition*', or how markets produced prosperity, if they operated without the interference of private monopolies. Impartiality dominates Smith's conception of Natural Liberty and was the key to his hopes for human and practical social improvement through morality, justice and prosperity.

Smith showed that serving oneself without concern for others is socially divisive and, ultimately, unsustainable. It breaches the ties of interdependence and justice that bind all members of societies. By serving others we lower barriers to others serving us. In the three fields of moral sentiments, justice and political economy, Smith showed how impartial forces impose a workable, though imperfect, social order on that most unpromising of entities, namely, the human species.

Adam Smith's Lost Legacy corrects the myths, misunderstandings and occasional outright fictions spread about him in the last two centuries. It reveals his radical ideas about society and how it operates, and from which he drew an optimistic vision. The distortion of Smith's ideas in the 19th and 20th centuries by politically inspired commentators obscures the real significance of his work in the 18th century. The first steps to restoring his original intentions begin with corrective comments from his life and Works that reveal his actual, not mythical, but very Scottish, contribution to the European Enlightenment.

His ideas are not obvious because he did not articulate them overtly as a system. That he had ideas is not in question. They are woven into his books and lectures for those who look for them. Once recognised for what they are your immediate reaction is likely to be: 'how did so many miss the obvious?' Mainly because those few who read his books for themselves succumb to the diversionary noises of the many who don't. False notions of what Smith was about crowd his ideas off centre stage. *Adam Smith's Lost Legacy* restores him to his proper place among the world's great thinkers for what he actually wrote, rather than for what he didn't.

Part I
The Man

Introduction

To appreciate the contributions of Adam Smith to philosophy, jurisprudence and political economy, to literature and letters, to the Enlightenment, and to discourse with his contemporaries, it is advisable first to know something about him as a man of the world he lived in.

There are several excellent biographies, the first written three years after his death and delivered as a paper to the Royal Society of Edinburgh (of which he was a founding member).[1] The second, just over a hundred years later, was the first full-length biography, by John Rae.[2] Ian Ross's, the most recent, is surely the definitive account of Smith's life.[3] In between there have been numerous short memoirs by people who knew him,[4] and some excellent and more reliable scholarly accounts of aspects of his life, of which Professor Scott's is pre-eminent.[5]

I cover swiftly those well-known aspects of his life (which because they are widely accepted as factual I have not referenced) and introduce some new, admittedly speculative, assessments of what appears to have been going on in the background of a man whose sense of privacy and prudence was well developed. I think these aspects explain something that tends to be passed over too quickly in standard treatments of his life.

1
Smith's Family Background

Adam Smith was born into a family of Scottish landowners and farmers, with connections to a fair sprinkling of educated functionaries of the State who had legal training and political ambitions. His father, Adam Smith senior, was a Scottish lawyer who had been one such functionary during the ill-tempered shenanigans over the Union of the English and Scottish parliaments in 1707, during which he became known to the important Argyll interest. He was a man of some distinction, originally from Aberdeen, and well enough connected to be awarded a post in the Customs service in return for his loyalty.

Smith senior married well (for the second time), aged 40. Adam Smith's mother, Margaret Douglas (1694–1784) was the daughter of Robert Douglas, a major landowner and MP for Fife in the Scottish parliament. In November 1720, aged 26, she married Smith, 14 years her senior (and a widower with an 11 year old son). But her husband suffered a 'premature' death, aged 43, six months before Adam junior was born in June 1723. She did not re-marry.

An unanticipated bereavement at any stage of pregnancy adds to an already emotional and stressful experience. In Smith's case, none of his biographers give the cause of his father's death. We know nothing of the circumstances, or of how his widow aged 29, and married for only three years, reacted. About the time of her husband's death she knew she was pregnant and, as the act of intimacy was not much more than 14 weeks earlier, the shock of his death may have been unusually burdensome. The baby was baptised Adam Smith and she devoted herself for 61 years to his welfare and loving comfort. Her portrait shows an almost masculine face, severe in countenance, with a large nose and a small book, perhaps a hymnal, held in her hand. (Her son's 'likenesses' or portraits resemble her in features remarkably closely.)

Mrs Smith was totally devoted to her son – as he was to her. Dugald Stewart's biography of Smith makes her devotion plain:

> His constitution during infancy was infirm and sickly, and required all the tender solicitude of his surviving parent. She was blamed for treating

him with an unlimited indulgence; but it produced no unfavourable effects on his temper or his dispositions:- and he enjoyed the rare satisfaction of being able to repay her affection, by every attention that filial gratitude could dictate, during a long period of sixty years.[1]

Smith grew up in a single parent household, making his domestic arrangements familiarly modern, except that 18th-century well-off single parents were more likely to be widowed rather than abandoned or divorced. Given his family circumstances he had a comfortable childhood – not that he was ever overly concerned with pursuing monetary gain. A plan of his mother's house and garden shows a substantial four-storey property fronting onto Kirkcaldy High Street, with a large, well-laid out narrow garden, stretching back to the shore of the Firth of Forth.[2]

Love interests?

Smith did not marry and of his love interests – or sexuality – we know next to nothing. Dugald Stewart says there was an early involvement with an unidentified young woman:

> it is well known to his friends that he was for several years attached to a young lady of great beauty and accomplishment. How far his addresses were favourably received, or what the circumstances were which prevented their union, I have not been able to learn; but I believe it to be pretty certain that after this disappointment he laid aside all thoughts of marriage. The lady to whom I allude died also unmarried. She survived Adam Smith for a considerable number of years, and was alive long after the publication of this memoir. I had the pleasure of seeing her when she was turned eighty, and when she still retained evident traces of her former beauty. The powers of her understanding and the gaiety of her temper seemed to have suffered nothing from the hand of time.[3]

There are other references to romantic, though apparently unrequited, episodes. Ian Ross, for example, refers to a French lady, a Marquise, whose 'love' remained unrequited because Smith was 'deeply in love with an English lady', 'a Mrs Nicol'. Ross reports yet another lady, a Miss Campbell, 'a woman of as different dispositions and habits from his as possible'.[4]

Not surprisingly, in the absence of definite evidence occasional speculation emerges that Smith's sexuality varied from him having an Oedipus complex to his being in a homosexual relationship with David Hume (another bachelor, but also one confirmed in various dalliances with named women; one young girl accused him of getting her pregnant). Given Smith's long association with Janet Douglas, his cousin, it is not surprising that she too has been the subject of gossip. Such speculation is a mite more tabloid than the evidence justifies and I agree with Ross when he concludes: 'It is to be feared that the biographer can do little more with the topic of Smith's sex life than contribute to a footnote to a history of sublimation'.[5]

In contrast, we do know something, but not much, of the two main women in his life – his mother and his cousin, Miss Janet Douglas, described as his 'housekeeper', though given his long absences from home, she was more of a live-in companion to his beloved mother. Dugald Stewart referring to his cousin, 'Jane' Douglas ('for whom he had always felt the affection of a brother'), says that she had 'divided with him those tender attentions which her aunt's infirmities required, reliev[ing] him of a charge for which he was peculiarly ill qualified, by her friendly superintendence of his domestic economy.'[6]

An anonymous editor mentions the death of his mother in 1784 and later 'his cousin, Miss Douglass, to whom he had been strongly attached',[7] but gives no source for his statement. Of Janet Douglas we know very little, but she lived all her adult life at his mother's house in Kirkcaldy, with his mother at his house in Professors' Close at Glasgow University and, until the day she died, at his home, Panmure House, Panmure Close, in Edinburgh (the latter still standing, just off the High Street in Edinburgh).

He gave a fulsome description of his feelings for his mother two weeks after she died. She was someone:

> who certainly loved me more than any other person ever did or ever will love me; and whom I certainly loved and respected more than I ever shall either love or respect any other person, I cannot help feeling, even at this hour, as a very heavy stroke upon me.[8]

2
Disease of the Learned

His universities

Smith went to Glasgow College, or University, in 1737, aged 14, as was the norm in those days for bright male students, and he studied moral philosophy for three years under the 'never to be forgotten' Professor Francis Hutcheson, an Ulster Protestant of liberal rather than rigid theological views. Having just turned 17 he won a Snell Exhibition to Balliol College, Oxford in 1740 and took up his place in August, leaving Glasgow University without graduating. Snell Exhibitions, worth £40 a year for up to nine years, were keenly contested at Glasgow and Smith received the support of Professor Hutcheson for his coveted place. Snell students solemnly promised to be ordained into the Church of England and take an appointment in the Episcopalian Church in Scotland.

Unlike the University of Glasgow, which conducted a heavy schedule of taught classes and tutorials each week, Balliol College disappointed Smith in its lack of teaching. Students were largely left to their own devices and apart from twice-daily prayers they received little instruction from their teachers. Years later in *Wealth of Nations*, he commented: 'In the university of Oxford, the greater part of the publick professors have, for many years, given up altogether even the pretence of teaching'?[1]

What happened?

Something happened at Oxford that caused him to abandon his studies and to break his promise to join the Church. Smith did not tell us what it was and neither do his early biographers. We do know he did not have a happy time at Oxford, in part because he and his fellow Scottish Snell Exhibitioners were the butt of some 'anti-Scotch' harassment.

Sticking closely to the bare facts, we can summarise the most important career forming years of his life: he attended Glasgow College from 1737 to 1740, then Balliol College, Oxford until 1746. He lived with his mother in

Kirkcaldy before moving across the Firth of Forth to Edinburgh in 1748. In January 1751 he became Professor of Logic at Glasgow University and in April 1752, Professor of Moral Philosophy.

Thus, a typical bland résumé of a critical period in his life that took a troubled 17-year-old at Oxford in under twelve years to the prestigious Chair of Moral Philosophy at Glasgow, aged only 28. So, what does his résumé leave out?

Scattered, half buried, and disjointed clues to what he did at Oxford are elusive. We fish in an almost empty ocean of uncertainty, marked by small islands called 'maybe', 'perhaps', 'possibly' and 'plausibly'. His first biographer, Dugald Stewart, in his 1793 eulogy, supplied a passport to travellers needing to cross such oceans. Stewart praises an early essay of Smith's as one of 'great ingenuity' because it 'provides a specimen of a particular form of enquiry' that must be used when all we have is 'a few insulated facts' but no 'direct evidence' and:

> we are under the necessity of supplying the place of facts by conjecture; and when we are unable to ascertain how men have actually conducted themselves upon particular occasions, of considering in what manner they are likely to have proceeded, from the principles of their nature, and the circumstances of their external situation. In such inquiries, the detached facts ... may frequently serve as land-marks to our speculations; and sometimes our conclusions *a priori*, may tend to confirm the credibility of facts, which on a superficial view, appeared to be doubtful or incredible.[2]

Stewart called this species of philosophical investigation 'Theoretical or Conjectural History.' It is how I suggest we proceed.

To assess what happened to young Smith we rely upon several sources and fill in the gaps as best we can. We are talking about a young student suffering a serious personal crisis, for which he deserved compassion. How close he came to doing serious harm to himself is not clear but later he wrote, knowingly, of the Stoical virtue of 'voluntary death', or suicide.[3] The personal traumas he endured in his years at Oxford changed his life.

In a search for fire we imagine smoke. He did not appear to make many life-long friends at Balliol College (in contrast to his crowded social life a few years later in Scotland), nor does he appear to have returned to Kirkcaldy during any of the six summer vacations. This separated him from the direct influence of his mother and allowed the seeds of liberal Christianity to flower, planted by Frances Hutcheson and watered by his lonely studies.

An important social contact

He made and maintained one important social contact while at Oxford, establishing a long lasting bond with the most powerful political family in

Scotland. This happy circumstance was of immense personal benefit to him, superseding even his genius as the main contributor to his early promotions.

Smith's cousin, William Adam Smith, on at least one occasion (October 1741) and possibly others, took him to Adderbury House (near Oxford) belonging to the 2nd Duke of Argyll, the leading Scottish 'fixer' for Prime Minister Walpole's faction in the House of Commons. This connection survived the Duke's death when it passed seamlessly to the Duke's younger brother, Archibald Campbell, Earl Ilay (also spelled 'Islay' in the literature; I shall follow Ross, 1995), after he became the 3rd Duke in 1743.

For Smith this was no passing social fraternisation. It was a political alliance, albeit one in which Smith played a bit part in the Earl's wider schemes. That it worked to Smith's personal advantage compensated for any awkwardness he might have felt. The 3rd Duke secured for Smith his Chairs in Glasgow University, and the 2nd Duke's grandson, the Duke of Buccleugh, became Smith's ward on his famous tour of France in 1764–6 and his life-long benefactor thereafter. The Duke of Buccleugh was also intimately associated with Adderbury House, as he, with his mother and famous stepfather, Charles Townsend (Chancellor of the Exchequer, and the man credited with causing the American rebellion), lived there.

William Smith had access to Adderbury House. His close connection as a private secretary with the Duke explains how Smith, in due course, became a long-term beneficiary of the Dukes' patronage. The Duke, however, was absent that October. Who else was at that 'agreeable enough' place and among the 'great deal of good company in the town' and what they did, is unknown.[4] The holiday did Smith good it seems ('the good company' contrasting with Balliol's stifling atmosphere). William Smith's kindness arose from his and his aunt's concern that his young cousin might 'endanger his health at Oxford by excessive study',[5] knowing only too well of his excesses whenever he had access to books. Smith was dangerously exposed to the self-imposed 'disease of the learned',[6] as Hume expressed it in reference to similar health problems he had experienced at the same age.

His depression?

Balliol's academic calendar accelerated his discomfort with his solemn promise to qualify for ordination into the Church. On 5th May 1744, Smith completed the requirements for his Bachelor degree[7] and a decision about his Church career now loomed in the guise of his following the syllabus leading to ordination.

Around 1744 he changed his mind about becoming a preacher: he no longer believed unconditionally in Church ritual, nor was its embrace congenial, and he was increasingly disenchanted with Balliol and the many Reverends who ran it. In the emotional turmoil provoked by these pressures and in his struggle to resolve the tensions associated with them, his spirit almost cracked and his physical health, already in question from his intense private studies, deteriorated.

From a letter to his mother we glimpse the state of his health in July 1744: 'Tar water is a remedy very much in vogue here at present for almost all diseases. It has perfectly cured me of an inveterate scurvy and shaking of the head.'[8] Alas, the symptoms returned and the tar water remedy failed.[9] The pamphlet prompting him to try tar water (written by the philosopher Bishop George Berkeley)[10] described his symptoms as 'lives that seem hardly worth living for bad appetite, low spirits, restless nights, wasting pains and anxieties' and Ross reports that modern diagnosis points to the symptoms of dyspepsia, 'spleen' and 'melancholy', and, perhaps, what we call today 'depression'.[11] Medicine, as practised in the 18th century, included a fair dose of quackery. Not all of the quackery was induced by fraudulent intentions; much of it was a result of medical ignorance, albeit dressed up in semi-scientific conjecture.[12] How clinically serious was his illness?

Interestingly, David Hume had fallen into similar conditions of 'laziness of temper' and scurvy, caused by the same tiredness induced by his over reading and lack of exercise.[13] Did Smith suffer something akin to the nervous breakdown that afflicted Hume ten years earlier?

Hume sought advice from 'a very knowing Physician' who prescribed anti-scorbutic juices and a course of Bitters & Anti-hysteric Pills' plus an 'English Pint of Claret Wine every Day', and long horseback rides. Hume, beset by health problems, kept notes on their effects. We may assume from them an insight into Smith's temper during his version of a similar illness Hume adopted the Physician's regime in total, including undertaking of 'a very laborious task' of travelling '8 miles every Morning and as many every Forenoon' and imbibing the bitters, anti-hysteric pills and anti-scorbutic juices. He did not let up on his studies. The disease, he noted, was a 'cruel Incumbrance'. He faced, he noted, his 'greatest Calamity' and in a flash of real depression he concluded, typically:

I had no Hopes of delivering my Opinions with such Elegance & Neatness, as to draw to me the Attention of the World, & I wou'd rather live & die in Obscurity that produce them maim'd & imperfect.[14]

It may be appropriate to insert here a short comment on the relationship between Smith and Hume. That they became and remained good friends is not in question. That Smith behaved less than loyally to Hume is also not questioned. That he behaved in a shameful manner towards his 'dear friend', Hume, is controversial, but for balance I refer to it.

These incidents place a question mark over Smith's loyalty to a man with whom he was closely associated for over twenty years. The first is an example of Smith not using his interest to help Hume with his application for a chair at Glasgow. Having been turned down for a chair at Edinburgh, Hume had hopes of taking over Smith's vacated chair in Glasgow in 1751, but Smith wrote privately to William Cullen, secretary to Glasgow University Senate:

> I should prefer David Hume to any man for a colleague; but I am afraid the public would not be of my opinion; and the interest of the society will oblige us to have some regard to the opinion of the public.[15]

Smith was concerned that Hume's public reputation as a critic of religion would damage the University. And it was because of views attributed to Hume on religion that Smith let him down at least twice more, not because he disagreed with his views. By publicly expressing them Smith considered him imprudent, and by associating himself with Hume's views it would complicate Smith's public persona.

Approaching his death in 1776, Hume wanted to appoint Smith has his literary editor and, in particular to see that his *Dialogues Concerning Religion* was published in the event of his death. Smith equivocated on accepting this responsibility and it clearly disappointed Hume,[16] who had agreed to publish Smith's *History of Astronomy*, in 1773, when asked to do so, when Smith was anxious in case he died while away in London.[17] Hume was frank in that he felt Smith's 'Scruples groundless' and that he thought that they had a 'specious Appearance and referred to the 'sacred regard to the Will of a dead Friend'. He amended the instructions (dropping his usual 'my dear friend' salutation for 'My dear Sir') in his will in May 1776 to acknowledge Smith's 'situation' on 'account of the Nature of the Work' and that it 'may be improper to hurry on that Publication'.[18] By October Hume had made separate arrangements with his nephew to publish the *Dialogues*.[19] Smith's reply was guarded, saying, he was 'very happy to receive a copy of your dialogues; and, if I should happen to die before they were published, I shall take care that my copy shall be carefully preserved as if I was to live a hundred years.'[20] What he plainly did not do was undertake to publish the *Dialogues*.

This episode can be put down to Smith's lifelong aversion of courting controversy over religious matters. It still leaves a bad taste, though Hume was reconciled because his last letter to Smith, three days before he died, is addressed to 'My Dearest Friend' and ends 'Adieu My Dearest Friend'.[21] To some extent Smith recanted by renouncing Hume's bequest of £200[22] (which renouncement Hume's brother John rejected)[23] and he wrote a moving statement (published with Hume's *My Own Life*), of Hume, as 'approaching as nearly as the idea of a perfectly wise and virtuous man, as perhaps the nature of human frailty will permit'.[24] However, he remained determined that the *Dialogues* should never '[be] published in my lifetime.'[25]

The *Dialogues* was published in 1779. It did not cause the stir that Smith expected; at least not half as much as the stir caused by numerous reverends of the Church towards Smith by his 'single, and as I thought a very harmless Sheet of paper' written as tribute to Hume, which 'brought upon me more abuse than the very violent attack I had made upon the whole commercial system of Great Britain'.[26]

3
His 'Juvenile Work'

Surprisingly, Smith took an early interest in astronomy. It was the source of his doubts about the religious approach to knowledge. Even more surprising was his life-long determination to preserve *The Principles which lead and Direct Philosophical Enquiries: illustrated by the History of Astronomy*.[1] He intended it for publication only after his death because he feared religious persecution. He called it a 'juvenile work',[2] and it was probably compiled between 1743 and before 1748, though there is more certainty of the latter date than the first.

His modern editors, W. P. D. Wightman and J. C. Bryce, state that 'it has been fairly generally assumed that he at least laid the foundation of the History of Astronomy at Oxford' because he 'could hardly have written' that 'chemical philosophy in all ages crept along in obscurity' when William Cullen, a distinguished chemist and future close colleague at Glasgow, had begun 'his epoch-making "popularisation" of chemistry' in 1748. Smith had also noted that Newton's 'followers from his principles, ventured even to predict the returns of several [comets], particularly one which is to make its appearance in 1758'.[3]

By taking such great pains to preserve a 'juvenile work' it must have had lasting emotional significance for him, perhaps because it was the cause of the beginning of the decline in his religious fervour.

'Philosophy,' writes Smith 'is the science of the connecting principles of nature.'[4] An everyday example is the observation that the sun 'rises' in the east and 'sets' in the west, supposedly 'proving' to generations of priestly authorities that God's will made the sun revolve round the Earth. The hidden connection of the revolution of the Earth and its orbit round the Sun took mankind millennia to unravel. Eventually, increasingly precise data of the movements of the planets showed that the Earth revolved round the Sun. By its trenchant denials, revealed religion exposed itself to an embarrassing error.

Surprise, wonder and admiration

'Mankind,' Smith writes, 'in the first ages of society, before the establishment of law, order and security, have little curiosity to find out those hidden chains of events which bind together the seemingly disjointed appearances of nature.'[5] The subsistence of 'savages' (a contemporary term without its 19th-century racist opprobrium)[6] being precarious, and their exposure to the rudest of dangers of the instant, gave them neither time nor inclination for idle speculation about the oddities of nature. Only after the acquisition of law, order and security, did the age of the philosophers commence, with their curiosity the busy companion of wild, often superstitious, speculation.

For Smith three everyday words, 'Wonder, Surprise and Admiration', summarised how curiosity reaches its highest refinement in philosophy. What is new excites Wonder; what is unexpected, Surprise, and what is great or beautiful, Admiration.[7] Hardly scientific definitions but we know what he meant.

Philosophers were interested in the connection between events even if the rest of humanity was not. Popular imagination ascribed hidden connections to 'magic' or to the 'hand of God' – but what easily satisfies the popular imagination, torments Philosophers. What the eye cannot understand or explain the Philosopher grieves about, as he wrestles with the absence of an explanation.

Discovering the connecting chain of intermediate events calms the emotional passions of Surprise and Wonder and makes way for the emotional tranquillity of Admiration. One senses Smith's mounting enthusiasm for the exhilarating effects on those who practise Philosophy. To know nature is to admire it by rendering it 'a more coherent, and therefore a magnificent spectacle, than otherwise it would have appeared to be.'[8]

Philosophical discovery is not easy. Smith cites the eclipses of the sun and the moon, which once 'excited the terror and amazement of mankind' and now 'seem no longer to be wonderful' since the connecting chain of events was discovered,[9] a theme tackled recently by Richard Dawkins.[10] But, in a strange outburst of ageism, he added that no matter how much is explained, attempting to discover the connecting chains of events can be dangerous for those 'somewhat advanced in years', because they risk 'lunacy and frenzy' from too severe a study of abstract science![11]

Philosophy was for young, not old, minds. Had he realised that he was brighter than his elderly Oxford tutors and certainly better able than they to tackle difficult problems in philosophy? In an extraordinary outburst, he alleges that those whose 'imaginations, from being late in applying, have not got those habits which dispose them to follow easily the reasonings of abstract science' should not try to do so, because they risk becoming 'first confused, then giddy, and at last distracted'.[12]

Invisible chains

The young Smith saw philosophy as 'representing the invisible chain which binds together all those disjointed objects' which 'disturb the easy movement of the imagination' and, by introducing 'order into this chaos of jarring and discordant appearances', allays 'this tumult of the imagination' and restores it to 'that tone of tranquillity and composure, which is both agreeable in itself and suitable to nature',[13] provoking a memorable quip from James Buchan: 'Philosophy as tranquilliser'.[14]

Smith's links Earthly phenomena to superstitious myths about the indulgences of the gods:

> Hence, the origin of Polytheism, and of that vulgar superstition which ascribes all the irregular events of nature to the favour or displeasure of intelligent, though invisible beings, to gods, demons witches, genii, fairies. For it may be observed, that in all Polytheistic religions, among savages, as well as in the early stages of Heathen antiquity, it is the irregular events of nature only that are ascribed to the agency and the power of their gods.[15]

Philosophers should not indulge in such evasions. If not the work of pagan gods, or magic and miracles, or God, what were the connecting causes of these irregular events? Nobody knew the answers for millennia, though some knew that superstition was no answer at all.

Regular events of nature pass unnoticed. Everybody knows that fire burns – if in doubt touch it. Water refreshes and puts out fires by the necessity of its own nature. Heavenly bodies descend – look at the sky at night – and the wind makes lighter substances fly upwards. No invocations of the whims of the gods were necessary to 'explain' the properties of fire, water, heavenly bodies or leaves. And, Smith notes, using his (now) famous metaphor to reinforce his assertion that primitive religion did not invoke the wrath of supernatural gods to explain everyday ordinary phenomena: 'nor was the invisible hand of Jupiter [the Roman god, Jove, not the planet] ever apprehended to be employed in these matters'.[16]

Invisible gods were employed for unusual events beyond our current understanding. While Smith focussed his spirited attack on primitive pagan religion, which he could do safely without earning the wrath of his tutors, religious explanations were his implied target.

The philosopher's vocation

Sentient beings act to alter events threatening to do them harm. As they had no knowledge of what caused thunder, lightning, and storms or sudden illness, bad fortune and other unexplained calamities, their imaginations created invisible beings – the gods – and supposed them to thwart the normal course of events. All irregular events were thus 'explained' in the first 'ages of the world' producing 'the lowest and most pusillanimous superstition' in 'place of philosophy.'[17] Ignorance fed primitive fears. But once subsistence ceases to be precarious, enlightenment follows – in theory, and then only relatively.

When we think of the Earth, we envisage a blue sphere held in the ultimate vertigo of space, circulating the Sun, a tiny speck in a Universe of unimaginable size. We recall photographs of Earth from the surface of the Moon, and close up shots of the moons of Jupiter and the surface of Mars, to which manned space flights are expected this century.

In the context of the times, their perceptions of the world were very real. Heaven was above, and Hades below and invisible gods roamed the land, intervening for good or ill and at will. The ignorant mob slept soundly, protected by illusory certainties about their world and their places in it. But little discrepancies remained a problem for the minority minded to worry about them. And that minority, worrying away, slept less soundly.

In the ancient version of the world, the ground around where you stood was all you would ever tread, the people you knew were all you would ever know, and the gods you feared were ever present, threatening and bountiful in perplexing measure.

You could neither run nor hide from the gods who ruled your fate, nor from their Earthly servants, the Kings, Priests and Soldiers, who could rule or ruin your life if you came to their notice – better to remain quiet and out of sight. Fantasy, on a scale we barely comprehend today, ruled every aspect of your life and 'explained' all you ever wanted to know about Nature. Read George Frazer's *Golden Bough*[18] to glean something of the fantastic constructions created by primitive humans about nature, life, death, magic, myths and religion, and the gods and spirits that were said to guide human destiny.

His Newtonian destiny?

Professor Campbell noted how Smith attempted to bring to the study of morals the same methods that Newton employed in natural science:

> The superior genius and sagacity of Sir Isaac Newton, therefore, made the most happy, and, we may now say, the greatest and most admirable improvement that was ever made in philosophy, when he discovered that he could join together the movements of the Planets by so familiar a principle of connection, which completely removed all the difficulties the imagination had hitherto felt in attending to them.[19]

Newton's connecting principle was gravity, which met the criteria of a good explanatory theory (comprehensiveness, simplicity and familiarity). Young Smith, suggests Campbell, wanted to do the same for moral philosophy, and in this endeavour he followed a path trodden by David Hume during 1729–40,[20] the sub-title of whose book was '*an attempt to introduce the experimental Method of Reasoning into Moral Subjects*'.[21]

The application of the Newtonian method to man in society was first hinted at by Newton himself: 'If natural Philosophy in all its Parts, by pursuing this Method, shall at length be perfected, the Bounds of Moral Philosophy will also be enlarged'.[22] Smith, reading Newton's *Optiks* (he had a copy in his library),[23] determined to look for a connecting principle akin to gravity in the moral arena and believed that he had found in *sympathy* a comprehensive explanation of moral phenomena, that 'acts here, as in all other cases, with the strictest œconomy, and produces a multitude of effects from one and the same cause.'[24]

Smith's peroration lauds Newton for his praise worthy system:

> Can we wonder then, that [Newton's system] should have gained the general and complete approbation of mankind, and that it should now be considered, not as an attempt to connect in the imagination the phaenomena [sic] of the Heavens, but as the greatest discovery that ever was made by man, the discovery of the immense chain of the most important and sublime truths, all closely connected together, by one capital fact, of the reality of which we daily experience.[25]

Before he started his essay he was destined for ordination as a Church Minister, not for a career as a Philosopher, therefore, two questions flow from his closing sentence.

First, to what extent did Smith see his quest – that of enlarging the bounds of Moral Philosophy by discovering its connecting principles – as a life-changing goal? Second, to what extent was Smith ambitious for the approbation accorded to Newton? Campbell's answer is unreserved: Smith's theory of sympathy demonstrated 'in detail that men *necessarily* approve and disapprove of certain types of behaviour' and from this premise, and in a roughly comparable way to Newton, he 'thought that he had discovered a key to moral "reality" in the sense of the morally proper standard of human conduct.'[26]

A decision to become a Philosopher does not of itself imply an ambition to emulate the great Newton, but his stubborn determination to preserve *Philosophical Enquiries* from destruction suggests that Smith on his deathbed felt more than merely a pressing need to preserve his adulatory praise of Sir Isaac Newton.

He advocated a no holds barred approach to the 'most sublime of all the agreeable arts', and he lauded its integrity with the claim that 'its revolutions have been the greatest, the most frequent, and the most distinguished of all those that have happened in the literary world' and, therefore, the 'most entertaining and the most instructive.' Boldly, he asserted that everything should be examined 'without regarding their absurdity or probability, their agreement or inconsistency with truth and reality' but only with respect to the 'particular point of view' of the history of philosophy. It was enough for philosophers to content themselves 'with inquiring how far each [theory/solution] was fitted to soothe the imagination, and to render the theatre of nature a more coherent, and therefore a more magnificent spectacle than otherwise it would have appeared to be.'[27]

He realised that he had either to sacrifice the Church or Philosophy. He could not combine both; he wrestled with his decision until he sacrificed the Church. With great caution he drafted his essay and hid it away in his bedroom cabinet for 40 years, occasionally taking it out and revising it, and, cautious to the end, he insisted it appeared before the public only after his death.

4
Bad Days at Balliol

Reading the lives of those Philosophers who had succumbed to the attentions of ignorant tyrants and their mobs, Smith saw the Philosopher's mission as dear to the meaning of his life as it could get. His tutors at Balliol, wearing the awesome faces of contemptible ignorance and, believing that they were doing the work of God, pushed young Smith over the edge.

Balliol's illiberal faculty entertained suspicions of young Smith's doctrinal soundness (he seldom kept his counsel when challenged by others). Without notice, they searched his college room and found (*quelle horreur!*) a copy of David Hume's *Treatise of Human Nature*. Their ire inflamed, they declared that it was wholly inappropriate for a candidate for ordination even to possess such a dreadful book, let alone for him to read it. They confiscated the book and severely reprimanded him in 'unceremonious manner'.[1]

We can only guess at the effect on him of this ill-considered censorship. Galileo's analogous treatment by the cardinals would not have been lost on Smith. Brought up in a Protestant Church, and in a country still embroiled in religious controversies with Rome, and with occasional unsettling disturbances over a deposed Catholic King, censorship was a bitter humiliation.

For Smith to become a Philosopher he needed to be familiar with philosophical controversies, no matter the discomfort suffered by the guardians of opinionated orthodoxy. Above all, he needed to be free from censorship by old men bereft of philosophical understanding and of insufficient intellectual capability for it. I conclude that this incident left him sorely angry and was the defining moment when his tutors lost his respect.

An extremely unsettled Smith grew less and less comfortable with his 'solemn promise'. By confiscating Hume's book, the College authorities disrupted his philosophical studies and challenged his vocation. Did his inability to see a way out of these happenings cause him, in tumult and disorder, to experience at first hand that 'confusion and giddiness' leading to the 'lunacy and distraction' discussed in his *Philosophical Enquiries*?

Were his memories of Oxford vivid enough years later for him to paint suicide in the sombre, and highly personal, colour of his discourse in *Moral Sentiments?*

> If your situation is upon the whole disagreeable ...walk forth without repining; without murmuring or complaining. Walk forth calm, contented and rejoicing, returning your thanks to the Gods, who, from their infinite bounty, have opened the safe and quiet harbour of death, at all times ready to receive us from the stormy ocean of human life; who have prepared this sacred, this inviolable, this great asylum, always open, always accessible; altogether beyond the reach of human rage and injustice; and large enough to contain both all those who wish, and all those who do not wish to retire to it: an asylum which takes away from every man every pretence of complaining, or even fancying that there can be any evil in human life, except such as he may suffer from his own folly or weakness.[2]

Was this his authentic voice, aged 22, recalling his outrage at the injustice he had suffered at Oxford while contemplating shelter in a harbour safe from the 'stormy ocean of human life'?

Smith also quotes a telling line: 'Never complain of that which it is at all times in your power to rid yourself'.[3] He had the remedy in his hands and the power to rid himself of his problem. Strictly, in this sense, he agreed with his tutors' assessment, but not their remedy: Hume's *Treatise* was not appropriate reading for a candidate for ordination, so he decided finally to cease to be a candidate.

Three obstacles

Smith had to overcome three obstacles before he could abandon his ordination in good conscience. The first was his 'solemn promise' to do so, backed by a £500 bond (an extraordinary large sum at the time – it was almost seven years wages for a Royal Navy Lieutenant); the second was his mother's predictable disappointment at him not becoming a Minister; and the third was the effect on his mentor, Professor Frances Hutcheson, who had been instrumental in gaining for him the much-prized Snell Exhibition, awarded only to the brightest and most promising of Glasgow's students. The strict chronology of their resolution, other than that they probably occurred at various dates between 1744 and 1746, remains uncertain.

The Lord Chancellor of England relieved him of his anxieties in one respect, only to intensify them in another, when, in rejecting an appeal in 1744 aimed at compelling Snell Exhibitioners to enter the Church, he removed the onerous burden of the £500 bond, clearing the way for Smith's resignation without financial penalty.[4]

The second pressure were his mother's wishes in matters of religion, albeit expressed passively in his anticipation that, as a passionately devout member of the Christian Church and who had brought him up in obedience to God's will, she would not approve.

Balliol was steeped in religion, not freethinking. 'Our only business here', he told his cousin 'being to go to prayers twice a day, and to lectures twice a week'.[5] What, besides the dreary ratio of 14 prayers to 2 lectures, he thought of the spiritual benefits of the tutors' prayers is not stated (we know he did not think much of their lectures).

While determined to leave Balliol, Smith wrestled with how to explain it all to his Mother. How could he induce her to forgive him (as she would eventually, from her 'unlimited indulgence' of his every step) without hurting her deeply held religious feelings, given her singular mind-set of conforming to Christian beliefs?

His *Philosophical Enquiries* testifies to his vision of the philosopher's vocation as one conducted for its own sake, as something good in its own right, and not something done for false pride or personal gain of any kind. And philosophy also was about the virtues of benevolence, sympathy, prudence, justice, beneficence, approbation and propriety, all of which he knew appealed to his mother's religious sensibilities.

The death of Frances Hutcheson in 1746 removed the last emotional barrier to his departure. Hutcheson himself had studied for the Ministry while at Glasgow between 1712–1716 and, having gained his licence to preach in the Presbyterian Church, he had to resign from his first posting following objections that his Irish background might dilute the Presbyterian interpretation of the scriptures for a Scottish audience. It must have been a rabid Kirk indeed that had no room for an Irish Ulster Protestant! Because Hutcheson had given up preaching to take up teaching, first at Dublin and then at Glasgow, he might have been more sympathetic than the young man anticipated.

In the event, with two of the three obstacles removed and one, his mother's disappointment mitigated, Smith left Oxford in August 1746 to explore his prospects for a career outside the Church. His decision meant following 'his own inclination' and not the 'wishes [of] his friends' who had sponsored his successful candidacy for a Snell Exhibition. By 'abandoning at once all the schemes which their prudence had formed for him' he limited 'his ambition to the uncertain prospect of obtaining, in time, some one of those moderate preferments, to which literary attainment leads in Scotland.'[6] His friends did not think he had made a wise choice at the time, considering his future uncertain, if not precarious.

Smith was not alone in his defection from the Snell obligations; of the ten Snell students at Balliol while Smith was there, only one was ordained.[7]

Tormented by a mob of young gentlemen

The last straw was the behaviour of his masters, backed by a raucous mob of English students. The Master of Balliol College, Reverend Dr. Theophilus Leigh, may have urged him to qualify for an early ordination if he perceived the incident over Hume's book as a sign that Smith's commitment was slipping away.

To escape what became an intolerable obligation and 'not finding the ecclesiastical profession suitable to his taste',[8] Smith sought a leave of absence to return to his mother's home during the August vacation of 1746. He had the perfect excuse in an urgent need to attend to his mother's safety in the aftermath of a civil war. Maybe Dr. Leigh was sympathetic enough to consider obliging young Smith with time to sort himself out. Masters of Colleges tend to take a relaxed view of the tribulations of overly serious, but bright, young scholars, in the hope that they may recover and rejoin the fold, especially if there are obvious signs of physical illness or, what they take to be, mental disturbance. Dr Leigh at the time had been Master of Balliol for twenty years, which included a three-year spell as Vice-Chancellor of the University. His length of service suggests much experience of individual students in their transition to adulthood.

Events in Scotland gave an unusual twist to an ordinary excuse for a leave of absence. Dr Leigh nursed, albeit romantic or sentimental, Jacobite sympathies favouring 'Prince' Charles' claims on behalf of his father to the British Throne. English Jacobites like Dr Leigh believed that the Church of England at the Coronation of the deposed Stuart King had sanctified publicly his divine right to rule and they were not yet reconciled to the claims of a foreign Hanoverian ruling by the mere fiat of mortal politicians. What pretence to Divine Right remained when God's choice was frustrated? While the warring armies were a long way from Oxford, the warring factions in Oxford University were right in the midst of it, albeit vicariously.

Balliol College was 'known in that age for the violence of its Jacobite opinions'.[9] Perhaps Leigh saw young Smith's doubts as further evidence of the unsuitability of the Scots to be flag carriers for the sacred Jacobite cause, mixed in with his own disappointments in the collapse of the Scotch Pretender's challenge. 1746 was the year of the brutal crushing of Charles Edward Stuart's Highland army at Culloden on 16th April. It was also the first year of the violent aftermath aimed at destroying for good the Highlanders' threat to the Hanoverian throne. Anti-Scotch feeling ran high at Balliol in that fateful year.

Additionally, despite English pro-Jacobite sentiments at Balliol, fairly virulent anti-Scotch sentiments prevailed among Leigh's colleagues, further unsettling Smith, especially because, as a convinced Unionist, he had no sympathies for rebellious Highlanders and their Stuart cause, merely sharing their nationality. Scott alludes to behaviour going beyond mere exchanges of rhetoric:

> When feeling is aroused, undergraduates can succeed in making the way of anyone unfortunate to be in a minority, exceedingly hard. Always Adam Smith spoke his mind freely, and in a College of seventy to eighty, his opinions in favour of the Revolution settlement were sure to have been known. If, as is not unlikely, his reading was made impossible and, perhaps, his books and papers injured, his position in the College would be difficult to maintain to any useful purpose.[10]

Balliol was a 'step mother to her Scotch sons' (of whom there were only ten at this time) causing 'their existence there [to be] made very uncomfortable not merely at the hands of the mob of young gentlemen among whom they were obliged to live, but more by the unfair and discriminating harshness of the college authorities themselves.'[11] Ross suggests that the 'sentimental Jacobitism' of the Balliol members 'would be at variance with the alarm felt by Lowland Scots over the fate of their country then at the mercy of the Highland army' and that this tension would 'deepen the ill-feeling' between them and the Snell Exhibitioners.[12]

Glasgow was strongly Unionist – it gained economically after the Union of Parliaments from access to trade with the American colonies – and the Snell students, Smith included, were by now quarrelling with the Balliol authorities about their treatment. They had complained about this to the Senate at Glasgow in February 1745. Dr Leigh took a take-it-or-leave it stance: if they had 'total dislike of the college' they should move elsewhere, he was to suggest.[13] Smith's request to return home was acceded to, with Leigh and his colleagues probably reconciled to his not returning.

5
A Game of Great Skill

The cultivation of interest

There must have been something about the 23-year-old Smith, displaying the polished erudition expected from a diligent student of Glasgow and Oxford, and bearing a gravitas beyond his years, which well connected family friends recognised as qualities worth nurturing. Smith spent two years in distant but not idle retreat at his mother's home in Kirkcaldy, quietly preparing to fulfil his post-Oxford ambitions and consoling her for her disappointment at his change in career.

Here we must appreciate how promotion was achieved in the 18th century. Merit played its part in promoting people for preferment, but so did what was called '*interest*', for without interest your chances of advancement were miniscule. Interest in the eighteenth century blurred the line between a convenience and corruption. Unhappily, in some appointments, where merit should have played the only part, it played none, with awful consequences for those who suffered the megalomania, and the crass stupidity, of those placed over them.

People in a position to award or influence a preferment had 'interest'. They relied upon people they knew, trusted or to whom they owed favours, to sponsor individuals worthy of their attention. Your influence with the people who had interest defined the extent of your interest too, and if important personages (usually aristocrats close to government) whom you knew, or could access, were known to exercise their discretion to advance the careers of those whom you recommended, your interest was known to be considerable and marked your social importance as someone to be cultivated, not offended.

Everybody who counted in Adam Smith's social stratum played the interest game, as did thousands in other professions. Interest was rife in the 18th-century Royal Navy for example, as illustrated by the careers of Captain James Cook, Lieutenant William Bligh, and Admiral Lord Nelson, among many others.[1] Competing networks of interest were interwoven across British society, each promoting aspirants, while blocking those of rival interest brokers, who interacted and counter-interacted in a ruthless contest of interest management. News of a death in service, or a demotion or the disgrace of someone in any position, from lowliest clerk to high members of the government, mobilised fiercely competing interest networks to secure the post for their nominee. Smith, for example, in 1784, responded to an urgent call from an aspirant who sought his interest the same night that the man in a lowly post died.[2]

Interest promoted and protected you, as long as your sponsors remained secure in their positions – the original greasy pole. Your channel of interest promoted you up whatever ladder of success you aspired to climb; as speedily, a lifetime of cultivation could crumble to dust if the head of your interest channel lost favour among those who had the ear of the King. You watched your rivals leap ahead whenever a friendly Minister 'fell', taking with him your aspirations too.

Interest was not just one way. Smith exercised his interest when the opportunity arose to work on behalf of others, showing that he understood and worked the system. In 1762, when referring to someone fumbling the unwritten code of unforgiving interest, he excused his embarrassment at this person's *faux pas* by noting that the young man he had recommended was 'not much acquainted with the way of the world'.[3] Smith certainly knew the 'way of the world' and made it clear that it was his way too. He knew of and accepted its limitations.

In another case he observed that 'our presentation [of Gabriel Millar] will be of little weight unless he is supported by better interest'.[4] He was also sternly circumspect. He warned one petitioner, harbouring a complaint involving the conduct of the Duke of Hamilton, that the 'subject ought to be talked of as little as possible, and never but among his most intimate and cordial friends'.[5] Hardly the conduct of a man alleged to be so 'absent minded' as not to know what he was doing!

The absent-minded professor?

Smith worked the interest system with consummate skill. He understood what was at stake for him and he made it happen. He also worked it for others. Years later, he set out how he saw the game of life should be played, borrowing from the Stoics their helpful advice in both a practical and a philosophical sense:

> Human life the Stoics appear to have considered as a game of great skill; in which, however, there was a mixture of chance, or of what is vulgarly understood to be chance. In such games the stake is commonly a trifle, and the whole pleasure of the game arises from playing well, from playing fairly, and playing skilfully. If notwithstanding all his skill,

however the good player should by the influence of chance, happen to lose, the loss ought to be a matter, rather of merriment, than of serious sorrow. He has made no false stroke; he has done nothing which he ought to be ashamed of; he has enjoyed completely the whole pleasure of the game. If, on the contrary, the bad player, notwithstanding all his blunders, should, in the same manner, happen to win, his success can give him but little satisfaction. He is mortified by the remembrance of all the faults which he committed. Even during the play he can enjoy no part of the pleasure which it is capable of affording. From ignorance of the rules of the game, fear and doubt and hesitation are the disagreeable sentiments that precede almost every stroke which he plays; and when he has played it, the mortification of finding it a gross blunder, commonly completes the unpleasing circle of his sensations. Human life, with all the advantages which can possibly attend it, ought, according to the Stoics, to be regarded but as a mere two-penny stake; a matter by far too insignificant to merit any anxious concern. Our only anxious concern ought to be, not about the stake, but about the proper method of playing. If we placed our happiness in winning the stake, we placed it in what depended on causes beyond our power, and out of our direction. We necessarily exposed ourselves to perpetual fear and uneasiness, and frequently grievous and mortifying disappointments. If we placed it in playing well, in playing fairly, in playing wisely and skilfully; in the propriety of our own conduct in short; we placed it in what, by proper discipline, education and attention, might be altogether in our own power, and under our own direction. Our happiness was perfectly secure, and beyond the reach of fortune. The event of our actions, if it was out of our power, was equally out of our concern, and we could never feel either fear or anxiety about it; nor ever suffer any grievous, or even any serious disappointment.[6]

By the time Smith summarised the game of life he had been playing it sufficiently long to know how much of a success he had made from it. He had done well by the standards he set himself when he left Oxford in 1746 for, by 1759, when he published *Moral Sentiments*, he had already more than exceeded his post-Oxford ambitions.

How did he achieve the far from moderate preferment of a professorship, and within only six years too? By playing well, fairly, wisely, skilfully and with propriety, and from applying proper discipline, education and attention to everything he did within his own power and direction. He did not trust to luck, though he enjoyed a fair bit of it, and he did not wait for it to fall into his lap. He worked hard for his success in a disciplined manner and paid attention to the small details of getting it right. Given his chance, he took it with both hands. Smith's diligence in pursuit of his personal ambitions is in contrast with the oft-repeated, stereotypical descriptions of his being an absent-minded professor, who, given to talking to himself and for being otherworldly in the extreme, was also given to lethargy and even to indolence in his demeanour. The latter reputation he cultivated by self-admissions in various letters (to his Mother in 1743–4 and to the Duc de La Rochefoucauld in 1784).[7] His 'confessions' are misunderstood. 'Workaholics' commonly feel stressed and neurotic over what they do not complete each day, no matter how much else they have achieved. For an alleged indolent man, Smith's literary and administrative output is impressive evidence against his self-image of idleness.

The famous oft-repeated anecdotes about him sit uneasily alongside the reality of Smith as a man who carefully planned and executed his moves. Either he was the awkward bumbling savant the anecdotes make him out to be,[8] or he grossly misled his contemporaries, perhaps, as he intended to do. Variously, he was absent minded at meetings of the Edinburgh literati; he is supposed to have fallen into a poisonous tanning pit in 1759 while conversing with a sponsor (Mr Townsend); he attempted to make tea by putting his bread and butter slice into a teapot and pouring hot water over it; one Sunday morning he walked 15 miles in his dressing gown while in deep thought (and, presumably, the 15 miles back?); he rubbed his head against the wall while dictating *Wealth of Nations* to his amanuensis; he 'stole' and ate sugar lumps at a tea party to the annoyed embarrassment of Miss Douglas; he was mistaken for a lunatic by two old women from his meandering walking style; he returned the musket 'salute' of a doorkeeper; and he copied the signature above where he was to sign a Customs paper instead of his own name.[9]

The anecdotes about him gained a wholly unwarranted, though understandable, credibility from the paucity of information that has survived (should he have conversed with the two old women on the natural price of labour?). Smith's alleged social gaffes amount to nothing more than misleading and inconsequential tittle-tattle, worth little in themselves and worth less from their repetition out of context with his other highly focused behaviours.

W. R. Scott understood the real nature of Smith's so-called absent-mindedness. The fault lies in those (not all of them friendly witnesses) who failed to understand the causes of Smith's aberrant behaviours. In place of absent-mindedness, with its implications that he had the concentration of a butterfly, we have, instead, a mind so focussed that he was not easily distracted from whatever he was considering at the moment.

Smith loved the company of like-minded intellectuals. He joined the many intellectual clubs of Edinburgh, Glasgow and London where the literati met and mixed convivially over a supper and tankards of wine (in Edinburgh's Oyster Club, which he frequented, served by very friendly ladies of wilful dispositions).[10] And, unlike many talkative contemporaries, he did not speak out on every subject or at all on many occasions. His physical mannerisms – shaking head, glazed stare into the distance and the mouthing of silent conversations with himself – stuck in the memories of contemporaries, many of whom misread them as a lack of social awareness (unlike the likes of Reverend Alexander Carlyle, Smith was not out to 'cut a figure' and impress young ladies or their mothers).[11] Those hostile to Smith used gossip about his mannerisms to damage his social reputation.

Scott ventures a more sympathetic assessment:

> at some stage in the conversation a remark caught his interest and he followed the thought on and on and became completely lost in the pursuit. Later, when he acquired some celebrity, it became usual to attract his attention and to draw him into the discussion by a direct question or by provocative statements. In such occasions he frequently explained his view in detail, which accounts for the reports that his conversation resembled a lecture. It is not improbable than on an average of a number of meetings, he spoke less than the majority of his fellow members.[12]

Scott attributes Smith's absence of mind to his 'power of intense concentration', a not uncommon faculty in men 'who have thought deeply'. It operated in two directions: when immersed in mentally processing something highly abstract and theoretical he would appear to be unaware of what was happening around him, and (a contradiction) when his attention was directed at something practical 'he saw much more in the situation than others who witnessed it at the same time.' He also had a formidable memory, especially for recalling the minute details of events occurring during his alleged wanderings in the suburbs of his attention, though he appeared not to be aware of the events occurring around him at the time.[13]

The contrast in the flimsy anecdotal impressions of Smith which, because baldly stated and bereft of explanation, imply that he was not safe to be let out on his own, and the Smith who was highly focussed on 'the proper way' of playing the serious game of life, could not be greater (his record as a policy maker, 'fixer' and administrator at Glasgow was outstanding; his manipulation of the interest system was no mean feat).

The anecdotal image of Smith became larger than it deserves and drove his truer persona into the background. I believe that a highly focussed Smith in control of his destiny is closer to the truth than surviving anecdotal detritus.

6

His Strategic Allegiance

Smith became a beneficiary of the 'Argyll' interest in the person of Archibald, Earl of Ilay and the 3rd Duke, who succeeded his childless elder brother to the title in 1743 (already a critical year for Smith). The Argyll brothers, as we have seen, were staunch supporters of the Union of Scotland with England, managed 'Scotch' affairs for the government and held onto their prominence from their ability to deliver the bulk of the 'Scotch vote' in the House of Commons to grateful ministries.[1]

The Argylls were born, and also spent much of their youth and most of their adulthood, in England. Archibald Campbell, the 3rd Duke, formerly Earl of Ilay, managed his affairs in Scotland through his resident and highly reliable retainer, Lord Milton, nephew of the famous Scottish patriot, Andrew Fletcher of Saltoun (who was, ironically, a prominent and articulate opponent of the 1707 Union).

Ilay maintained strong academic interests throughout his life, having a large home library and a 'thirst for books' according to his main ally, Walpole, the long serving British Prime Minister.[2] He was also handicapped in his quest for high office by two retarding influences on his life. One was his brother's behaviour as a political manager, of which Ilay remarked to Lord Milton: 'The great error in my brother's conduct was that he was too apt to quarrel and knew whom he fought against, but never considered whom he fought for'.[3] Ilay's other handicap was that he did not go to Oxford University.

Like most of the male elite in the Establishment, Ilay went to Eton, but then, unusually for a British aristocrat, he attended Glasgow College, not Oxford. His 'handicap' had nothing to do with the quality of his education at Glasgow – far from it, as Glasgow at the time was superior academically to Oxford or Cambridge. He missed out on something far more important for the game of life near the top of British politics – the lifetime male 'bonding' (and, of course, lifetime hatreds too) built up as 'the mob of young gentlemen' prepared to become men in the cloying intensity of their shared *alma mater*. In adult life, 'outsiders' were treated with a degree of suspicion by Oxbridge *alumni* (and still are) and, in the great crush for political position and place the 'insiders' were prone to indulge in orchestrated innuendo against 'Scotch' interlopers (a version of which Smith suffered at Balliol).

Not for the last time, events outside the control of Smith worked in his favour. He seized the opportunities provided by unexpected events, acting always with a deliberation, as he 'read the game' and played it with exceptional skill. On this occasion, fortunately for Smith, Ilay's career handicap was an advantage to Smith. Ilay, the semi-detached Establishment power broker, took a personal interest in the affairs of the Scottish universities, hence the strategic importance for Smith through the influence of his cousin, William Smith, of aligning himself with the Argyll interest as a student. Smith, to advance his career, chose his allies carefully.

Ilay was a Whig, not a Tory; he supported the Union, was loyal to the Hanoverian succession and he opposed the Jacobites. Ilay would see in young Smith someone of the same mould politically as himself, evidenced convincingly by his father's record of service to the Unionist cause (personally witnessed by the 2nd Duke), and by his suffering for his pro-Hanoverian stance at the hands of the 'mob of young gentlemen' at Balliol, a place widely known for its fanatical Jacobite prejudices. What a chord that image would strike with the Duke!

No matter that Adam Smith junior throughout his life regarded many of the British elite to be deficient in good sense, he also considered the Jacobite cause a dangerous regression into savage backwardness, and he offered no support for the irrational fiction of the divine rights of kings. Taking into account that English Jacobites drove Smith out of Oxford to return to the widow of a valiant servant of the Unionist cause, it is not difficult, if his attention was brought to consider Smith's merits, to appreciate how Ilay would see Smith as a victim of Tory intrigue and Jacobite subversion, and, therefore, a sound and safe man worthy of assistance. And, crucially, men of interest were available who both knew Ilay and Smith and they were positioned where they could gain Ilay's attention.

In short, the Argyll interest promoted people like Smith and 'without [Argyll] no preferment could be obtained in Scotland.'[4] But before he could benefit from the interest of his sponsors, Smith had to position himself as suitable for what he really wanted, namely, a professorship at Glasgow, preferably Hutcheson's Chair of Moral Philosophy. His horizon of ambition had moved firmly outwards after 1748 when he moved to Edinburgh.

Uncertain prospects

After six years in Oxford, Smith spoke English close enough to a dialect associated with 'modern' Britain. He sounded quite different from fellow home-based Scots with their multiplicity of related dialects, some remnants of which Robert Burns threaded into his poems forty years later. Smith's distinctive 'English' accent marked him out.

Smith had been educated at Glasgow University without graduating[5] and at Oxford University, where he took his BA in 1744, enhanced in 1749 to an MA on resigning his Exhibition.[6] Glasgow also awarded him a Doctorate of Laws in 1762.[7]

Impeccably well mannered and polite, in public he espoused no controversial views on religion. These attributes added greatly to his suitability to mix with and call upon influential persons in Fife and Edinburgh. He passed the social tests set for him, and among these was the social one of a suitable romantic courtship. Unfortunately, though smitten, nothing came of it and Smith and 'the lady from Fife' died unmarried, but, whether from unrequited love or from other incompatibilities, we do not know.

His thoughts, and those of others who knew him, turned to what he intended to do. How might he become a teacher? Professorial vacancies were rare events (assuming his ambitions at that stage stretched that far) and his six years away from Scotland were six years out of sight, place and mind. Beyond the environs of Kirkcaldy and Glasgow, how many remembered the studious teenager? Hence, he needed visibility to further his career.

An ingenious 'plan' for his promotion as a teacher was put into effect. What better way to promote his future than by public lectures? 'Demonstrate what you can do' are infallible tests of suitability, though no guarantee of reward. To report on this episode in his life as if it were merely a passing item in his résumé misses its social and personal significance. Smith's accent approximated to 'proper' English, and Scotland's educated youth (more importantly, their parents) were aware that without a similar accent they remained disadvantaged socially and politically in the New Britain. Ambitious Scots, fashionably keen to overcome their perceived disadvantages in elocution, sought to adopt the English style of speaking. David Hume went so far in 1751 as to provide a glossary of 'Scotisms' to be removed from polite speech. Such fads as these gave Smith a slight edge in his ambitions.

Henry Home (later, Lord Kames, on his becoming a Scottish Judge) was a prominent lawyer and advocate, and later Judge and Lord Commissioner of Justiciary, in Edinburgh. As Smith's immediate source of interest, and sharing the fad for English-style speaking, he conceived of the campaign and Smith's role in it.[8] Kames' role in Smith's plans is supported by other sources.[9]

Smith, no doubt, was motivated sincerely to help Henry Home fulfil his vision of educating Scots in 'proper' English, but there were also personal benefits for Smith in achieving public recognition as an accomplished academic lecturer. His alleged personal mannerisms did not discourage his friends' conception of the plan, nor its implementation.

Besides Henry Home, his sponsors included his boyhood friend, James Oswald of Dunnikier, Fife, an MP and later a Cabinet Minister and Privy Councillor, well known to the Argyll interest (he was also the son of Smith's guardian), and Robert Craigie of Glendoik, later a Lord Advocate, and Lord President of the Court of Session, whose daughter married Smith's cousin, Colonel Robert Douglas, and whose son in turn lived in Smith's household and later became his heir.[10]

This was no disinterested alliance solely to promote Home's ambitions for an Anglo-Scottish North Britain. The venture proceeded because, fortuitously, the parties' interests coincided. And the deal? Smith composed his lectures on 'rhetoric, belles-lettres and jurisprudence' and read them with care to sizable audiences of about 100, drummed up by his sponsors at a guinea per person, of which Smith received £100 per winter series,[11] a grand sum for his trouble.

His audience consisted mainly of young students of law and theology from Edinburgh University, plus several current and future Members of Parliament and assorted others, interested variously in improving their spoken English and in refining their literary tastes. In effect, Smith auditioned and submitted himself and his ideas to public scrutiny in front of many current and future powerful influencers and managers of interest networks.

And the plan worked!

7

Professor Smith!

On Tuesday 9 January 1751 Adam Smith, aged 27, was elected Professor of Logic at Glasgow University by the Faculty of Professors and, with remarkable speed for the postal services of the time, the very next day he accepted the Professorship by letter. From free-lance public lecturer to university professor in three years was no mean achievement.

The speed of Smith's election on the 9th to his admittance on the 16th hides the prodigious efforts required to arrange support for his candidacy. News of professorial vacancies at the Universities of Glasgow, Edinburgh, St Andrews and Aberdeen, sparked men of interest into action from amongst Scotland's small elite in support of favoured candidates. The relatively unknown Smith needed strong interest to win the election – and he had the strongest.

Lord Kames, originally of Jacobite sympathies but switching prudently to the Whig interest in the 1730s,[1] is barely visible in the mist surrounding what happened. All that is left of his presence is the outcome. Kames helped to place Smith's name before the one man in Scottish affairs whose support assured success to any professorial candidate. That man was, of course, the 3rd Duke of Argyll.

Circumstantial evidence suggests that James Oswald (1715–69) also brought Smith's name before the Duke: he co-sponsored Smith's lectures; he was a Member of Parliament (1741–68) and a member of Scotch faction in the House of Commons. Therefore he had regular access to the Duke, on whose behalf he voted for the government's Bills. When Smith was a candidate for the professorship at Glasgow, Oswald was 'Lord of Trade' in the cabinet (1751–9). As a Scottish MP he could speak favourably of Smith to the Duke. What better interest could Smith have behind him?

It is claimed that Ilay secured the appointment of 55 academic posts in Scotland between 1723 and 1761, including 20 in Glasgow University alone and, in further evidence of his power, he managed to block more than 30 other candidates from university appointments.[2] Among those appointed with Ilay's approbation were Francis Hutcheson (Smith's tutor and mentor) in 1729, William Cullen in 1747 and Joseph Black in 1756, all three of whom were close allies of Smith.

Smith's reputation from his public lectures in Edinburgh undoubtedly established his academic credentials (as a former Glasgow student, he was one of their own after all) but his academic excellence alone was not enough. University electors, however forlornly, eyed professorial vacancies as a means of settling past obligations, or of inducing future reciprocation, to or from other men of interest besides the Dukes of Argyll. University Senates, then as now, consisted of professors no less jealous of their independence and no less cantankerous at being out-voted by more powerful interests and, as ever within a University, its 'politics' were no less rife with troublesome rumours and affected disharmonies, slights and insults. Smith's passage was not smooth; it met with the usual minor upsets from those nursing bruised egos, easily irritated feelings and aimless grievances. In a short while though restless, it blew over, to be followed in time with the usual squabbles over somebody or something entirely different.[3]

Professor Loudon's death on 1 November 1750 had caused the vacancy.[4] Between news of his death and the meeting of the Faculty of Professors on 9 January, the first available Tuesday in 1751, the candidates' sponsors manoeuvred behind the scenes. Two serious candidates emerged, namely, George Muirhead, who became Professor of Oriental Languages in 1753, and Adam Smith. At the meeting, they elected Smith 'unanimously' and Professor Robert Simson, his former mathematics teacher, invited him to present himself 'as soon as his affairs can allow him.'[5] He replied immediately by return on the 10th![6] That the letters exchanged so quickly suggest an early confidence in what was to transpire and demonstrate the usual thorough preparation of matters under his control that were the hallmark of Smith's attention to administrative detail.

There are other indications that he was warned to expect the invitation. First, there was his ability at 'short notice' to attend the official admittance ceremony in Glasgow on the Tuesday following the meeting that elected him. Second, the ritual for admittance to a professorship included his reading a 'dissertation' in Latin and it is most unlikely that he wrote it in the few days between receipt of the invitation on 10th January and his attendance at the inauguration on the 16th. He prepared his thesis, entitled *'De origine idearum'* (The Origin of Ideas) in advance in anticipation of success, confirming that he focused on other things beyond his public lectures.

The rituals also included a formal requirement that he sign the Calvinist Confession of Faith before the Presbytery of Glasgow, and that he also swear an oath of fidelity (*Oath de Fideli*) to the University authorities, neither of which proved difficult for him.[7] With the formalities completed, he left Glasgow for Edinburgh as the newly created Professor of Logic. The 'plan' had succeeded.

In his letter of acceptance he warned that his attendance at the admittance ceremony in Glasgow would 'of necessity' have to be followed by a quick return to Edinburgh, presumably to prepare one of his Edinburgh lectures on the following Friday. He also mentioned enigmatically that he 'could not even be certain if that absence will be consented to by my friends here.'[8] His candour shows his confidence that the Argyll interest would push through his appointment whatever the intrusions of his private affairs on the University's convenience. But for all the speed with which he was catapulted into the Chair in January, Professor Smith took his time in assuming his duties. Though the University's year ran from October to June he did not begin lecturing until the following October.

Smith's remarkable journey to international acclaim and lasting fame had begun.

A macabre dance

As a new Professor, he was expected to lecture to the traditional syllabus, but he had reservations about the relevance of logic to learning. Clearly, he had not taken the Chair with a view to an academic career in Logic, which did not interest him. Accepting a Professorship in an unsuitable subject as a prelude to a more congenial chair was not unusual.[9]

Smith 'depart[ed] widely' from tradition and discarded much of the Logic syllabus left by Professor Loudon, replacing it with extracts from his 'more interesting and useful' Edinburgh lectures. He retained those parts of the old syllabus which gave 'a general view of the powers of the mind' and only 'so much of the ancient logic as requisite to gratify curiosity with respect to an artificial method of reasoning'. Professor Millar, a former pupil, added, wryly, that the parts Smith had dropped 'had once occupied the universal attention of the learned'.[10] Smith's interests focused well beyond a dry course in logic. Though an unpromising platform for his ambitions, he seized it with alacrity. Events flattered his ambitions.

Thomas Craigie had supported Smith in the minor upset following his Professorship but had fallen seriously ill in April 1751, forcing him to take sick leave.[11] Because Smith's friendly beneficiaries of the Argyll interest kept him abreast of the 'politics' of the College, he was aware that illness, unfortunate as it was for Craigie, was fortuitous for him. An ill professor occupying a coveted preferment was news in a society where the ambitious, as if carrying empty coffins on their backs, shuffled impatiently and stalked the dying.

Craigie's indisposition continued over the summer months. Smith, prompted by his informers, wrote to the Clerk to the Senate (Professor Cullen) to say he was 'very glad' that Craigie had 'at last resolved to go to Lisbon' on sick leave. Smith did not have long to wait. On 11 September 1751, the University re-allocated the indisposed Craigie's lectures, giving the Natural Theology class to the Professor of Divinity (Mr. Ross) and the Natural Jurisprudence and the Politics classes to Smith, who, typically absent from the meeting (confirming that the collective noun for professors is 'an absence of'), intimated by letter that he would 'willingly undertake both' classes. Smith accepted these extra responsibilities 'with great pleasure'.[12]

And 'good' news for Smith soon followed; Craigie died in Lisbon on 27 November 1751. The new Professor of Logic, barely completing his first month's lectures, immediately set his sights on the now vacant Chair of Moral Philosophy. He gained the support of the Principal, Dr. Neil Campbell, who in turn spoke to the Duke of Argyll. For Smith it was important enough to his prospects for him to take two days to travel through to Edinburgh for a brief social introduction to the Duke, who feigning not to recognize or recollect his name gave him his all-important support.[13] Seven months later on 29 April 1752, and before he had completed his lectures to Craigie's class, he was elected Professor of Moral Philosophy.[14]

This success crowned the plan begun in 1748 to allow his talents to flower. And flower they did. He wrote *Moral Sentiments* and published it almost seven years to the day after he became Professor of Moral Philosophy.[15] Smith had played the interest game with great skill and was now in the right Chair and in the right place, ready for his next steps.

Part II
Impartial Spectators

Introduction

In Part II I discuss selected ideas from Smith's philosophy in plain language. Philosophical ideas can seem unconnected with the real world but my treatment is selective, not comprehensive, and I miss out a great deal from the contents of his *Moral Sentiments*.

Moral Sentiments covers the first of the three pillars of Smith's legacy. It discusses the moral sentiments that constrain individuals living as strangers in close proximity in society. The net effect of his imaginative construct, the impartial spectator, means they live in relative harmony (nothing human is perfect). Moral sentiments alone are not enough.

By itself, *Moral Sentiments* is ignored as a lasting contribution to a science of morals and this probably accounts for its relative obscurity. Certainly, without Smith's *Wealth of Nations* and the fame that it engendered for its author, *Moral Sentiments*, much like George Berkeley's book on Tar Water,[1] would be a scholarly curiosity on the fringes of the attention of specialists in 18th-century minutia.

8

The Religious Climate

The great issues in moral philosophy in the 18th century reflected major changes in British society. Christian moral precepts were more concerned with preparation for the afterlife in heaven than with this one on earth, except indirectly: what you did in this life determined what happened to you in the next. Residual grievances about others were comforted by what would happen to them for their earthly sins.

This mixture of 'moralistic exhortation and the threat of damnation'[1] was under siege because the power of religion to curb amoral behaviour declined slowly from doubts about the Christian monopoly of truth. Young Smith's essay on the *History of Astronomy* may have lain in his bedroom cabinet for forty years, but the evidence contained in it was public and others, beside Smith, talked of similar themes.

The world he lived in experienced the unsettling effects of social changes that were occurring at a gradually accelerating pace, exciting the passions their effects aroused. For example, the expansion of commerce at the time gave topicality to the age-old moral dilemma: is virtue consistent with material wealth? Ministers and Priests in their Sunday sermons reminded rich and poor alike of the problems for rich men and camels in the vicinity of the eyes of needles[2] and pointed the finger at those who, in their quest for wealth, forgot the quest for God.

In so far as intellectual discussions ever reflect the temper of the times, *Moral Sentiments* addressed very practical questions: 'How is it that people live in relative amity with each other; why were they not at each other's throats?' Smith was not the originator of the dilemmas. With his knowledge of Christian theology from a Calvinist Protestant viewpoint, he joined the slipstream of a wide-ranging debate, contributing to a crowded library of books and pamphlets by other people from clergy and laypersons alike. From his background and former ambitions, he was steeped in religious knowledge and practice. His mother was seriously religious, as was his schoolmaster too, and all classes began with prayers at University (Smith proposed, unsuccessfully, that he be allowed to abandon this requirement).

Noticeably, his Professor, Francis Hutcheson, switched from lecturing in Latin to English, a remarkable change in scholarly practice and a sign of the changing times, and one which Smith followed when he took over his classes.

Smith learned his Bible at his mother's knee. No room for ambiguity here. Strangely, it is seldom mentioned as a prominent feature of Smith's intellectual make-up and cause of his circumspect behaviour, yet at the time religion dominated social, family and academic life in Scotland to a degree unappreciated in today's secular society. Religion was ubiquitous in 18th-century Scotland and it dominated his family life through his mother and his cousin. His mother's abiding presence throughout his adult years restrained his public utterances when, intellectually, but never publicly, he moved away from orthodox Christian revelation, though not necessarily from belief in a Deity. He was mindful neither to show the slightest disrespect for his mother's deeply held beliefs nor to give her cause to doubt his piety. David Hume, his closest friend, on occasion teased him about his 'double-life' but, ever the gentleman, he never publicly questioned Smith's belief that a son's duty to a devoted mother preceded his scholarly duty to philosophical exactitude.

Smith knew the Bible's views of the iniquities of money wealth. And this had to be the starting point for his addressing questions of whether virtue was compatible with a desire to make money. If wealth and bettering oneself were incompatible with virtue, then a philosophical case for the expansion of the commercial society was stymied. There was no doubt that Smith recognised the signs of economic growth – they were all around him in Edinburgh and Glasgow, and he could read about similar trends in England. Most telling, his second book was about the 'nature and causes of the wealth of nations'. He no longer needed to look up to the night sky to practise the philosophical method; his mind's eye was fixed firmly on what was happening around him on earth.

He knew the relevant biblical verses too: 'Lay not up for yourselves the treasures upon the earth, where moth and rust doth consume, and where thieves break through and steal'; 'You cannot serve God and mammon';[3] 'And I shall say unto you, It is easier for a camel to go through a needle's eye, than for a rich man to enter into the kingdom of God';[4] 'For what doth it profit a man, to gain the whole world, and forfeit his soul';[5] 'The bishop therefore must be without reproach ...no lover of money' (some translations give 'filthy lucre' for money); 'For the love of money is a root of all kinds of evil: which some reaching after have been led astray from the faith'.[6] Such themes brook no compromise. For many, the commercial ethos was incompatible (and, for some, it still is) with the Christian life, and that was that.

Christian theologians were not alone in their suspicions of commercial activity. The classical (pagan) tradition was suspicious of, and in some sense as hostile to, the debilitating influence of wealth on the practice of virtue, as were communities still in thrall to primitive superstition.[7] For the Church, the decline and fall of Rome was a long tale of the corrupting dissolution of virtue under the relentless spread of the iniquities of greed and sexual profligacy, and the brutal evil of naked violence. Smith, and others,[8] saw a different explanatory consequence for the same events. The fall of Rome destroyed its commercial system and sent Europe into the thousand years of the 'Dark Ages'. These centuries were equally dissolute in their post-Roman rapine and violence, and they were incomparably poverty ridden too. It was not the Age of Commerce that destroyed Rome with greed, profligacy or awesome violence; it was the destruction of Rome that destroyed the peaceful commerce of Roman Europe. The Age of Commerce, Smith believed, was not the cause of the problem; it was its solution.

Religious hostility to the green shoots of trade illuminated what was at stake in the contest between the idea that commerce was a source of evil and greedy corruption, and the new ideas favouring wealth creation as a material benefit for ordinary people, who were otherwise condemned to a (short) life of poverty and misery. Those favouring the new ideas re-cast Mammon as having, unlike the leopard, changed its spots. For Smith, in re-casting God's answer in this manner he breached the walls of Christian absolutism with radical philosophical relativism. He could not help but know what he was doing and also know that for a 'quiet life' he had to keep this a secret from both his mother, who would be disappointed, and the vigilance of religious zealots who could do him harm.

Debates over the merits of the social changes occurring around them encouraged those who theorised about their consequences. So, long before Smith joined the debate, it had been underway inconclusively for more than a century.[9] The re-emergence of commerce, first imperceptibly, later like an incoming tide, spread through the heartland of Europe and, as Braudel showed in his magisterial *Wheels of Commerce*,[10] the changes continued at different rates and took different forms, but everywhere they were in the same direction towards greater wealth, as ever mal-distributed. For the vast majority of the people, wealth creation started from an extremely low base.

These new trends re-constituted the commercial society of Europe that had been lost in the violent disruptions of the post-Roman era. They also took new forms from improvements in technology and from the spread of networks of markets. Their causes and effects were spiral rather than cyclical.

If religious precepts and exhortations were insufficient to ensure that harmony prevailed across society, Smith's had to explain what might be done to curb unruly and vicious passions arising from greed and selfishness. If exhortations to virtue and reason failed to curb the vicious passions, could they be curbed by other, more virtuous less vicious, passions, as naturally as Newton's laws of gravity bound everything within its scope? It is from Smith's explanations and answers to these questions that the contribution of his *Moral Sentiments* to his legacy is best understood.[11]

9
On Benevolence

Did Smith's books contradict each other? 'Yes,' said critics in Germany, calling it 'Das Adam Smith problem'. Specifically, *Moral Sentiments*, allegedly, was based on *sympathy* and *Wealth of Nations* on *selfishness*. Neither charge is true. Yet, no matter how often the 'Das Deutschland problem' is refuted it keeps re-appearing – like that 'grassy knoll in Dallas'.

For Smith, sympathy was about moral judgement; it was not a motive for behaviour. Self-interest, not selfishness, was one among several motives for economic behaviour. Selfishness causes harm to others, but self-interest (not selfishness!) benefits others.

It is appropriate that we focus on Smith's criticism of benevolence as the 'supreme virtue'. Smith wrote that Christian philosophers had asserted that benevolence ('that most graceful and agreeable of all the affections') is the 'supreme virtue'. Opening his book at random and reading sentences like that might explain why three bishops bought copies of *Moral Sentiments* from Millar's London bookshop in one day. David Hume teased Smith with his observation that he 'may conclude what Opinion true Philosophers will entertain of it, when these Retainers to Superstition praise it so highly'.[1]

From a rigid sense of prudence, unlike his good friend David Hume, Smith tended to leave Christian assertions unchallenged, because he preferred to be left alone to teach what became his legacy rather than spend time defending himself against charges of heresy (a fate his mentor, Professor Hutcheson, had not managed to avoid, though, thankfully, he was found not guilty; David Hume, who was under constant pressure from similar harassment, was another example of the reality of Smith's fears).

Critics who read *Moral Sentiments* carelessly think that because Smith believed that benevolence was 'the supreme and governing attribute'[2] of all actions of the Deity it *necessarily* followed that he thought benevolence ought to be the 'supreme virtue' for mere mortals too. This is not what he said, however. He simply asserted that 'many ancient fathers of the Christian church'[3] believed that virtue consists of benevolence (love or charity). He did not share their views; he described them accurately.

Smith used the phrase 'according to these authors' (i.e., according to the Christian divines), men who acted from benevolence 'were alone truly praise-worthy, or could claim any merit in the sight of the Deity'.[4] Having merit in God's sight, it should be noted, was a self-proclaimed attribute of the true believer. Indeed, Christian divines believed it was from actions of charity and love that men imitated the conduct of God, and by assuming a greater resemblance of His holy attributes they become worthy of His love and esteem.

Crucially, 'it was the great object of this [Christian] philosophy to raise us' so that 'at last' we were worthy of 'communication' with the Deity.[5] True believers sought to talk to, if not walk with, God! Smith, however, added that 'this system', by which he meant one that saw its highest goal as 'communication with the Deity', was 'adopted by several divines'[6] – those distinguished servants of the Church, among which number he had volunteered at Oxford not to be included.

'Proper benevolence,' writes Smith, presenting Hutcheson's views:

> is the most graceful and agreeable of all the affections, that it is recommended to us by a double sympathy, that as its tendency is necessarily beneficent, it is the proper object of gratitude and reward, and that upon all these accounts it appears to our natural sentiments to posses a merit superior to any other.[7]

Even the weaknesses of excessive benevolence, he continued (still reporting the views of Hutcheson) are highly regarded, unlike excessive malice, selfishness or resentment, which 'are always extremely disgusting'.[8] Benevolence bestows a 'beauty superior to all others' and its absence 'communicates a peculiar deformity' to those whose actions lack it.[9]

Smith's next paragraph says 'Besides all this':

> Dr Hutcheson observed that whenever in any action, supposed to proceed from benevolent affections, some other motive had been discovered, our sense of the merit of this action was just so far diminished.[10]

Hutcheson took his argument to an extreme, which undermined the practical relevance of benevolence as the supreme virtue to be practised by mortals, because no mortal could act from pure motives on all occasions. The Protestant Church in 18th century Scotland was no place for half measures.

It was no longer sufficient, according to Hutcheson, to consider an action alone to be benevolent because the motivations of the person acting in a benevolent manner had to be questioned too. While benevolent actions merit the high regard in which they are held, he warned that benevolent actions motivated by the expectations of a favour, or the hope of a pecuniary reward, would 'entirely destroy all notion of merit or praise-worthiness'. He states[11] unequivocally that the 'mixture of any selfish motive, like that of a baser alloy', with benevolence debases whatever merit the apparently benevolent act attracts:

> It was evident he [Hutcheson, not Smith!] imagined that virtue must consist in pure and disinterested benevolence alone.[12]

Hutcheson had left his Chair to return to his Pulpit. His pupil chose not to follow him.

Smith's critique of Hutcheson's theory of benevolence

Hutcheson believed firmly that selfish motives corrupted benevolent actions and were deservedly condemned. But, somewhat strangely, he also believed that selfish actions could be motivated by hidden motives of benevolence! This was the gap in Hutcheson's argument into which Smith advanced his arguments.

Hutcheson clearly distinguished between the visible behaviours of a selfish player and his hidden motives of benevolence. We see the behaviours and assume them motivated by selfishness – we cannot see into the player's mind – but we find out later that the selfish behaviours were motivated by benevolent intentions. That alone changes everything about them and 'greatly enhances our sense of their merit'.[13] It seems that an angel is absolutely corrupted by a single sin, but a multiple sinner is saved by a single benevolent action!

There is a strange asymmetry in the assertion that selfish motives deserve condemnation, while selfishness deserves praise when motivated by benevolence. This exception included someone endeavouring to increase his fortune (a selfish action) with no view other than to do good services to his fellow men or to repay his benefactors. Benevolence was denied if his motive was merely to increase his wealth for himself. Hutcheson concluded that 'it was benevolence only which stamped upon any action the character of virtue' and not in any measure its selfishness.[14]

In this context, self-love, asserted Hutcheson without a hint of qualification, was a principle that could 'never be virtuous in any degree or in any direction', and 'it was vicious whenever it obstructed the general good.'[15] He left no room for confusion about where he stood on benevolence, as was only to be expected from an Ulster Protestant.

Smith criticised Hutcheson's 'amiable system'[16] that virtue consists of both the purist of motives for, and the unsullied actions of, benevolence alone, but never when corrupted by 'self-love'. He noted that 'regard to our own private happiness and interest' appears on many occasions a 'very laudable' principle of action, and he lists other laudable and praise-worthy habits which serve self-interested motives, such as 'economy, industry, discretion, attention, and application of thought'.[17] To see Smith's point, think of opposites for these self-interested motives: spendthrift; indolence; indiscretion; distraction and mindlessness. None of these qualities serve any beneficial purpose for others, yet the self-interested qualities he quotes do.

Smith concedes that selfish motives 'often seem to sully the beauty' of benevolent affections but insists that this was not to be taken to show 'that self-love can never be the motive of a virtuous action' Selfishness, he opines, is neither 'the weak side of human nature' nor is it lacking in virtue.[18] As always with human behaviour, it depends, and he gives an example.

It was from a man's unselfish regard for his family, and not just selfishly for himself, that he takes 'proper care of his health, his life and his fortune, to which self-preservation ought to be sufficient to prompt him'. A man, who neglected himself and put his family at risk, renders himself a pitiful object, not to mention our feelings of pity for his family in their straightened circumstances. When we disapprove of his 'carelessness and want of economy' it is not that person's 'want of benevolence' that we criticise, but his want of a proper attention to 'his self-interest.' Once an exception is accepted in philosophical debate, Hutcheson's general proposition to the contrary – selfishness sullies the beauty of benevolence – is under siege. Contributing to the welfare of society is not the 'sole virtuous motive'. It has to be weighed alongside all other motives.[19]

Hutcheson's proposition on benevolence was impractical. Smith questions whether imperfect humans could ever approach, by inclination or circumstance, the demands of perfection. And because it is an unrealisable state for humans it was, therefore, defective as a virtue because it was an unattainable standard.

Smith broadens his attack on benevolence as a supreme virtue to humans. Benevolence, he writes, may be the 'sole principle of action of the Deity', but:

> It is not easy to conceive of what other motive [besides benevolence] an independent all-perfect Being, who stands in need of nothing external, and whose happiness is complete in himself, can act from. But whatever may be the case with the Deity, so imperfect a creature as man, the support of whose existence requires so many things external to him, must often act from other motives. The condition of human nature were peculiarly hard, if those affections, which, by the very nature of our being, ought frequently to influence our conduct, could upon no occasion appear virtuous, or deserve esteem and commendation from any body.[20]

Hutcheson's benevolence is not relevant for humans. By definition, God the Creator already has the entire Universe and all within it at His disposal and, needing nothing from anybody else, He is able to be benevolent in the infinite extreme. No matter how much He gives to all the entities in all of His Kingdoms ('In my Father's house are many mansions'),[21] He has infinite amounts more of everything (love included) to give away than any man has or could have, and greater amounts in his gift than all the riches and love of mankind put together. To see the religious duty of mankind to imitate the perfect standards set by God sets all men an impossible and utterly unrealistic goal.

This has to be a debilitating blow to Hutcheson's benevolence as man's supreme virtue. What is Smith's alternative? He writes: 'whatever may be the case with the Deity', man's very many imperfections, including his having many needs and scarce resources, means that his conduct will of necessity always fall short of the ideal and, therefore, he 'must often act from other motives' besides perpetual and pure benevolence. The human condition, asserts Smith, would be 'peculiarly hard' if we could upon no occasion act from motives, which lacked virtue.[22] The very nature of our condition may drive us to act in this manner from inferior motives, and as he points out elsewhere, our motives, despite their lack of pure virtue, may produce unintentional virtuous outcomes.

In *Wealth of Nations* he developed this theme in harmony with, and not in contradiction to, *Moral Sentiments*. There is absolutely no doubt, from the clear internal evidence in *Moral Sentiments*[23] that Smith loyally presents his teacher's views, not his own. Das Adam Smith problem is buried (yet again).[24]

10
A Poem about a Louse

One way to pass through your mind's window into Smith's theory of the impartial spectator is to start with a poem by Robert Burns:

> 'O wad some Pow'r the giftie gie us
> To see oursels as ithers see us!
> It wad frae monie a blunder free us,
> An' foolish notion;'[1]

Translating Scots into English drains its poetic power: 'We would save ourselves from many a blunder and foolish notion if only we could see ourselves as others see us.'

Robert Burns (or Burness) was born in 1759, the same year Smith published *Moral Sentiments*. He was a young contemporary of Adam Smith and, during the winter of 1786–7, Burns tried to meet him in Edinburgh but Smith was too ill to socialise, though they were at the same meeting of a Masonic lodge on at least one occasion.[2] It is said that *Moral Sentiments* influenced Burns composition of the above lines.[3]

Unlike Smith, who theorised about the consequences of imagining how other people in the persona of 'impartial spectators' might judge our behaviour, Burns wrote of our blindness to the perceptions of others and how our vanity masks our imperfections. In truth, others who weigh us in the balance find us wanting (as we do them). Powerful poetry indeed! On hearing Burns' lines we often assume that his poem applies to others, not ourselves. How vulnerable we are to foolish and petty vanities!

Burns' poem is a way into Smith's 'impartial spectator'. Both men would have agreed that 'to see oursels as ithers see us' expresses their different perspectives; Burns, pessimistically, reminding us of human frailty and its consequences, and Smith, optimistically, mapping how humans develop and maintain their moral senses. Smith, contrary to the poet's assertion, says we do have the power 'to see oursels as ithers see us' and he explains how. We have this power, if we wish to use it, from what we may crudely describe as akin to a conscience (though it was much more) in a weak resistance to self-deceit.

Smith is explicit and his stance inspired Burns' verse:

... self-deceit, this fatal weakness of mankind, is the source of half the disorders of human life. If we saw ourselves in the light in which others see us, or in which they would see us if they knew all, a reformation would generally be unavoidable. We could not otherwise endure the sight.[4]

Burns' editors (Messrs. Noble and Hogg) comment that his poem:

should also remind us not to read 'O was some Pow'r the giftie gie us/*to see oursels as ithers see us*!' as a piece of sententious sentimentality but Burns' two line demolition of Adam Smith's concept of the creation of [an] internalised spectator in his *Theory of Moral Sentiments* as a form of secular conscience adequate to controlling our materialism and social pretentiousness.[5]

The editors, unlike Burns, forgot Smith on 'self-deceit, this fatal weakness of mankind'.

It is not enough for sentiments to depend on the dictates of proper conduct, such as a virtuous sense of propriety, duty, prudence or benevolence, and it certainly is not enough to depend on rational exhortations of the 'right' thing to do for the 'good' of society. Nor are virtuous sentiments dictated by our fear of transgressing God's laws in the hope of His promises of Heaven or our fear of Hell's fire. Something much stronger is needed to bind people to proper conduct, for in its absence we become a rude and fractious people. *Moral Sentiments* was the theory of that 'something much stronger'!

Hobbesian nightmares?

Moral Sentiments explains why some people abide by and practise the manners and associated politeness conducive to civil peace. While the prevalence of moral sentiments aided social stability in civil society, Smith acknowledged the necessity for civil magistrates to resort on occasion to dreadful punishments against those who flouted the law and disturbed the peace.

Every man, Smith asserted, is:

no doubt, by nature, first and principally recommended to his own care; and as he is fitter to take care of himself than of any other person, it is fit and right that it should be so.[6]

We are deeply interested in whatever concerns ourselves and less concerned with others. We are not best judges of the interests of anybody else. However, the pursuit of self-love is not a licence to violently plunder others:

> To disturb [a neighbour's] happiness merely because it stands in the way of our own, to take from him what is of real use to him merely because it may be of equal or more use to us, or to indulge, in this manner, at the expense of other people, the natural preference which every man has for his own happiness above that of other people, is what no impartial spectator can go along with.[7]

If we are solely concerned with ourselves is mankind incited to the permanent war of the egos? Not at all! Raging self-love does not dominate the social intercourse of mankind, because, paradoxically, no ego can acquire what it wants without the peaceful co-operation of other egos, and it is that dependence, effectively total, that safeguards society from self-destruction (though a megalomaniac can do a lot of damage until restrained).

Smith did not subscribe to an apocalyptic 'war of all against all' and neither should you. Human behaviour curbed outrageous expressions of egoism, enabling mankind to live in society, and it was human nature, not government, which preserved us from the Hobbesian nightmare of lives that were 'solitary, poor, nasty, brutish and short'.[8]

Every person knows that no matter how egoistic we feel, others do not share our feelings; they care for themselves with the same degree of passion as we do for ourselves. For a tiny minority, untrammelled egoism leads to degrees of psychopathic paranoia, but the majority of us express concerns for others and temper the grosser manifestations of our egos.

Each of us may be a lonely ego in a sea of indifference to others but none of us dare assume that other people are indifferent to the impact of our actions on them. If we do, the brute course of retributive events soon educates us otherwise. Where our actions impinge on their self-love they react with the same hostility as we might towards anybody impinging on ours. Observation of how others react to our intrusions on them, compared to how we react to the intrusions of others, eventually informs the dullest that mindless egoism breaches acceptable behavioural norms and provokes dangerous hostility and harmful counter-measures. We easily spot the relationship between their inflicting behavioural atrocities on others and the retribution of those so affected.

Smith asserted that no man would dare to look mankind in the face and declare his intention of acting according to the dictates of his self-love. His fellows could never go along with such an explicit, 'excessive and extravagant' disregard for their interests and such a person risked severe disapproval. The perpetrator 'must, upon this, as upon all other occasions, humble the arrogance of his self-love' and, in consequence, bring public displays of his undoubted self-love 'down to something which other men can go along with'.[9]

The majority of people, whose egos are humbled by acknowledging in their behaviour the legitimacy of the self-love of others, thrive in socially stable societies in the sure and safe knowledge that their person, property, possessions and rights are secure from the depredations of neighbours.[10]

In the personal struggle for the place, position and prizes in life there are constraints on each person's conduct. Blatant disregard for others invites retribution and disapprobation in defence of their legitimate self-love:

> In the race for wealth, and honours, and preferments, he may run as hard as he can, and strain every nerve and every muscle, in order to outstrip all his competitors. But if he should justle [sic], or throw down any of them, the indulgence of the spectators is entirely at an end.[11]

People cannot abide foul play. They sympathise with the injured and the offender suffers the hatred and indignation bursting out from all sides against him. The game of life has rules and norms, and players are expected more or less to abide by them. Society, for peace to prevail, ruthlessly remedies defections from its norms by submitting solitary egoists to an impartial system of justice.

The shameless individual who intrudes upon the persons, property, possessions or rights of others and who is careless of the 'shame, horror and consternation' he causes, suffers from those he provokes because his crimes 'call loudest for vengeance and punishment'. In the extreme, the unremitting hostility, vengeance and punishment he suffers causes him the 'greatest and most dreadful distress' and 'incomprehensible misery and ruin'.[12]

The only way out of constant isolation and prolonged pariah status is that deep feeling of regret or 'remorse', which Smith thought was the most dreadful of 'all the sentiments', and he agreed with Lord Kames, who called it 'the most severe of all tortures.'[13] Smith acknowledged that there were individuals with untrammelled egos and a determination to ride roughshod over others, but he regarded them as in a minority.

11

The Impartial Spectator

Smith's impartial spectator contributed to the debate on why society held together despite all the dreadful things that humans living in close proximity could do to each other. It fits into his general model of society.

All men are selfish, yet all men take an interest in the fortunes of others and are happy when other men are happy and derive some pleasure from their happiness, and also derive sorrow from the sorrow of others. So obvious are these sentiments, Smith claimed they required no proof. Yet this theme pervades all of his philosophy. And, by appealing to your common experience that did not need proof, he had a point. He assures us that even 'the greatest ruffian, the most hardened violator of the laws of society,' is not altogether bereft of universal sentiments.[1] There are some principles so deep in man's nature that all men feel them to some degree. Neither governments nor preachers invented goodness.

We cannot see inside the minds of other people, or have direct knowledge of how they feel or what they intend. Our mind's limitations imprison us. We can only imagine what we would feel if we were in their situation.[2] When we observe incidents affecting other people, we imagine ourselves in their situation. And when we observe a particularly dramatic situation – someone about to suffer a blow to their arm or leg, or a dancer on a tightrope swaying to hold proper balance, or the exposed sores of a beggar in the street, or someone with sore eyes – we draw back the same limb, sway slightly in like manner to the tightrope dancer, feel an itch in the same places as the beggar's bodily sores and feel a soreness in our eyes too.[3]

Smith introduces his 'attentive spectator', or the 'bystander', whose sympathetic emotions always correspond to what we imagine should be the sentiments of the persons we observe in their various situations. And what is true for us is true for everybody else!

As Shakespeare wrote:

> All the world's a stage,
> And all the men and women merely players:

They have their exits and their entrances;
And one man in his time plays many parts.[4]

Smith's world is about real players, not 'actors', though he makes full use the imagery of the theatre to help his readers understand his message.[5]

Everybody playing is aware of others watching, as if players are also spectators and spectators are also players. Players imagine how spectators regard whatever they do or experience; spectators imagine how players feel about their experiences. Whichever role we play, as player or spectator, and no matter how many times we switch between them, sympathy is the common factor in both.

Smith takes the notion of the spectator a step further. He asks us to think of the spectator as present 'in the breast', in our imagination, and operating on our behaviour as if we know he watches what we are doing. This imaginary spectator, no less real in his effects on our behaviour, has the same characteristics as an anonymous stranger, specifically in his disinterest for or against our fortune or misfortune. He is neither disposed in our favour nor ill disposed against us. He is *impartial*, and acts at all times as the *impartial spectator* of our conduct, and whose approach to us is one of impartial human sympathy.

It is most important that you understand that Smith refers not just to the human sympathies of 'pity or compassion' associated with a deep and genuine understanding of the sorrows and sufferings of others. Smith specifically uses the word sympathy to denote our feelings for any human passion 'of which the mind of man is susceptible,' including sympathy for the great joy someone experiences from a happy event.[6] And to make sure that this is clearly understood, he repeats himself by using sympathy 'to denote our fellow feeling with any passion whatever'. Sympathy, then, is not confined to the commonly accepted sympathetic passions of 'benevolence' or 'altruism'.[7] Smithian sympathy applies to every passion we can experience. Perhaps the ability to share or understand another person's feelings, irrespective of their causes and mood, or *empathy*, is a better name for his meaning than sympathy, though not all would agree with me on that.

The spectator's compassion is limited to how he imagines he would feel if he was in our situation and, because he cannot have a perfect understanding of how we feel about our situation unless he was in it, we cannot expect him to feel as strongly as we do about the source of our feelings. And that is the edge Smith develops to explain how humans find harmony in their relationships. How, for instance, can someone else, even a friend, feel as we do in matters of love and romance? His imagination does not contemplate our lover in the same light and to him our passion appears 'ridiculous', though we are pardoned because 'love' is considered natural to persons of a 'certain age'. A lover, notes Smith somewhat sardonically, 'may be good company to his mistress, he is so to nobody else.'[8]

When the spectator contemplates impartially the object of his observations, as most spectators must do because we have fewer friends – even counting distant acquaintances – than the rest of mankind added together, his compassion is unlikely to be swayed by positive or negative prejudices for or against us. But such sympathy as he expresses is enough to enliven our joy or alleviate our grief, though the benefits of the latter are much stronger than those of the former.[9] To share sympathy for something that already brings us great joy, enlivens our joy but does not change it. His sympathy when something untoward or unpleasant happens to us lessens our grief because we feel better for knowing we share our burdens. Rehearsing the causes of our grief reminds us of the pain we felt and, sometimes, the very tears we shed. But in the process of retelling and receiving the sweetness of sympathy we are compensated for the bitterness of our sorrows.[10]

Harmonising influences of impartial spectators

Feelings of sympathy are proportionate. If we approve of the intensity of the passions exhibited by other persons in their reaction to a joyful or a grievous incident, we sympathise entirely, but not so when they over react. Those observing or hearing of our outburst at some trivial or imagined affront would not regard it to be proportionate if we threaten suicide or murder. The propriety or proportionality of over-reactive behaviour, remember, is judged by the impartial observer not by the player.

The greater or lesser the dissonance between my sentiments and yours, the lesser or greater the sympathy we feel for each other.[11] In common life, we observe in others their 'excesses of love, of grief, of resentment' and we contemplate the 'ruinous effects they tend to produce', especially when we also observe the 'little occasion which was given for them.' Nothing we see justifies 'so violent a passion' as is exhibited. In contrast, when we find that the sentiments 'coincide and tally with our own, we necessarily approve of them as proportional and suitable', but when they do not we 'disapprove of them as extravagant and out of proportion.'[12] In the extreme, if it's my love, grief, or resentment I feel and you do not have any feeling for my evident distress, I am not going to tolerate your company. You are 'confounded by my violence and passion and I am enraged by your cold insensibility and want of feeling.'[13]

Experience of dissonance in feelings is common. Everybody has occasion to be angry at someone else's behaviour and, when we recount the cause of our anger, we sometimes find others less sympathetic to our sense of outrage. Social pressures reduce the heat of passion. A friend's sympathy calms our anger or grief somewhat, because we expect his sympathy and if it is given even in some small degree (the 'but' comes later!) it reduces our outrage. The sympathy of an acquaintance to a lesser degree has a similar effect because we expect less from them; if they proffer total sympathy we recognise them in a new, friendlier, light. The way we express our feelings to a group of strangers, from whom we expect minimal sympathy, calms us yet further but for different reasons. Anticipating minimal sympathy we try to 'maximise' what little we anticipate, by reducing the vehemence of our passion to a pitch with 'which the spectators are capable of going along'.[14]

It is exactly the same when someone exhibits joy at an event that is way beyond what we consider it to be worth and continuing the celebrations for months would tire even the most sympathetic person, let alone an impartial spectator. Proportionality is the rule for both sorrow and joy. Modesty in both sorrow and joy is expected if you expect the approval of the impartial spectator.

While reporting to a close friend an incident that hurt us, privately we might express emotional outrage, but we will be less emotional when explaining our distress to an acquaintance, and probably we will speak with measured calmness when explaining what happened to strangers in public. The observable fact that feelings are lowered in intensity as social distance increases is the harmonising mechanism ascribed by Smith to the impartial spectator. It makes it possible to live in society with strangers, even though each individual looks after his or her own interests first and foremost.

The idea that the ego seeks to gratify self-love does not account for the predicament of the individual living in a society of strangers, with few friends or family. Smith's contribution was to realise that the existence of the self-love model, while plausible for the individual, as if on a desert island, was not plausible for individuals living in close proximity and almost totally dependent upon each other.

The key to how this predicament could function without society tearing itself apart lay in the simple observation of how the intensity of feelings about anybody else's behaviour diminished as the irate individual in search of sympathy interacted with others further from his or her immediate circle of family and friends.[15] Sympathy is given or withheld according to how the cause of the grievance justifies its intensity and the individual can only obtain the sympathy he seeks 'by lowering his passion to that pitch, in which the spectators are capable of going along with him.' He has to flatten the 'sharpness of its natural tone, in order to reduce it to harmony and concord with the emotions of those who are about him.'[16]

While perfect harmony of the passions between the affected individual and an impartial spectator is unlikely, the fact that the intensity with which the passions are expressed is reduced is sufficient for a degree of (workable) harmony to prevail. The individual moderates his or her ego-driven behaviour towards a level likely to be accepted as proportionate by the unaffected spectators who, in turn, moderate their criticism of the individual's behaviour. The spectators constantly re-consider what they would feel if they were in the position of the players they observe and, crucially, the players under observation constantly moderate what they would feel if they were only spectators and not players.

Each reciprocal review of the appropriate amount of sympathy and degree of passion serves to abate the violence of the individual's passions and reduce the criticism of the spectators, particularly if this interchange of views is facilitated by 'society and conversation'.[17] We are compelled thereby, and almost in spite of ourselves, to 'see ourselves as others see us.' The result for society is a greater degree of tranquillity than would be thought likely in a society composed of individual egos who ignore (or defy) their spectators.

The impartial spectator restrains individuals from unbridled expressions of their passions in pursuit of their interests and confines them only to pursue their interests to the extent that is equitable and proportionate to what indifferent persons 'would rejoice to see executed.'[18] From this binding relationship, for example, we restrain our selfish aspirations and indulge our benevolent affections, and through this harmony of the sentiments and passions, if we succeed, we move towards, without ever reaching, the perfection of human nature, which alone produces in mankind that harmony of the sentiments and passions, and its 'grace and propriety.'[19]

12
The Looking Glass

Smith asserts that we approve or disapprove of our conduct according to how we imagine others see, or are likely to see, our behaviour. In short, we try to anticipate the views of the 'fair and impartial spectator' and only approve of our conduct if it receives 'the approbation of this supposed equitable judge.' Otherwise we condemn and restrain it.[1]

It is from the social pressure of living in society that we obtain our judgement as to the merits or demerits of our behaviours. It would be easy to overlook this observation. Smith dramatises it neatly. Suppose a person grew to adulthood without contact or communication with fellow members of the human species. In these circumstances, asserts Smith, 'he could no more think of his own character, of the propriety or demerit of his own sentiments and conduct, of the beauty or deformity of his own mind, than of the beauty or deformity of his own face.'[2]

Why? Because he has 'no mirror to present them to his own view.'[3] And the mirror in this sense is Smith's powerful metaphor for what living in society does to a person's sense of character and beauty. Society mirrors our person, giving feedback on what is and what is not acceptable in our behaviour.[4] What disgusts our neighbours cautions us; what pleases them, satisfies us. We 'endeavour, as much as possible, to view ourselves at the distance and with the eyes of other people.'[5]

Contrary to Burns, we are not indifferent guardians of our reputations. Other people, in practice, are the 'looking-glass' by which we see ourselves through their eyes, not ours. Once satisfied with what we believe they see (beware hubris!), we are less flattered by the applause of some and less bothered by the censures of others if, in the main, what we believe they see indicates natural and proper approval of our behaviour.

In like manner, we criticise the moral character and conduct of others in so far as they might affect us and we are 'very forward' in expressing our views. But this traffic is not all one-way. We soon learn that others are equally forward in their criticisms of us! This causes us to review our conduct by imagining how we appear in the eyes of others. If we wish to become less worthy of censure and more worthy of praise, we must discover how we might improve our behaviour. In effect we become 'the spectators of our own behaviour' and we imagine how other people 'scrutinize the propriety of our own conduct' in their eyes, not ours.[6]

When other people sharply divide in their sentiments towards us, whom do we believe, our friends or our critics? If we believe what we see in the looking glass of the spectator, we are 'tolerably satisfied' and can discount the applause and downplay any censure. On the other hand, we may be doubtful about the merits of their disapprobation, and provided we know we have not already 'shaken hands with infamy', we are doubly struck with the severity of their disapproval. But if we are secure in our beliefs that we are 'the natural and proper objects of approbation', because our imagined spectator's view of us is 'tolerably satisfied', we may reject misunderstandings and misrepresentations of our conduct by others.[7]

Smith's argument takes us right back to Burns' scepticism: can people really see themselves as others see them? Smith's response is ingenious, though perhaps a trifle laboured.

The two in one persona

It is not enough to deny the existence of Smith's impartial spectator. He admits that they are imaginary constructs in the mind. Nor can we simply assert that people who do not know us cannot judge our conduct. We know that people do observe others, including strangers, and we know that they judge, as we do, their conduct. True, the judgements of people who know us are often coloured by their views about us for good or ill, but that is why Smith points to the impartiality of his imaginary spectators, which mutes their prejudices for or against those whom they observe.

Imaginary impartial spectators are projected as both external to the persons influenced by their presence and internal to the same persons. They have a dual existence in the imagination. Using the first person, he describes the division of himself into two persons: one is the 'examiner and judge'; the second is the self who 'is examined and judged'. The first self is the spectator, whose sentiments Smith endeavours to 'enter into' by 'placing myself in his situation, and by considering how it would appear to the spectator, when seen from that particular point of view'; the second self is the 'agent', the person called Smith, i.e., himself, about whom the first self was endeavouring to form an opinion. The first 'judges', the second, is judged.[8]

That all persons in society consist of two such personae in one is the source of 'that inward tranquillity and self-satisfaction' which arises from the belief that our virtue is meritorious in the eyes of others. If we had suspicions or doubts to the contrary, our suspicions would be 'torments of vice'. Smith was not so inept as to fail to see where his argument could lead in the hands of a hostile critic. Virtue, he states, is not meritorious because it is the object of 'self-love' but because 'it excites those sentiments in other men.' You cannot pronounce yourself virtuous anymore than you can pronounce yourself dead. To be 'beloved' and to know that we 'deserve to be beloved' is the source of 'great happiness'; to be 'hated' and to know we 'deserve to be hated' is the cause of great personal misery.[9]

In society, we are aware of each other's views and we are careful to act in a manner that gains the approval, and avoids the disapproval, of others. Making a conversational gaffe is disconcerting in any social situation and the consequences are not confined to any particular social class. A gaffe in a group of social misfits can lead to a life threatening violent outburst; in a middle class drawing room the outcome may be just as serious in their terms from the social ostracism it may provoke; and in all cases it is treated as personally humiliating and long remembered by companions, hostile and friendly, as a source of mocking humour and embarrassment. In French, *faux pas* signifies this experience, and the avoidance of a *faux pas* with its unintended disapproval by others is a strong social imperative.

We care about what other people think of us, especially if we have high regard for their views. And this leads to that most powerful mechanism in Smith's impartiality model based on the difference between being praised and being praiseworthy.[10]

Each person desires not just to be praised but also to be 'praiseworthy' and not just to avoid blame but also to avoid being 'blameworthy'. The impartial spectator observes our behaviour as if through the eyes of others, or as they are likely to view our behaviour, and this constrains our behaviour within tolerable limits. If we note that our behaviour meets with approval, we become happy and content and if we observe others confirming our views of how the impartial spectator views our behaviour, we strengthen our sense of praise-worthiness. Those others, of whose character and conduct we approve, are models of behaviour worthy of emulation, which is founded in our admiration of their excellence. This turns us into impartial spectators viewing our own character and conduct 'with the eyes of other people, or as other people are likely to view them'.[11]

But what constrains us from self-delusion or of undeserved self-approbation by our acting the impostor and seeing ourselves through our own eyes and not those of a genuine impartial spectator? Surely his impartial spectator could derive any conclusion any person felt inclined to accept about his conduct and character. Smith responds by distinguishing between the consequences of love of praise and the love of praise-worthiness.

'If we are conscious that we do not deserve' praise and that 'if the truth were known, we should be regarded with very different sentiments' then 'our satisfaction is far from being complete'. Anybody who 'applauds us' for 'actions we did not perform' applauds 'another person'. Being thought of that 'other person' is 'more mortifying than any censure'.[12]

Smith is quite strident about the discomfort of receiving praise for which we are not worthy. Clearly, the distinction was important to him. It is 'proof of the most superficial levity and weakness', he says and it is 'vanity' and the 'foundation of the most ridiculous and contemptible vices, the vices of affectation and common lying; follies which, if experience did not teach us how common they are, one should imagine the least spark of common sense would save us from'. Smith accurately describes the sentiments repeated in Burns' poem:

> Their superficial weakness and trivial folly hinder them from ever turning their eyes inwards, or from seeing themselves in that despicable point of view in which their own consciences must tell them that they would appear to every body, if the real truth should ever come to be known.[13]

What if we are applauded for things we did not do or deserve? Such vanity arises from 'so gross an illusion of the imagination, that it is difficult to conceive how any rational creature should be imposed upon by it.' Praised people who are not praiseworthy know in all conscience that others view them as despicable (even laughable) but they persist with the illusion that they are viewed differently. Little wonder that Smith did not hide his contempt for such silly people, and in this he concurs completely with the sentiments of Burns about the silly lady with the louse on her silly hat.

13
Social Cohesion

From self to society

Truly, man shall not live by bread alone,[1] but neither does he live alone. All 18th-century explanations for why humans *first* grouped together in society are redundant; humans have always lived in societies. There never was a time when individual *Homo sapiens* lived alone – except for a handful of 'eccentric' individuals and outcasts. The vast majority lived in extended 'families' or small bands. Humans lived in 'families', which grew into bands and regularly split apart in high dudgeon (human nature being what it is).

Humans had the warmest affections, after themselves, for their parents (or at least for their mothers, whom they could reliably identify), brothers and sisters, 'spouses' and their children. Their sympathy for them approached what they felt for themselves,[2] though feelings were uneven (human nature again!). While exhibiting gratitude for their parents, their affections for their children were, or ought to have been, stronger. The human child is absolutely helpless for its first years and relatively so until maturity. An old man can die lonely and unlamented; and in an age of high child mortality, scarce a child can die 'without rending asunder the heart of somebody.'[3]

People living in the same house develop appropriate affections for each other, though Smith, fully informed on family 'politics', recognised that all may not be right in every household. We are shocked, he says, to discover discord in the affections that members of the same family feel for each other and we may well regard signs of this discord as of 'the highest impropriety, and sometimes even a sort of impiety'.[4]

From society to strangers

Ties of blood bind people (i.e., 'blood is thicker than water'), though Smith mocked authors of 'tragedies and romances' who imagined a 'force of blood' being so powerful that it manifested itself even before the relations knew they were related! He said that 'such mysterious affection' was 'too ridiculous' to imagine.[5] Neighbours have a similar effect, provided no offence is committed (because neighbours can be 'very convenient' or 'very troublesome'). Smith's assertions were born of realism: a 'bad neighbour is a very bad character', he declared.[6]

People who associate with the 'wise and the virtuous' cannot help but pick up some of their habits and those who associate with the 'profligate and the dissolute' lose their original abhorrence of profligacy and the dissolution of manners.[7] The virtuous have an important role for it is from beneficence, or kindness and generosity properly distributed among others, that Nature's intentions are fulfilled. And Nature, which intended man to be mutually kind, arranges it so that men are most kind to those who are kind to them, which, in turn, renders each man the object of the kindness of others to whom he has been kind. Reciprocal kindness ('one good turn deserves another') binds men to society; reciprocal enmity dissolves it ('one bad turn deserves another').[8]

There were people distinguished by 'their extraordinary situation', which Smith described as 'the greatly fortunate' rich and powerful, matched by 'the greatly unfortunate' poor and wretched. The former are respected because 'the distinction of ranks' and the 'peace and order of society' are founded on respect of the less 'great' for the truly 'great'.[9] His pupil, John Millar, took up this theme and, way ahead of his time, expressed sympathy for female inequality.[10] For Smith, being fortunate or unfortunate had nothing to with fairness; it was how it was, that's all.

Again, being pragmatic more than sympathetic, our benevolence towards the greatly fortunate and the rich and powerful is more important than it is to the greatly unfortunate and the poor and wretched, because 'the peace and order of society is more important than even the relief of the miserable.'[11] Smith was not saying that the 'relief of the miserable' was unimportant and not a proper object of policy. He simply meant that 'peace and order', if threatened, should take precedence over poor relief, an altogether different proposition.

It is easier for the 'mob of mankind' to recognise the 'plain and palpable difference of birth and fortune' (they behave differently) than for them to recognise the 'invisible and often uncertain difference of wisdom and virtue' (which even the wise and virtuous had difficulty in discerning). Nature's 'benevolent wisdom' makes the distinction in ranks and the peace and order of society a consequence of the people's 'fascination for greatness'.[12]

The human need for society

Why then do we live with others? Notwithstanding a few hermits, a singular society must end inevitably in the barren life and lonely death of the one who forms it. Smith, therefore, insists that man 'can subsist only in society' and that man was 'fitted by nature to that situation for which he was made'.[13]

There are significant benefits from living in society. All humans need the assistance of others and all are exposed to mutual injuries. Societies may flourish where mutual assistance is reciprocated from 'love, from gratitude, from friendship, and esteem' (high expectations, indeed!),[14] but those who live in flourishing, stable societies, may not reciprocate mutual assistance and be bound together at all times by 'the agreeable bands of love and affection'. The necessary assistance which each requires is not absolutely dependent on the dictates of mutual love and affection; these dictates, in fact, can be absent without society dissolving into a 'fratricidal' bloodbath.

Smith foreshadows where his thinking was to take him in the opening chapters of *Wealth of Nations*. Societies can hold together and

> may subsist among different men, as among different merchants, from a sense of its utility, without any mutual love and affection; and though no man in it should owe any obligation, or be bound in gratitude to any other, it may still be upheld *by a mercenary exchange of good offices according to an agreed valuation.*[15] [emphasis added]

The binding link is a 'mercenary exchange' (bereft of positive feelings) 'according to an agreed valuation' attained by means of voluntarily negotiated agreements that define the ratio of the exchange of the 'good offices' to their 'valuation.' In short, the binding essence of society is negotiation between strangers, who may not, and need not, feel 'mutual love and affection'.

However, Smith hasn't finished, because while 'mutual love and affection' are never essential, though they may be desirable, what is certainly essential is that no society can 'subsist among those who are at all times ready to hurt and injure one another.' A society of robbers and murders must at least 'abstain from robbing and murdering each other' and, therefore, 'beneficence is less essential to society than justice' because, though society can subsist uncomfortably without beneficence, 'the prevalence of injustice must utterly destroy it.'[16] We can live in a stable society without mutual love, but not with mutual hate.

Mankind is exhorted to beneficent acts but is not punished for their absence because, while beneficence is not the foundation of society; justice, on the contrary, is:

> the main pillar that upholds the whole edifice. If it is removed, the great, the immense fabric of human society ... must in a moment crumble into atoms. In order to enforce the observation of justice, therefore, Nature has implanted in the human breast that consciousness of ill desert, those terrors of merited punishment which attend upon its

violation, as the great safe-guards of the association of mankind, to protect the weak, to curb the violent, and to chastise the guilty.[17]

As shown in *Wealth of Nations*, reciprocal mutual assistance to meet essential (even frivolous) needs can be accommodated at a highly complex level between persons who scarce, or don't, know to whom they provide mutual assistance and from whom they receive assistance in return. Economic transactions differ from personal relationships because economic transactions, by persons unknown and at great social distance, can affect anonymous beneficiaries far removed socially and geographically from each other.[18]

We live in societies because we thrive in the company of others and because we cannot survive easily or for long on our own. We benefit sufficiently from the universal human habit of living in societies to compensate for its, sometimes, serious disadvantages, among which we observe that wherever humans congregate there is always a risk of depredations and harm of various kinds from neighbours. In need of each other's assistance we expose ourselves to mutual injuries.

In the ideal world, as imagined by utopians, like the gentle anarchist, Peter Kropotkin, mutual assistance could be proffered by reciprocal gestures and by the pure motives of love, gratitude, friendship and esteem.[19] If it were so arranged, human society could flourish and enjoy mass uninterrupted happiness, with everybody striving for the common good. Unfortunately, neither humans nor their societies are like that, though some individuals may be so inclined, perhaps a few on all occasions, but most unlikely for all of them on all occasions. Something else was needed.

If the intensity of affections declines from self to family, to friends, to acquaintances and to strangers, actual, as opposed to idealistic, societies need something to sustain the exchange of mutual assistance. Imperfect societies survive from the poverty of alternatives and there is a high threshold for sub-optimal mutual behaviour before they become dysfunctional and self-destructive failed societies. Flourishing societies can succumb, there being nothing inevitable about continual progress, or about the perfectibility of humanity.

We do not assist others from some general notion of our love of humanity; we assist strangers, for whom we feel nothing special (and may not even know) from the anonymous assistance we give in reciprocation of the anonymous assistance given to us. Mutual assistance, without the need for mutual affection, is one of the unnoticed benefits of commercial society and, once we recognise this, as shown in *Moral Sentiments*, then Smith's connecting principle in *Wealth of Nations* takes shape. The theme of his Legacy is defined.

If we cannot rely on the 'love and affection' of others for our needs and if men were determined to harm their neighbours, how can we live safely in close proximity to others whose dispositions towards us are not easily discernible? Men feel so little for each other, compared to what they feel for themselves, that they have the power to hurt each other and have many temptations to do so, and, Smith adds sombrely, unless they were somehow overawed to respect each other, they would 'like wild beasts' be ready to attack each other violently, and each man would join an assembly of men 'as he enters a den of lions'.[20] (A simile owed to Montesquieu: 'Without [justice] we would be in continual terror; we would move among men as among lions'.)[21]

Adequate as Smith's arguments and assertions are, they seem to dissolve into doubts, like a sauce hiding temporarily what it disguises. Some people become overawed at the thought of the dependence of all upon all, assured only by 'mercenary exchanges' and not by sentiments. Attempts to bind society by sentiments, and hostility to 'mercenary exchanges', inevitably leads to unsentimental tyranny, of which the communist experiments of the last century were potent examples.

14
The Ends of Nature

If we wish to understand human nature we have to visit the guiding principle of human existence.[1] Smith anticipated this notion and it brought him closest to a religious explanation of the themes of *Moral Sentiments*. Smith, however, ducked a potential religious challenge to his ideas by writing in an overtly religious 'code' that appeared to accept the Deistic verities. By doing so he escaped the morbid attention of zealots.

Smith was talking about matters of fact and not about matters of right.[2] He was not interested in how a perfect being would approve of the punishment of bad actions. He was interested in the principles upon which 'so weak and imperfect a creature as man'[3] in practice approves of those punishments, 'wisely ordered' by Nature (and, variously, the 'Author of Nature'; the 'Director of Nature'). Nobody needed to be a philosopher to know that the very existence of society required that unmerited and unprovoked malice be properly punished and that the infliction of punishment to this end was laudable and proper.

Smith resorts to referring to 'the Author of nature', who chose not to rely on man's rational faculties to discover by trial and error over long periods that only punishment can protect society's welfare and preserve its existence. Instead, 'the Author of nature' chose to endow man with 'immediate and instinctive'[4] approval of proper punishment to attain the desired end of preserving society. It was as if He had hard-wired this endowment into our brains, so to speak. Moreover, the 'economy of nature', in this and other instances, endowed man not just with an appetite for the end its Author had intended, but He also endowed him with an appetite for the means by which alone this end could be brought about. In this, the Author of Nature acted in the best interests of man so that, independent of any man's intentions, men will act to attain the two great ends intended by Nature, namely that of 'self-preservation' and 'the propagation of the species'. Thus, he disguised his radical ideas in Deistic code.

Man desires Nature's ends and is averse to contrary outcomes. He is imbued with a 'love of life' and a 'dread' of death, with a desire for his species to continue in perpetuity and an aversion to thoughts of its extinction. The 'desire for his species to continue in perpetuity' seems a rather unreliable way of expressing the 'Author of Nature's' intentions; is it credible that the average individual had such an exalted notion of his life's mission? More likely, as Smith concedes, the instrument to achieve 'the Author's' purpose was the human indulgence in the sex instinct for its own sake, rather than a mission driven by notions of species propagation through pregnancy. Whether it would be appropriate for Smith to say so to his younger students probably prompted his aversion to such blatant impropriety.

The closest Smith gets to raw bluntness is to say that to have left the beneficent ends of self-preservation and the propagation of the species to the 'slow and uncertain determinations of reason' would have been too risky, hence, by entrusting them to the more certain 'original and immediate instincts' of 'hunger, thirst, the passions which unite the two sexes, the love of pleasure and the dread of pain', the 'Director of nature' allied ordinary men to His intentions without them having to know anything about rational philosophy.[5]

Life itself is the great objective of Nature and the 'Author of Nature' instilled basic instincts for which man has a permanent appetite. Threats to these ends produce in man the 'passions' that cause countervailing acts to protect the self from destruction and dissolution and, by so doing, enable the two sexes to live long enough to breed and nurture their offspring. It was not 'reason' that enabled our ancestors, in an unbroken chain from them to us, to live long enough to breed, but their pursuit of their natural 'passions' for their own sake. Smith neatly avoids elaborating on the original cause of 'Nature's ends'!

As the same instinctive rules for the preservation of life and the propagation of the species apply to all societies, even those of 'robbers and murderers', and, by legitimate extension, those of all forms of governance, monarchical, aristocratic, democratic, republican, barbarian and savage, Smith shows that men act to preserve society from self-destruction under the imperatives of nature, not their faculties of reason. 'No social intercourse can take place among men who do not generally abstain from injuring one another'[6] and all societies, in their way, punish those who violate their laws and their systems of justice. As the destruction of a society is abhorrent to all men, they will do all they can to 'hinder so hated and dreadful an event', including the use of 'force and violence.' In a passage dripping with rage at lawbreakers, he sanctions the mob's blood lust:

Injustice necessarily tends to destroy [society]. Every appearance of injustice [i.e., criminals 'getting away' with their crimes, not breaches of their human rights!] therefore alarms him, and he runs, if I may say so, to stop the progress of what, if allowed to go on, would quickly put an end to every thing that is dear to him. If he cannot restrain it by gentle and fair means, he must beat it down by force and violence, and at any rate must put a stop to its further progress. Hence it is, they say, that he often approves of the enforcement of the laws of justice even by capital punishment of those who violate them. The disturber of the public peace is hereby removed out of the world, and others are terrified by his fate from imitating his example.[7]

Rage cools, the troublemaker is contrite and terrified of his approaching punishment and the 'generous and humane' are 'disposed [to] pardon and forgive him', and they wrestle with their feelings of pity and their consideration of the 'general interest of society', reflecting that 'mercy to the guilty is cruelty to the innocent.'[8]

But few men reflect on the necessity of justice for the existence of society, though 'even the most stupid and unthinking, abhor fraud, perfidy, and injustice' and delight to see offenders punished.[9] Assertion that nature guides men unintentionally on their own account, though consistent with the intentions of the Author of Nature, raises other questions, at least of clarification. If the preservation of society was a sufficient objective for societies since before civilisation, and was effected without reason or moral principles, what role did virtue play?

Smith suggests that because the world judges the outcome of a man's behaviour and not his design (intention), it is a 'great discouragement of virtue'. In practice, he adds, the intentions behind an action have been ascribed to good or bad opinions of its prudence, and our ascription of intention almost always generates our gratitude or resentment and excites our sense of merit or demerit.[10]

Hence, the Author of nature prescribed that it was safer for justice that only a person's actions were subject to approbation or punishment. All sentiments and intentions were taken out of the remit of earthly courts and reserved for the 'unerring tribunal' of 'the great Judge of hearts'.[11] Society dealt with actions in this life, the Deity with intentions in the next.

The virtuous man was made for action and action consists of doing good, and doing good consists specifically of exerting his faculties to change 'the circumstances of both himself and others as may seem most favourable to the happiness of all.'[12]

It is not enough to wish the world prosperity by benign benevolence; the virtuous man must bring this about. And Smith is absolutely insistent on deeds not words.

Like the ripples in a pond, as we act first to do good for those nearest to us (our family), then outwards to the vast body of strangers of whom we know next to nothing. Cropsey writes:

> Nature has disposed us toward individuals and societies in the order of
> their proximity to ourselves; so that we wish most strongly to do the

best first for ourselves, then for our immediate families, then for remoter relatives, next for strangers; and we naturally desire the well being of our own society first, and so on. The rule is proximity, not desert.[13]

Now, as the same imperative of nature operates upon all, it follows that all, or almost all, benefit from the good actions of those to whom they are nearest and they benefit others from their good actions towards them. Everybody is both a friend to some and a stranger to others, living in interlinked and overlapping circles of good and beneficent behaviours that connect us all.[14] The good motives and actions of the virtuous align with society's better interests and where good actions are not linked between persons in close proximity, they are governed by 'mercenary exchanges' which act as surrogates for the good actions of the virtuous. The harmonious essence of *Moral Sentiments* and *Wealth of Nations* is revealed.

Part III
Impartial Jurists

Introduction

After *Moral Sentiments*, Smith remained Professor of Moral Philosophy at Glasgow University for five years. For many years he claimed he was writing 'two other great works', a 'Philosophical History of all the different branches of Literature, of Philosophy, Poetry, and Eloquence; the other is a sort of theory and History of Law and Government'. In 1785 he claimed that 'the materials of both are in good measure collected, and some Part of both is put into tolerable good order.' His explanation for their non-completion at that time was 'the indolence of old age, tho' I struggle violently against it, I feel coming fast upon me, and whether I shall ever be able to finish either is extremely uncertain'.[1] He also hinted at plans to write a treatise on the Greek and Roman Republics.[2]

In the first, and the sixth last edition of TMS that he edited, he announced his intention 'in another discourse' to 'endeavour to give an account of the general principles of law and government, and of the different revolutions which they had undergone in the different ages and periods of society; not only in what concerns police, revenue, and arms, and whatever else is the object of law.'[3] He stated in the 6th edition that he had 'partly executed this promise' in *Wealth of Nations* but what remains, the theory of jurisprudence, which I have long projected, I have hitherto be hindered from executing, by the same occupations which had till now prevented me from revising the present work'. Again he gives the reason as his 'advanced age', which does not explain why he did not complete the work in the thirty one years since his announcement of it in the first edition. He had not 'altogether abandoned the design' and at the time 'entertained no doubt of being able to execute every thing as announced'.[4]

An alternative explanation for the non-appearance of the general principles of law and government is discussed in Part III. I shall refer to the proposed book below as *Jurisprudence*. His ideas on jurisprudence had been given as lectures in Glasgow from 1751 to 1764, and for a century they were believed to have been lost.

However, two sets of student notes for the 1762–3 and 1763–4 academic sessions were discovered, one in 1895 and another in 1958, and from these we get a sense of his theories of justice.[5] His lectures dealt with the general principles of law, illustrated with general points to contemporary practice and discourses on 'the different revolutions which they had undergone in the different ages and periods of society'. We can safely take the notes of his lectures as representative of the contents of his unpublished *Jurisprudence*. While second-hand lecture notes are a barely adequate substitute for his considered prose, they contain surprisingly strong sets of ideas, recognisably smithian in scope, and they are thoroughly consistent with *Moral Sentiments* and *Wealth of Nations*.

Since my purpose is to show Smith's distinctive approach to the history of human society and the evolution of its laws (his Legacy), I extract brutally from the lectures, leaving out most of his detailed arguments. I establish Smith's democratic credentials and his support for the rule of law not men. Government and justice to be trusted to work fairly and not arbitrarily when directed by men required checks and balances, which became an implied though dominant principle of his moral sentiments and, later, his Age of Commerce.

Smith's views on jurisprudence and government, because they are less well known, have not attracted the kind of misinterpretation common to his other books. By presenting them relatively unadorned, we hear the authentic voice, if not the prose, of Smith, a moral democrat and lover of liberty and justice.

15

Justice as a Negative Virtue

Justice is different from the other virtues.[1] It is not about what people should do, such as in acts of benevolence (be more benevolent more often) or of prudence (be more prudent). These are positive virtues that are voluntary, not forced. You cannot force people to be virtuous. Flogging someone for failing to be beneficent (acting kindly) makes nonsense of the virtue in which she is defective!

Justice, on the contrary, is about what people on pain of punishment must *not* do. Justice is a negative virtue. Compliance is enforced by compulsion. A violation of justice causes injury – food is stolen, a family member murdered, a house burnt down, a debt not paid, or a magistrate not obeyed. It is because violation positively hurts someone in ways that are disapproved of by the impartial spectator that, in response to violation, guilty persons suffer punishment, ranging from verbal chastisement to lawful execution. The number of crimes attracting the extremes of capital punishment, incidentally, increased as the 18th century closed.[2]

In contrast to breaches of the negative virtue of justice, breaches of the positive virtues cause disappointment and degrees of disgust, not grievous injury to the guilty. Even the 'blackest ingratitude' only causes the disapprobation of the impartial spectator. Ingratitude, an offence against propriety, does not warrant grievous punishment and nor does its absence warrant the use of force to compel a person to be grateful. Punishment would be as improper to enact as was occasioned by the original impropriety. Gratitude cannot be extorted. You either express it, or you don't.

Note how Smith expanded the spectator's role to that of the preservation of society through the negative virtue of justice. Smith's unequivocal belief in the pivotal nature of justice in society is as clear and unambiguous as David Hume's assertion that 'without justice, society must immediately dissolve.'[3] This is what is meant by 'the break down of society' – a total absence of law and order, or justice.

Justice as a negative virtue draws out the distinction between its general principles (the preservation of the foundations of society) and how it operates in practice. Justice is essential for the survival of society but, in practice, people who break the law are dealt with by due legal process. Guilty individuals caught up in the system might generate personal sympathies for their plight and what may happen to them, merely because they are our fellow creatures, without undermining the regrettable necessity of their self-generated predicament.[4]

Because 'the violation of justice is what men will never submit to from one another, the public magistrate is under a necessity of employing the power of the Commonwealth to enforce the practice of this virtue [duty]', otherwise 'civil society would become a scene of bloodshed and disorder' with 'every man revenging himself at his own hand whenever he fancied he was injured.' All governments, which achieve sufficient authority to enforce their writ, endow their magistrates with authority to 'do justice to all', under the promise that they will 'hear and redress every complaint of injury',[5] and they produce rules regularising the decisions of the judges with the intention that they coincide with the principles of natural justice.

Sometimes governments rule in their own interests; sometimes particular groups of men (e.g., monopolists) badger the government into bending the laws away from what natural justice would prescribe, and sometimes 'the rudeness and barbarism of the people hinder the natural sentiments of justice' compared to those of civilised nations, making 'their laws' like 'their manners, gross and rude.'[6]

Generalising, Smith states that:

> The most sacred laws of justice ... whose violation seems to call loudest for the vengeance and punishment, are the laws which guard the life and person of our neighbour; the next are those which guard his property and possessions; and last of all come those which guard what are called his personal rights, or what is due to him from the promises of others.[7]

He adds that 'the greater and more irreparable the evil that is done' the greater the degree of the 'resentment of the sufferer' and 'the sympathetic indignation of the spectator, as well as the sense of guilt in the agent'.[8] He draws the impartial spectator into the ambit of jurisprudence because justice involves the conduct of the perpetrator and the resentment of the victim, with the impartial spectator impartially observing how they behave.

Unlike the positive virtues, which are 'loose and inaccurate' and 'admit of many exceptions' and 'modifications', the rules of justice are 'accurate in the highest degree, admitting of no exceptions or modifications' and flow from a common set of principles. The rules of justice are like the formal rules of grammar, while the rules of the positive virtues are more about the elegance of composition and style.[9]

The impartial spectator influences the application of the virtues but the 'rules' are fuzzy. In the case of justice, the impartial spectator influences the chosen conduct of the individual where the rules are not in doubt. The individual, in consultation with the spectator in the breast, is not left alone to judge privately his potential or past breaches of the law; he may also be subjected to the impartial members of a jury, who determine the facts in his case, and to the impartial judgement of a magistrate, who decides his punishment.

Jurisprudence is the theory of the general principles of law and government and Justice is about rights, both 'natural' and 'acquired.' Of our natural rights, nobody doubts that 'a person has a right to have his body free from injury, and his liberty free from infringement unless there is proper cause'. Our acquired rights are less obvious. Property (what we acquire) is linked to civil government, for they 'very much depend on one another.'[10] Property begets government, which begets property.

Justice enforces acquired property rights and protects natural rights. But enforcement is not enough, for justice cannot rely entirely on the terrors of enforcement to cower determined and persistent challenges to other people's property, even were a sufficiency of means and the will to use them available. It required two other principles defined by Smith as 'authority' and 'utility', to ensure majority compliance with, and acceptance of, the laws of civil society.

People tend to defer to those they feel are of 'superior' rank and abilities to themselves. Authority acquires it own legitimacy, be it from superior strength, intellect, wealth, or recognition (i.e., from an ancient family).[11] Of course, we are all descended from 'ancient' families, but Smith alludes to our deference towards those who are descended from the few 'distinguished,' as opposed to the many 'obscure' families from which most of us descend and belong.

Because even the ignorant easily recognise the attributes and appurtenances of superior wealth, and with difficulty recognise the subtler (perhaps hidden) characteristics of personal superiority in strength, intellect and lineage, he found the majority of people readily deferring to those with wealth, however acquired, and not to those who might be worthy of admiration because of their superior character, intelligence or manners (to which small elite, Professor Smith surely believed he belonged!).

Utility, or the perceived general benefits of justice, are less reliable than authority as an inducement to obey the civil magistrate. Smith says of utility that 'everyone is sensible of this principle to preserve justice and peace in the society.' He asserts that 'the poorest may get redress of injuries from the wealthiest and most powerful' and concedes, though, that there 'may be some irregularities in particular cases, as undoubtedly there are', but we 'submit to them to avoid greater evils'.[12]

In the abstract of what *ought* to be, as opposed to what *is*, the practice of justice, Smith was correct, but Scotland in the mid-18th century was no place for the 'poorest' to challenge the injuries they believed the 'wealthiest and most powerful' inflicted on them. In theory, it could be done, and perhaps in some cases it was done, as in the successful case of Joseph Knight, an African freed from slavery by the Court of Session in Edinburgh in 1777,[13] but Smith exaggerates if he regarded redress as more than a principle.

Parenthetically, the application of law in 18th-century Britain tended not only to be biased in practice against the 'poorest' majority, but was also biased against at least half of the population (i.e., women) across all social classes, both in principle and in practice. For Smith's very evident biases in his non-recognition of, but not necessarily his hostility to, women's rights (natural or acquired) we do not have to look too far in any of his Works![14] He was an 18th, not a 21st, century man (hence, I have left his terminology intact because it would rapidly become tiresome to soothe today's sensibilities).

16
Constitutional Monarchy

Smith's assessment of the development of constitutional government in Britain was consistent with his thinking about the democratic process. He drew attention to what he considered to be the necessary elements of liberty and which, with hindsight, we can recognise as being developed in constitutional practice in the two centuries that followed the American and French Revolutions.

The democratic forms that he highlighted in the 18th century were comparatively primitive, but they were to be broadened and deepened, rather than radically changed or discarded, in modern secular democratic constitutions. In short, smithian constitutional monarchy, advanced as it was in his day, was not the culmination of the democratic process; it was nearer to its beginning than to its end. That itself was an implicit Legacy, left as such for reasons of his prudent political sensitivity. The 18th century was not the time or place to challenge the status quo in matters of constitutional governance. He was not a revolutionary in constitutional matters.

Whigs and Tories

In monarchies, which prefer 'peace and order', the guiding principle of government is its 'authority' over its subjects; in republican democracies, which prefer 'liberty', the guiding principle is its 'utility', or whether it works in a beneficial sense for its citizens.[1]

Britain was a constitutional monarchy, with two competing political tendencies, Tories and Whigs (much looser coalitions of MPs than we find today). The Whigs, says Smith, were for submitting to government on grounds of utility because of the advantages they derived from it; the Tories submitted to government because they 'pretended that it was of divine institution' and to rebel against it was as criminal as a child rebelling against a parent.[2] This last taunt at Jacobite sympathisers might also be taken as a subtle explanation for his prudence in not challenging the established order.

Men, he opines, of a 'bold, daring and bustling turn' tend to Whig-like utility; men of a 'peaceable, easy turn of mind' tend to a Tory 'tameness'.[3] His caricatures reveal his 'sceptical Whig' credentials.[4] Whether he would ever have allowed such impolitic remarks in his lecture to go into print is another matter!

The British monarchy was quite different from monarchies on the continent and from those in Britain's recent past. Britain's was a constitutional, not an absolute, monarchy. The British sovereign ruled under a modest balance of legal constraints and the King acted within a primitive form of constitutional checks and balances and not, as kings might elsewhere, solely on whim and fancy. Britain's 'system of liberty', Smith claimed, had been established, at least in outline, before its governments had funded and formed a standing professional army. As an associated protection against tyranny, the nascent democratic parliament, by its control of the army's finances, could prevent or at least inhibit the army undoing the steps taken to ensure the general liberty of the king's subjects. Lack of independent sources of money limited a potential tyrant's recourse to the armed intimidation of his subjects.

Smith's history of the steps taken from absolute monarchy towards constitutional liberty, whatever the individual intentions of those who took them, provides an interesting insight into his view of public liberty and its manifest values, demonstrating that whatever else Smith was politically he was not what his century understood as a Tory. He saw nothing 'divine' in the exercise of tyranny.

For Smith, a 'system of liberty' was a constitutional arrangement secure from tyranny from a king, parliament, judges, officials of the state, or any private person. In 18th-century Britain, its government was founded on a system of liberty, confirmed by 'many Acts of Parliament'. While this was liberty by legal fiat and not by universal franchise, it was nevertheless in advance of what happened elsewhere, before the founding of the United States of America in 1783. Consequently, he asserted confidently that Britain's liberties were so entrenched that 'every one would be shocked at any attempt to alter this system' of liberty and such attempts 'would be attended with the greatest difficulties'.[5]

Threats to liberty

Smith deliberated on two threats to constitutional liberty, specifically in the form of the Civil List covering the Monarch's personal expenses in support of the 'dignity of his office' – a euphemism for his extravagance on his person and his mistresses. Fortunately, instead of spending these monies on a Standing Army willing to do the sovereign's bidding, kings chose to spend it on personal extravagances. Smith writes: in the hands of 'designing, vigorous and ambitious princes [the Civil List spent on a standing army] might give them an influence superior to that which the dependence on a few officers about the palace can bestow.' In Smith's view, individual army officers, lounging about the Palace and amusing the king, were hardly the men liable or able to lead a royalist putsch.

Smith felt that princes would have great difficulty changing established customs; besides, I suggest, lives of pampered indolence flatter, but do not embolden, ambitious vanities. Bluntly, a Civil List, through affording the Sovereign an all expenses paid free ride on the 'dignity of his office', inevitably corrupted tentative temptations to his dabbling in returning Britain to absolutism.

A Standing Army 'might also without doubt be turned against the nation if the king had attained great influence with it.' But this was unlikely because many of the senior ranks in the army had large estates of their own and some were members of the House of Commons, which gave them influence and power independent of the king. Pure self interest prevented their joining a vainglorious king attempting to enslave the nation as nothing 'he could bestow on them' would 'turn their interest to his side', no matter, added Smith, displaying a keen sense of the shallowness of their loyalties, 'however mercenary we should suppose them' to be. Smith had the measure of these men.[6]

17
Foundations of Liberty

Certain constitutional features acted as barriers to tyranny. The courts of justice, for instance, secured the liberty of the people. He detailed his confidence in the courts in six parts.

First, judges held office for life entirely independent of the king and accountable under law for their conduct. Self-interest prevented judges from acting unfairly against defendants if by such acts they would endanger the loss of their regular, and relatively high, personal incomes from their 'profitable offices' and their reputations too. Crucially, nothing a king could offer the judges would tempt them to act outrageously in his favour.[1]

Second, because judges had little power to explain, alter, extend or correct the meaning of laws they must, with 'great exactness', strictly observe the literal meaning of words as intended by parliament.[2] Judges did not make the laws they enforced, though in England they interpreted the 'common law'.

Third, the *Habeas Corpus* Act ('you may have the body') was a 'great security against oppression'. In the past, the Privy Council (a meeting of the king's appointees) could put anyone into prison and detain him without trial for the uncertain duration of the king's (dis)pleasure. In the 18th century, prisoners had to be jailed locally or, if they could afford the transport, had a right to be tried at Westminster within 40 days and no judge would oppose *Habeas Corpus* on pain of 'infamy and a high penalty'. *Habeas Corpus*, asserted Smith, 'will never be allowed to be reppealed [sic], as it would destroy in a great measure the liberty of the subject.'[3]

Fourth, juries heard the evidence and decided on the facts. Smith developed a brief history of the jury system from *Magna Carta* (regularising the relationships between the king and the barons, including a person's 'right to legal judgement by his peers'). He explained the differences between jury practice in England and Scotland – rights to challenge potential jurors, jury size and the acceptability of majority verdicts in Scotland as opposed to the requirement of unanimity in England. He was, we must always remember, lecturing mainly to local Scottish students and a sprinkling of visitors.

He concludes, however, that 'the liberty of the subjects was secured in England by the greater accuracy and precision of the law' and that the 'courts of England are by far more regular than those of other [continental] countries.'[4]

Fifth, the powers of the House of Commons to impeach the king's ministers for mal-administration also 'secures the liberties of the subjects.' Henry VIII – 'that tyrannical prince' – conceded this privilege to the Commons as a convenient device for him to dispose of his out of favour ministers. When he wanted rid of one he simply got his 'servile' Commons to impeach the minister, knowing that he could not pardon a minister if parliament found him guilty. The convenient device used by Henry VIII to intimidate his ministers, remained a power of the House after his death and became a power available to parliament to deter the king's ministers from attempting any act against the commonwealth. A minister's 'fear of disgrace and loss of reputation', as well as a possible guilty verdict leading to capital punishment, from which there was no appeal or pardon, was a powerful sanction against those who eroded the 'great rights' of liberty enjoyed by the king's subjects.[5]

Sixth, the frequency of elections was 'also a great security for the liberty of the people' because, unless the representative serves his country or 'at least his constituents', he will be in 'danger of losing his place at the next election.' The more frequent these elections, the more dependent were parliamentary representatives.[6] True, of course, but in practice it was a long time before elections in Britain became free of corruption and fairly reflected the general will.

Smith asserted that Britain's constitutional arrangements in the mid-18th century 'secure[d] the liberty of the subjects.' He repeats this each time he covers one of his points, to make sure his young audience understood that liberty was closest to perfection where a society's legal system matched those arrived at after centuries of development in England. He comments more favourably on England's parliament than he does on Scotland's former parliament (of which his grandfather had been a member), and considered England's parliamentary elections more democratic than Scotland's (which is not saying much by modern standards).[7] Smith develops the historical evidence in a masterly analysis, well worth reading in the original.

Smith's six characteristics for constitutional liberty are:

1 An independent judiciary holding office for life
2 Laws made exclusively by the legislature, not judges or the Executive
3 *Habeas Corpus* ('you may have the body') to ensure timely due process
4 Juries of the defendant's peers to hear the evidence and decide on the facts.
5 The legislature to have powers to impeach the Executive
6 Regular and frequent elections to the Legislature

By modern standards, these are fairly modest institutional instruments for securing liberty but in their absence the effectiveness of markets in securing general opulence would be compromised, as would governments following inappropriate policies. Smith believed that commerce flourished under the rule of law and personal liberty.

He conducted a vigorous polemic against mercantile ideas (too vigorous for some), making the essential point that the existence of constitutional liberty does not of itself secure general wealth if Governments pursue wrongheaded policies. You could have liberty without opulence; manifestly it was better if you had both.

Smith's lectures on *Jurisprudence* were a *tour de force*. His clear views on liberty made clear the impartiality of justice and contributed to 18th-century constitutional theory. Glasgow University awarded him its degree of Doctor of Laws (LL.D) in 1762 and the citation for it mentions Smith's 'acknowledged Reputation in letters' and that 'he has taught Jurisprudence these many years in this University with great applause and advantage'.[8]

18
History as Imagination

Origins of societies

What passed for law before our predecessors wrote about it? This led in the 18th century to imaginative debates on society's origins. Most contributors believed that humans were induced (by social contracts) or coerced (by violence) into forming societies. Views of society's origins were fuelled from contemporary accounts of the 'savage' societies in America, Africa and the Pacific islands, compared to both modern and classical Europe.[1] Enlightenment readers were fascinated by the differences between human societies and to the errors, confusions and false conclusions about them they added an absence of evidence.

The first explorers of the Americas considered the people living there to be 'Indian'. Despite the geographical error, the name stuck. Recently, 'Indian' changed to 'Native American', even though over 13,000 years earlier the 'native Americans' were the continent's first immigrants – and from far away Asia after all![2]

Prior to travellers' accounts, educated Europeans only knew of predecessor societies from the ancient Greco-Roman classics and the archaeological detritus scattered across the European continent, north Africa and near Asia, and of course, from their Hebrew Bibles. Now they read about even older societies from across the Atlantic.

In fact, the larger part of the known world consisted of 'pre-civilised' societies and stagnant civilisations in states of arrested development (India and China) and, because no civilisation was as advanced as parts of Europe, a racist interpretation of human progress was bound to gain ascendancy in the manner it did in the mid 19th century. But the savage societies in North America posed a particular problem. The authors of the Bible knew nothing of them because God had not enlightened them.

How did the Americas fit into the Eden-to-Europe progression? Even the Bible's accounts of the Eden Garden showed the existence of shepherd and farming societies, against which the North American Indians were truly primitive, though at higher levels than the so-called 'brutes', because they had language, art and dance cultures, and a hunter-gatherer economy. John Locke popularised the notion that 'in the beginning all the World was America' – every human society had started of by living the savage life.[3] The rude societies of America were a veritable theme park on the lives of our distant ancestors. Some compared then to Germany in Roman times and more recently to parts of the Scottish Highlands.

The Hobbesian imagination

The debate had serious defects, not the least the constraint imposed by religious theories of a Creation, imagined by authors (from c.8000 BCE), who had no knowledge of human societies in sub-Saharan Africa, Australia or the Americas. The Eden Garden was conveniently located somewhere in the Middle East.

Imagination led to different conclusions, by which, for example, savage men passed power to a 'sovereign' who kept the peace by civilising its members through the terrors of being without society and subject to a 'war of all against all'.[4] An alternative view had society corrupting the freeborn, self-reliant man, who then degenerated into a servile dependence on others for his every want.[5]

Just how his imagination misled him can be seen in what Hobbes actually wrote about the 'war ... of every man against every man':

Whatsoever therefore is consequent of a time of war, where every man is enemy to every man; the same is consequent to the time, wherein men live without other security, than what their own strength, and their own invention shall furnish them withal. In such condition, there is no place for industry; because the fruit thereof is uncertain; and consequently no culture of the earth; no navigation, nor use of the commodities that may be imported by sea; no commodious building; no instruments of moving, and removing, such things as require much force; no knowledge of the face of the earth; no account of time; no arts; no letters; no society; and which is worst of all, continual fear, and danger of violent death; and the life of man, solitary, poor, nasty, brutish, and short.[6]

That this is pure imagination and not a description of historical fact, is evident from the next but one, seldom quoted, paragraph:

It may peradventure be thought, there was never such a time, nor condition of war as this; and I believe it was never generally so, over all the world.[7]

That ought to be clear enough. Hobbes concedes that the 'life of man, solitary, poor, nasty, brutish and short' – his most quoted reference – never happened. It was merely his imagination of 'what manner of life there would be, where there were no common power to fear, by the manner of life, which men had formerly lived under a peaceful government, use to degenerate into, a civil war.'[8]

Purely to emphasise the point about his imagination, I quote part of a sentence, which undoes what was clear from Hobbes' statement. It reads:

> … but there are many places, *where they* [the Brutes] *live so now*. For the savage people in many places of America, except the government of small families, the concord whereof dependeth on natural lust, have no government at all; and *live to this day in that brutish manner*, as I said before.[9]

The imaginative construct that 'never' existed becomes a description of brutish humans in America! He compounds the confusion by repeating: 'But though there has never been any time, wherein particular men were in a condition of war one against another', society's kings, through their 'continual jealousies', are in a constant 'posture of war' towards their neighbours.

So, men 'outside' society would be, but never have been, in a state of perpetual war, but 'inside' society under a sovereign they are compelled to chastise their neighbours in wars sanctioned by their kings. What an irony for men, desperately wishing to avoid the misery of permanent war, choosing to live inside society to endure permanent wars with neighbouring societies!

Actual life of the brutes

Now take Smith's innocent belief that 'the pulling of a wild fruit can hardly be called an [e]mployment.'[10] He had rephrased a statement taken from Grotius (cited by Meek): The 'first men lived easily on the fruits which the earth brought forth of its own accord, without toil'.[11] Clearly, Smith had no idea of the sweated reality of living solely by gathering the bounties of nature. To pick an apple in his mother's Kirkcaldy garden, Smith took a short, safe walk from her house to her orchard without fear of being attacked by a predator, stretched up to a bough laden with apples and exerted the easiest of pulls on the fruit, and enjoyed his leisurely snack as he strolled back a few yards to his home.

The lives of the brutes in the open savannah from three million years ago were nothing like he imagined, or could imagine. Truly, he took the admonitions of God in expelling Adam and Eve too literally.[12] If 'toil … all the days of thy life' and 'in the sweat of thy face thou shalt eat bread' was

God's punishment, it must be true that the gatherers 'lived easily', otherwise expulsion from the Eden Garden was insufficiently severe. To assert anything to the contrary was heresy. There was never any question about what it was like *before* man lived in society. Man has never lived alone. Sociability is a constant both for our species and our primate cousins. The first appearance of property – 'this is mine, not yours' – pre-dates by many hundreds of thousands of years the relatively cultured (in language and ritual) 18th-century hunting societies of North American 'Indians', which Smith and others took mistakenly to be 'the lowest and rudest state of society.'[13]

While Hobbes 'war of all against all' never happened, in reality there were 'wars' of tiny bands of humans against other bands, not wars of all individuals against each other. Fortunately, given the extremely low human population densities and the vastness of the empty habitable landmass of the Earth until fairly recent times, the incidence of war must have been rare indeed (not because of universal pacifism – there has always been violence *within* and *between* societies). Most beleaguered bands and breakaways could move into empty territory. Moving a few kilometres a generation took mankind from Africa to the rest of the world. Humans reached Australia only 40,000 years ago and only about 13,000 years ago they reached the Americas.[14]

Female gatherers fed their children and themselves. Males fed only themselves. The burden of feeding solely by gathering became more onerous as the brain size of the hominids, and the brain's ravenous appetite for energy inputs, ramped up as its size quadrupled from a chimpanzee's of 300 cc to 1400 cc in three million years.[15] Either males helped to feed the bands, mainly by supplementary scavenging and, later, hunting, or the bands perished (as many probably did). Not, of course, that people would see the problem as survival of the species (natural selection works on the individual, not the species). Those individuals that adapted continued to breed and successfully nurtured their young; those that maladapted suffered local extinctions.

Smith's stage of the Hunter was preceded by tens of thousands of years of the scavenger. Scavenging, like gathering, was no mere stroll to feast on plenty. What was scavenged usually had to be taken from highly dangerous rivals intent on eating what was theirs and killing anything trying to stop them, just as pulling fruit exposed people to prowling predators.

Speed of access and egress to and from the carcass was essential. Too slow or too timid, and the scavengers risked being scavenged themselves. Stone cutting tools (growing intelligence) proved invaluable for butchering a carcass speedily, while the rest of the band (a nascent division of labour) distracted deadly predators by noise, stones, heavy clubs and, later, fire. It was much easier to be disembowelled by hungry lionesses than it was to succeed in taking their kill. Carelessness was suicidal and scavenging required co-operation.

When humans graduated from scavenging to hunting, new levels of expertise and technology supported by increasingly sophisticated forms of co-operation added to the knowledge base. With uniquely a human speech, knowledge accumulated (plus a great deal of superstitious fantasy) that was passed on through the generations. Teamwork and knowledge of the habits and behaviour of fauna altered social structures and increased the divisions of labour. It also drove the growth in hominid intelligence, which in turn, drove the application of intelligence to subsistence gathering. The combination of the social evolution of co-operation, teamwork, division of labour, intelligence and speech, set the scene for the evolution of the smithian 'propensity to truck, barter and exchange.'[16]

19
The Four Stages

Long before Smith sat in awe in Dr. Hutcheson's class and heard him on the 'Stages of Society', he was already familiar with the Bible's allegory for the origins and ages of mankind in the fable of the expulsion of Adam and Eve from the paradise of the Eden Garden for eating the fruit of a forbidden tree.[1]

Smith learned his Old Testament from his mother's knee. Cain, Eve's first born, 'a tiller of the ground', murdered Abel, his younger brother, 'a keeper of sheep'. Encapsulated within the Bible fable, the 'Garden of Eden' represents the age of the Gatherers (Adam and Eve), followed by Abel's age of the Shepherds and Cain's age of Agriculture.[2]

God ended the mythical 'Golden Age' and its 'easy' lifestyles; Cain murdered the Shepherd, and Cain's Agriculture flourished in a land called 'Nod, east of Eden,' where he was exiled.[3] The Bible gives a religious motive for the murder – a jealous dispute over God favouring Abel's to Cain's offering. A more likely motive for the violent discord between the shepherd and the farmer was a murderous row after sheep ate the crops, an event sure to strain brotherly relationships.

Cain also prospered in Nod and built the 'City of Enoch',[4] symbolically significant, because agriculture led to permanent settlements, which led to Smith's fourth age, the Age of Commerce. But the Bible's authors implausibly compressed a process lasting many hundreds of millennia – from gathering to shepherding to farming – into a single generation from Adam and Eve to their adult sons.

Smith taught a stages theory in Hutcheson's classrooms confident that they were confirmed by Biblical evidence. His four stages (Hunters, Shepherds, Agriculture and Commerce) thematically underlay jurisprudence and political economy.[5] However, Smith did not originate the theory of stages – he derived 'vague hints' of it from attending Dr Hutcheson's lectures (who derived his ideas from Pufendorf.)[6]

Lord Kames, Smith's patron and leading Scottish Judge, published his *Historical Law Tracts* in 1758, in which he advanced a Four Stage theory, causing a minor academic problem of scholarly precedence.[7] The precedence dispute turns on whether Smith used a Four Stages theory in the lectures he began in the early 1750s (for which there is only conjecture and circumstantial evidence), or whether Kames' publication in 1758, or even Dalrymple's in 1757, is decisive proof of their precedence. Some attribute precedence of Kames or Dalrymple, some to Smith,[8] but the anonymous authors of Genesis trumped them all.

The stages in the literature had the benefit of real world examples, and numerous versions of them were circulating (e.g., Rousseau, who was closest to an evolutionary theory of mankind long before Darwin and hominid fossil data were available).[9]

Smith's island of stages

Smith's exposition of the age of hunters shows his acquaintance with 18th century literature – from voyages, travellers and explorers – and he quotes from Charlevoix's description of societies of North American 'Indians' and a few African tribes.[10]

Smith invented a story to show what people in each stage might have done. This is fine for his purposes (and for the attention span of his young audience) but it tempts him into gross simplification.

He supposes that a dozen people of both sexes settled on an uninhabited island and co-operated to support themselves. What would they do? Smith says that initially they would rely only upon 'wild fruits and wild animals'. 'Their sole business would be the hunting of wild beasts or catching of fishes.' It is the age of the (male) hunters; the (female) gatherers were disregarded, though providing most of their band's diets.

A nation of hunters had 'no government at all'. It consisted of a few independent families, living in the same camp and speaking the same language. When disputes broke out the whole society deliberated on the alleged offence and, where possible, reconciled the parties, but failing reconciliation it could banish the miscreants, kill the arguers or permit a party to obtain violent redress. But this was not government, because any deliberate action required the entire society's consent, and they lived, according to the laws of nature.[11]

Population growth on the 'uninhabited island' drove humans through the four stages. As 'their numbers multiplied,' he noted, 'they would find the chase too precarious for their support.'[12] In contrast to Smith's imagination, in real islands dispersed across the Pacific, when isolated communities faced population pressures they resorted to infanticide and quasi-judicial murder (meaningless 'taboos' caught the unwary for which 'offences' the careless were killed). The chiefs also engaged in stylised warfare, using surrogate 'soldiers', who killed each other (almost like gladiators), thereby limiting populations to what could be sustained on the islands.[13]

Absent knowledge of such real world options in 1763, and illustrating the risks of deductive reasoning without data, Smith suggests that 'the most natural contrivance they would think of, would be to tame some of those wild animals they caught' and, by affording the community better food than obtained by hunting for it, they would continue to occupy the island and 'multiply their kind'. Hence, 'would arise the age of shepherds'.[14] It would have to be a large island for shepherding to function as a source of food. Sheep and cattle required large land areas to prevent over grazing.

Societies of shepherds 'first gave rise to regular government.' Until there was property, asserts Smith, there could be no government, the purpose of which is to 'secure wealth, and to defend the rich from the poor'. In the inequality of fortune we find the rich having great influence over the poor. Smith adds a subtle touch. A nation of shepherds has no means of spending their sheep having no domestic luxury, and can only give them away as presents to those who are poor. This creates dependence and with it influence of the rich over the poor, making them 'slaves'.[15] He illustrates this by reference to the Biblical account of Abraham and Lot, calling them patriarchs acting 'like little petty princes.'[16]

Smith asserts confidently that the age of shepherds preceded the age of agriculture, because the 'Tartars and Arabians' subsisted entirely on their flocks and knew nothing of agriculture. He insists that 'whole savage nations' which subsist by flocks have no notion of cultivating the ground'.[17]

He makes two notable points; first, the loose sequence of his stages, gives them an air of an ideal type, rather than a dated historical sequence, and second, that the replacement of shepherding by agriculture was not a 'revolution', as is normally implied, taking a few generations, or even a case of the physical elimination of troublesome shepherds by vengeful farmers (Genesis writ large). It was a long drawn out process of technological and economic change, with hunting, shepherding and agriculture co-existing side by side, for many millennia, until agriculture triumphed.[18]

Population growth once again drove Smith's next stage on his mythical island. '[W]hen a society becomes numerous they would find difficulty in supporting themselves by herds and flocks' and 'would naturally turn themselves to the cultivation of land.'[19] This may have happened but not without the usual problems of transition. Free ranging herds and flocks in close proximity to growing grain and vegetables are not comfortable neighbours. Where there is discord there is a need for peaceable dispute resolution (laws) and, for longer-term tranquillity, a proclivity among the parties for dispute avoidance (religion, moral philosophy and justice).

Agriculture, Smith says, was discovered by observing accidental contamination and by deliberate experiments. He knew his Bible and he paraphrased the 'some fell on stony ground' parable.[20] Some of the seed would come to nought, but other seed would enter the soil and proliferate, reproducing what was planted and creating a surplus for consumption (and, in time, for sale). Observation, he said, showed that certain trees produced nourishing food, as well as certain plants, and by this means 'they would gradually advance into the age of Agriculture.'[21]

Agriculture helped develop a division of labour, presaging the coming commercial age. Society developed arts and skills in the production of a range of produce, enabling some persons to cultivate one kind of produce and others to cultivate different produce. People, said Smith, thinking rationally, would then 'exchange with one another' their surpluses over what 'was necessary for their support' and 'get in exchange ... the commodities they stood in need of and did not produce themselves'.

What began as an occasional exchange between individuals within the same society, would become an exchange between individuals 'of different nations' (presumably societies living close to the mythical island) and with this development '*at last* the age of commerce arises.' In the words 'at last', Smith heralds a culminating development, not one presaging another stage yet to come.[22]

He concluded that a society stocked with all the flocks and herds it can support, and its land cultivated so as to produce all the grain and other commodities necessary for its subsistence that its lands can bear, or at least sufficient to support its inhabitants, plus the surplus it exports in exchange for its imports, is a society that 'has done all in its power towards its ease and convenience.'[23] For Smith, this happy situation was the limit of his ambitions for society, which is a long way off from two centuries of economic change from the commercial society he analysed in *Wealth of Nations* and the corporate capitalist society that was just around the corner, but which he neither foresaw nor anticipated.

The fundamental question faced by a society aspiring to 'its ease and convenience' was: in what circumstances and under what social arrangements would a society be most likely to achieve its aspiration?' Smith gave his answer in *Wealth of Nations*.

20
Was He Aware of a Fifth Stage?

The Age of Commerce was Smith's fourth stage. Beyond the age of commerce he mentioned no fifth, or later, stage. This is significant.

Smith was aware that it was possible for any of the four stages to be reached and for its people to suffer from events provoking a relapse into a degenerate form of earlier stages. The collapse of the Roman Empire from the invasion and rapine of the barbarian warlords caused the virtual collapse of the original age of commerce in Europe. This collapse heralded not the birth of a new age (e.g., 'feudalism') in Smith's sense of a stage. Post-Roman Europe was a degeneration of agriculture and shepherd societies under various forms of tribal barbarism, which slowly led to a rebirth of the agricultural age, this time based on, first, regional and local war lords, and, later, on feudal political structures dominated by kings.

Smith's stages were not mere changes (who should rule?) in the governance of societies. They represented changes in the underlying 'means for pursuing the requisites of preservation' of life and reproduction of the species. Feudalism was a political not an economic change. Grains grow the same way whether the political regime is allodial, feudal, oriental despotism, Yeoman farmers or capitalist agribusinesses (a point missed by marxian stage theories, which mix economic stages with political regimes of which they disapprove).

Smithian stages, within the limits of the existing knowledge and technology suited to the particular environment and climate, address the question of which economic 'system of organisation supplies the means of preservation in greatest abundance?' In this sense, the question of 'who should rule' compared to 'what is the most productive economy' is not an issue for Smith. Smithian stages are compatible with various political regimes.[1] 'Feudalism', therefore, was not a stage in a smithian sense; nor for that matter did 'mercantile' governments become a sort of successor stage to feudalism. These mix a form of governance (feudalism) and economic policies (e.g., mercantile) with the underlying, albeit degenerated agricultural and commercial stages.

To conceive of political forms as stages only confuses their smithian meaning with other, later, often marxian, stage models, and distort Adam Smith's strictly limited intentions of determining the economic characteristics of the age he lived in.[2]

Smith taught that property evolved through four distinct stages (hunting, shepherding, farming and commerce) and each stage had connected legal ideas of what constituted property. These ideas varied because property rights varied, causing competing claims to ownership to grow more complex through each stage as legal norms adapted to new and varying circumstances. For Smith, the 'new circumstances' appeared to be how humans responded technologically to population pressures on the existing means of subsistence, in contradistinction to Nature's Malthusian remedies for over-population: starvation, disease, pestilence, and war, which together or separately reduced the birth rate and increased the death rate.[3]

Each of the Four Stages, or ages of man, exploited the existing dominant method of production up to some optimal level because no stage expanded output indefinitely. When the subsistence claims of a growing population exceeded that which an existing method of production could support, the necessity to expand subsistence occasioned a search for a different, more productive, method, leading in turn to a new stage in the ages of mankind. Gavin Reid has provided an elegant exposition of Smith's stages model in a modern context.[4]

Smith focused on whether 18th-century Britain was uniquely placed to provide for continuous improvement in the material well being of its population, the advancement of knowledge and science, stable governance, security from the depredations of neighbours, and personal and social tranquillity. If Britain was not so well placed, what arrangements in society contributed to these ends? *Wealth of Nations* was his answer to such questions, using materials and narrative structure from his lectures delivered from 1748 to 1764, and from selected accounts of his contemporaries.

Part IV
Impartial Competition

Introduction

It is often fashionable to accuse Smith of taking his economics from the French economists whom he met during his tour of France with the Duke of Buccleugh. Smith did not publish *Wealth of Nations* until 1776 and he visited France in 1764–6, ergo, the French economists (the Physiocrats) must have been the source for his economics because he showed no interest in economics before he met them. But two plus two does not equal five.

Moral Philosophy courses in Scottish universities from the early 18th century included lectures on political economy. Smith, for example, took Francis Hutcheson's classes in political economy as part of Hutcheson's moral philosophy course between 1737–40. A comparison of subject headings in Hutcheson's posthumous book, published in 1755, shows many identical topic headings to those in *Wealth of Nations* (see Appendix).[1]

The anonymous students who transcribed Smith's lectures between 1762 and 1764 showed that he lectured on economics over 14 years before he visited France and met the French economists. That French intellectuals like Montesquieu, Cantillon, Quesnay, Mirabeau and Turgot had influenced him is undoubtedly true (he had copies of their works in his library),[2] but claims for a French origin for his economics are undoubtedly exaggerated. For an authoritative summary of what Smith added to and developed independently of the theories of the Physiocrats, Professor Walter Eltis supplies guidance at the end of his study of classical growth theory.[3] However, Smith was so impressed with Francois Quesnay[4] that he intended to dedicate *Wealth of Nations* to him but, unfortunately, Quesnay died before it was published.[5]

The more serious transformation of his political economy from what he wrote originally to what he was represented to have written, which started within years of his death, persists today, namely that he was the progenitor of the economics of capitalism, especially in its laissez faire variations. This is an embarrassing error. We get closer to the authentic Smith by integrating the two pillars of his ideas – the cohesion and relative harmony of society – with the third pillar of his political economy, and find that modern derivations of his legacy are not his ideas at all.

21
A Linguistic Osmosis

What we are up against

The following examples reveal that a kind of osmotic linguistic imperialism has almost conquered modern interpretations of *Wealth of Nations*. Words that Smith wrote have been replaced by words he didn't write or mean, and wholly different meanings have been given to words he did write. The assimilation of Smith's legacy into stances, oft times totally alien to his intent, has reached such a pitch that whether anything can be done now to rescue it from its modern misuses is open to various answers, of which this essay, though, is one attempt:

Classical economics: Smith the prophet of laissez-faire[1]

The Wealth of Nations is a stupendous palace erected upon the granite of self-interest.[2]

After all, in a book [WN] which has been regarded as the *locus classicus* of the *laissez-faire* ideology for 200 years, a book which shook the world by recommending a maximum degree of freedom for business enterprise – in such a book surely the entrepreneur would play a major role.[3]

The capitalist division of labour which in Smith's treatment is used interchangeably with the word 'commerce', is a necessary condition for such progress.[4]

The term 'laissez-faire' also provides a means of understanding an important aspect of the complex and detailed account of the commercialisation of Western society that we find in the Wealth of Nations. ... In helping us to understand [the transition to industrial capitalism], the views of commerce in Hutcheson, Hume, and Smith can be said to form an important part of the intellectual history of capitalism.[5]

In the two hundred years that have passed since the publication of the *Inquiry into the Nature and Causes of the Wealth of Nations*, Adam Smith's reputation as a pioneering exponent of, and leading spokesman for, the principles of liberal capitalist society has become firmly established.[6]

From the time of publication of the *Wealth of Nations* in 1776 until the middle of the twentieth century, Adam Smith has been viewed primarily as the source of *laissez-faire* ideas.[7]

Capitalism as defined by Adam Smith is a world ruled by exchange based on money: exchanges devoid of either sympathy or morality. Adam Smith built a model of a modern economy in the belief that it could only work if all transactions were perfectly amoral and selfish in nature. And Smith's model assumes that morality and mutual support would automatically emerge from such selfishness.[8]

One axiomatic premise of this study is that capitalism is an embodiment of smithian principles. Hence the interpretation of Smith's teaching must be an interpretation of capitalistic society.[9]

On this basis, Smith argues that a necessary prerequisite for increasing wealth and prosperity is extensive markets, which leads him to recommend that market restrictions such as tariffs, regulations, and taxes be abolished or significantly reduced. It is principally because of these recommendations that Smith has come to be considered the father of laissez-faire economics.'[10]

Not all authors perpetrate linguistic distortions of Smith's political economy. Scholars sometimes merely pass on factual statements taken to be the considered views of the profession. Two of them, Tribe and Griswold, thankfully, report the problem without adding to it, providing a welcome respite from the barrage of misinformation.

By the mid nineteenth century this 'system' [natural liberty] had been transmuted into a doctrine of *laissez faire* which had not been part of Smith's intention, a doctrine which allied simplified principles of free trade to conceptions of minimal government intervention into the economic process.[11]

In spite of his influence and fame, Smith's fate has for some time resembled that of Epicurus. Epicurus became known as an 'Epicurean,' and so today as an advocate of an hedonism at odds with his true teaching... [Adam Smith] is seen solely as an economist, to the exclusion of his work in ethics, moral psychology, jurisprudence, rhetoric and belles lettres, as well as political, economic, and intellectual history. Even worse, he is seen as an economist of a particular ideological bent. In short, he tends now to be known just as an advocate of crude laissez-faire capitalism and, to add insult to injury, of a capitalism inseparable from imperialism and colonialism.[12]

Rothschild revealed the takeover of Smith's radical criticism of imperfect markets and his posthumous transformation into a voice for 19th-century ill-liberalism. There are others too whose approach to Smith's work, by no means reverential, at least in good measure is respectful and recognises his intentions, if not wholly agreeing with them.[13] Would that there were more like them.

Occasionally too, we come across green pastures in the usual deserts of mindless repetition of Smith's alleged laissez faire views. One such patch of green is found in Jacob Viner's admirable essay on 'Adam Smith and Laissez Faire':

He had little trust in the competence or good faith of government. He knew who controlled it, and whose purposes they tried to serve, though against the local magistrate his indictment was probably unduly harsh. He saw, nevertheless, that it was necessary, in the absence of a better instrument, to rely upon government for the performance of many tasks, which individuals as such would not do, or could not do, or could only do badly. He did not believe that laissez-faire was always good, or always bad. It depended on circumstances; and as best as he could, Adam Smith took into account all of the circumstances he could find. In these days of contending schools, each of them with deep, though momentary, conviction that it, and it alone, knows the one and only path to economics truth, how refreshing it is to return to the *Wealth of Nations* with its eclecticism, its good temper, its common sense, and its willingness to grant that those who saw things differently from itself, were only partly wrong.[14]

The misrepresentation of Adam Smith continues. Two of the authors quoted above, Nobel Prize winners, Paul Samuelson and George Stigler, have formidable reputations in the history of economic thought and their inclusion suggests this is not just a problem of uninformed ignorance. It has become a wholesale, often innocently camouflaged, but nevertheless mistaken distortion of Smith; in some cases a parody.

The distortion takes two forms: first, the misappropriation of Smith's ideas, beginning in the early 19th century, by sleight of mind for political purposes opposite to that which he had intended, using the authority of his name in pursuit of policies, the like of which he expressed severe reservations; and second, a completely different rendering of his main hypothesis, specifically that we serve our own interests best by serving the interests of others, which was transmuted into the falsehood that selfishness necessarily is the guiding motive of commerce. This was and remains a fundamental error.

The fundamental error is analogous to a 'flat earth' view and I shall engage the error by examining Smith's original ideas. At least flat earth-ers were daily witnesses to the visual illusion upon which they perpetrated their erroneous theories and, it can be said in their favour, that they confirmed the source of their illusions everyday. The distortion of Smith's ideas, promoted by endless repetition of the fundamental error, indicates a failure to check on his books regularly or at all. They may have accepted on trust what others have told them about *Wealth of Nations* and failed to examine for themselves how Smith described the interactions of people in the markets he knew and wrote about.

One outstanding example of a critical mind reviewing the evidence of what has happened to Smith's legacy is that of Vivienne Brown and her formidable challenge to the misreading of his texts. She writes:

> There are many ironies to note in the historical outcomes of Adam Smith's discourse and the canonisation of WN [Wealth of Nations], as has been evidenced by the history of more than two centuries since WN was published. The argument of WN against the undue expansion of trade and manufacturers has come to be interpreted as an argument in favour of such expansion. The invective against merchants and manu-facturers has been construed as an apologia for the new capitalist class that emerged in a later age. But one of the greatest ironies is that Adam Smith's discourse – indebted as it was to stoic moral philosophy – has contributed centrally to the de-moralisation of economic and political categories and to the construction of an economics canon in which moral debate has virtually no place.[15]

22
Insufficiency of Self-love

I shall begin by examining one of the most quoted passages from *Wealth of Nations*:

> It is not from the benevolence of the butcher, the brewer, or the baker, that we expect our dinner, but from their regard to their own interest. We address ourselves, not to their humanity but to their self-love, and never talk to them of our own necessities but of their advantages.[1]

Clearly, Smith said that self-love drove behaviour in markets. But no, he does not quite say that! And to see why, read on:

> This division of labour, from which so many advantages are derived, is not originally the effect of any human wisdom, which foresees and intends that general opulence to which it gives occasion. It is the necessary, though very slow and gradual consequence of a certain propensity in human nature which has in view no such extensive utility; the propensity to truck, barter, and exchange one thing for another.[2]

This passage is not about the motives of one selfish man acting alone. The 'propensity in human nature' is common to all humans. It is the interaction known as negotiation, involving a minimum of two persons acting in concert (though not necessarily in tune). And, once you go beyond one individual to two, their transactions involve more than one ego and expression of self-love or self-interest. If self-love drove their behaviour, the propensity to 'truck, barter and exchange' would be limited. Negotiators, locking horns, would never let go and would never conclude their bargains.

Asserting that humans are driven solely by self-love, self-interest or selfishness ignores the process that intervenes between the clash of the passions initiating the interaction (at least two solutions are proposed for every negotiation problem) and the outcome that decides it. All humans breathe but breathing does not drive their interactions. True, they cannot interact without breathing but the necessity of their breathing is independent of whether they bargain. All people experience self-love or self-interest, but, to achieve an outcome agreeable to their selfish self they must modify their self-love to find an outcome agreeable to the other party too. For be clear, truck, barter and exchange requires the acceptance of both parties of what ever they agree is the solution. Negotiators square the circle by simultaneously suppressing their selfish passions (of each wanting it all) as they approach the moment of agreement. Selfishness is not the driver of joint decisions.

Smith's next sentence is revealing:

> Whether this propensity be one of the original principles of human nature, of which no further account can be given; or whether, as seems more probable, it be the necessary consequences of the faculties of reason and speech, it belongs not to our present subject to enquire.[3]

In his jurisprudence lectures he had envisaged a dozen humans adapting their food production to their increased numbers and in his *First Formation of Language*[4] he presupposed a time when humans did not have language. The propensity to 'truck, barter and exchange' was a necessary consequence from 'the faculties of reason and speech' and, because these faculties pre-date the commercial age, he infers that humans acquired language and developed these propensities in the earlier ages.

To gather food for collective consumption requires co-operation, aided by language, or at the very least some form of communication and an acceptance of the dictates of the group. The band could scatter for gathering but it was safer for them to agree to limit their search to smaller areas for safety in numbers when predators were in the neighbourhood. Bands disregarding safety risked local extinctions.

To scavenge meat required complex forms of co-operation between at least three groups in the band: the makers of sharp stone tools for speedily butchering large carcasses;[5] those good or lucky at carcass finding; and those defenders of a kill site from dangerous predators. Sharing tasks in this manner developed a high level of co-operation at a low technology level.

Because co-operation requires agreement on who does what and in what order they do it, negotiation, which is implicit in reciprocation and explicit in exchange, appeared in the countless interactions among intermittent co-operators. These considerations underline the significance of co-operation implied in the meanest of negotiations.

Long before the age of commerce, zero sum ('what you gain, I lose') was not the only outcome. Mixed motives and co-operation go together. Violence in pursuit of plunder is an alternative to peaceful trade. The violent plunderer gains everything; his victim loses everything (on occasion, life itself – the ultimate zero sum). But while violence re-distributes the bounties of nature and the fruits of labour, it cannot create them. A selfishly successful society of robbers impoverished itself by creating grave-yards out of plundered orchards and fields.

Placing the 'certain propensity in human nature' into this context reveals why we must 'address ourselves, not to their humanity but to their self-love, and never talk to them of our own necessities but of their advantages.[6] Selfishness is never enough to obtain what we want because, to obtain our wants peacefully, we have to consider unselfishly what the other party wants too.

Smith's rendering of the above passages in 1763 included:

Man continually standing in need of the assistance of others, must fall upon some means to procure their help. This he does not merely by coaxing and courting; he does not expect it unless he can turn it to your advantage or make it appear to be so. Mere self-love is not sufficient for it, till he applies in some way to your self-love. A bargain does this in the easiest manner. When you apply to a brewer or butcher for beer or for beef you do not explain to him how much you stand in need of these, but how much it would be in [his] interest to allow you to have them for a certain price.[7]

Smith places limits on 'self love' as a motive. Could it be clearer? 'Mere self-love is not sufficient'! And the price of the exchange constrains the selfishness of the bargainers, for no matter how high the agreed price the seller will always prefer a higher price and no matter how low the agreed price the buyer will always prefer a lower price. Neither buyer nor seller can get unilaterally the price they prefer because they must take account of the price the other will accept.

23
Self-love and Conditionality

In a 1764 lecture Smith spoke of 'self-love' three times:

> Man, in the same manner, works on the selflove of his fellows by setting
> before them a sufficient temptation to get what he wants; the language
> of this disposition is, give me what I want, and you shall have what you
> want. It is not from benevolence, as the dogs, but from the selflove than
> man expects any thing. The brewer and the baker serve us not from
> benevolence but from selflove. No man but a beggar depends on benev-
> olence, and even they would die in a week were their entire dependance
> [sic] upon it.[1]

Smith's reference to self-love does not give it the role some claim for it. To
see why, we must look into a two-party negotiation more deeply.

Man's propensity to 'truck, barter and exchange' formalises and
entrenches dependence on others but it does not eliminate attempts on
occasion to act in the manner of a spaniel endeavouring 'by a thousand
attractions to engage the attention of his master who is at dinner.'[2] Man
'when he has no other means of engaging [his brethren] to act according to
his inclination, endeavours by every servile and fawning attention to
obtain their goodwill',[3] illustrated in the saying that a 'friend in need is a
friend indeed'.

Whatever the opportunities for fawning, few have enough time to practise whenever they have occasion to want something. A man's needs are
multiple and 'he stands at all times in need of the co-operation and assistance of great multitudes, while his whole life is scarce sufficient to gain
the friendship of a few persons.'[4] Nor, as shown above, is violence an
optional alternative to fawning. This leaves many opportunities for the
more certain prospect of negotiation, because:

> man has almost constant occasion for the help of his brethren, and it is
> in vain for him to expect it from their benevolence only. He will be

more likely to prevail if he can interest their self-love in his favour, and shew them that it is for their own advantage to do for him what he requires of them. Whoever offers to another a bargain of any kind, proposes to do this. Give me that which I want, and you shall have this which you want, is the meaning of every such offer, and it is in this manner that we obtain from one another the far greater part of those good offices which we stand in need of.[5]

Smithian truck, barter and exchange introduced the conditional proposition: 'if you give me what I want [the condition] then I will give you what you want [the offer].' Negotiation, a two-way transaction, is dominated by conditionality, preferably stated explicitly, and 'it is in this manner that we obtain from one another the far greater part of those good offices which we stand in need of'.[6]

Smith illustrates the role of self-love in truck, barter and exchange, in the following passages:

This he does not merely by coaxing and courting; he does not expect it unless he can turn it to your advantage or make it appear to be so. Mere self-love is not sufficient for it, till he applies in some way to your self-love.[7]

Man, in the same manner, works on the selflove of his fellows, by setting before them a sufficient temptation to get what he wants; the language of this disposition is, give me what I want, and you shall have what you want.[8]

He will be more likely to prevail if he can interest their self-love in his favour, and shew them that it is for their own advantage to do for him what he requires of them.[9]

We address ourselves, not to their humanity but to their self-love, and never talk to them of our own necessities but of their advantages.[10]

Notice that it is the other party's self-love to which he refers. He excludes using 'coaxing and courting' or appealing to their 'humanity', or, of course, depending on their 'benevolence'. Does this mean that selfishness drives the transaction? Not at all!

Just as you must go beyond your selfishness by offering them some of what they want, they too must go beyond their selfishness by offering you some of what you want. Absolutely selfish people cannot conclude deals. Both parties simultaneously modify their selfish motivations to conclude their bargains ('Give me that which I want, and you shall have this which you want'). Mutual selfishness ('give me that which I want') expresses only half of the conditional proposition. Remain selfish – and the result? Deadlock. Like two dogs arguing over bones, the strongest, or wiliest, wins what the other loses. Or, as Smith eloquently put it: 'Nobody ever saw a dog make a fair and deliberate exchange of one bone for another with another dog.'[11]

Now, some very brilliant scholars have never considered the dynamics of exchange relations that they study. Uncomfortable with processes, they focus on outcomes, the latter being more easy to cast as equations. The mid-20th-century tortured genius, John Nash, typified in his classic contribution, 'The Bargaining Problem',[12] the non-process focus popular with many economists; he assumed away the *process* of bargaining to define the optimal *outcome*. Thousands of graduate economists who can reproduce the Nash Theorem in all its simplistic elegance (Nash was a genius!) cannot discuss Adam Smith's presentation of the process.

Even with the evidence from markets they access daily, they completely miss what is staring them in the face. One such talented and distinguished political economist, a decade after Smith died, was Frances Horner (1759–1823) (later a corresponding friend of both Thomas Malthus and David Ricardo). He wrote in his *Journal* in 1801, in reference to Smith on exchange, an amazing statement for someone credited with drafting the Bullion Report that led to the Bank of England taking responsibility for controlling the money supply:

> This is a very superficial and unnecessary chapter; all that is valuable in the doctrine of it stated in a single sentence. The disquisition belongs rather to the philosophy of the mind than to political economy: and as a metaphysical investigation, it is treated in a very slight and unsatisfying manner. The first paragraph, however, of the chapter expresses an important truth in political philosophy.[13]

Horner, like many economists since, neglected the very essence of commerce bound in the transaction. He read Smith's words, but to little effect. He saw commerce in its outcome as the total of the money value of its output and the process that created it. If this was how the 19th century opened, is it any wonder that the next century closed with Smith's insights still ignored, only more so?

For example, Philip Wicksteed, a leading figure in academic economics in the early 20th century, unnecessarily complicated Smith's exchange model. Wicksteed modified the accusation that self-love dominates exchange transactions. He re-defined self-love into an unselfish act by supposing that a negotiating party may act in the interest of himself (self-love), or in the interest of his family (family love), or in the interest of his friends (friendship), or on behalf of people with whom he has no connections, such as customers. He acknowledged that the other party with whom he bargains may act for his family too, but he need not.

Wicksteed characterised this as 'non-tuism' (i.e., the inclusion of every-one's interests in your motives except those of the person, and the people he represents, with whom you are negotiating) and he suggested that this is the essence of business transactions.[14] Professor Tom Wilson, sixty years later, commented that Wicksteed's hypothesis is 'not without sub-stance', but resorts to defending markets by relying on the strange and irrelevant, though true, grounds of the poverty of state planning as a worse alternative.[15]

Wanting something for ourselves is selfish, yet we all want things we do not have, hence we all have selfish wants. That is a fact, which does not mean we are not nice persons. It most certainly is selfish, and not *nice*, however, to demand that others supply us with what we want *without offer-ing to give them something in return* (especially if we back up our demands with a threat of doing them harm – the 'offer they should not refuse'). Our wants are infinite, our means are scarce; Nature is niggardly, and so are people.

24
Of the Process of Negotiation

In negotiation, voluntary exchange is free of coercion. Both of us transact not because we like or love each other (though that is not precluded), but because we want something from each other. The negotiated decision settles the terms of exchange. I can only get what I want (my selfish side) by giving to you what you want (my unselfish side), and you can only get what you want (your selfish side) by giving me what I want (your unselfish side). The transaction transforms our selfishness into a mutually wilful exchange (unless either or both of us declines the terms of the transaction). Each of us in the content of our offers exhibits our unselfish side in exchange for our selfish demands.

Neither party is impartial at the start of a negotiation; the seller of labour, say, seeks the highest wage he can get from the employer; the employer, the buyer of labour, seeks the lowest wage he must pay to labourers. But partiality, where there is a conflict of interest, is either resolved by relative bargaining power (too few or too many labourers for hire at that moment), or by the impartiality of competition. Itinerant migrants lower the price of labour, and competing employers raise it. Smith commented (somewhat sarcastically) on the imbalance of Britain's laws against labourers combining to raise wages and the absence of laws against employers combining to lower them. Be clear, he sympathised with the labourers.

Negotiation integrates the essential linkage in what Smith described as 'a mercenary exchange of good offices according to an agreed valuation'.[1] It is the necessary means by which people, who need have no cares for each other (they may not even know each other), engage in peaceful transactions in society to secure each other's co-operation:

> Negotiation is the process by which we seek for terms to obtain what we want from someone who wants something from us.[2]

The fundamental error of mindlessly repeating that self-love is the defining characteristic of the universal practice of the voluntary negotiation of commercial transactions shows a lack of awareness, bordering on other world-liness, of what these behaviours involved. Given that the systematic study of the negotiation *process*, as it was practised, only began in 1960s in the US[3] and in the mid-1970s in the UK[4], why applied economists (but not social and behavioural psychologists) showed so little interest in negotiation as a process, despite it being the subject of Smith's opening chapters, remains a mystery.

Negotiation as a process

Smith's model of the mediation between self and the impartial spectator usefully describes how an analogous mediation of the conflicting passions of the negotiating parties by the transmutation of selfishness into an 'agreed valuation' is found in all negotiation processes.

Recall how individuals seek sympathy from others and the impartial spectator recoils from overly extravagant expressions of their passions. Our tolerable demeanour in front of our close friends is less tolerable to the impartial spectator who disapproves of extravagant expressions of partial-ity. This prompts us to 'lower [our] passions to the pitch' which 'the specta-tors are capable of going along' with.[5]

In a remarkably apposite passage for negotiation, Smith adds:

> Society and conversation, therefore, are the most powerful remedies for restoring the mind to its tranquillity, if, at any time, it has unfortunately lost it; as well as the best preservatives of that equal and happy temper, which is so necessary to self-satisfaction and enjoyment.[6]

Negotiation is one such purposeful conversation where the parties propose different solutions to the same problem (be it a price, terms of a contract, disposition of rewards and penalties, competing outcomes, or whatever), and construct, iteratively, a single solution acceptable to both. Negotiation requires communication; nobody negotiates by brooding.

In disputes, tones and tempers can be fraught. People passionately express their demands, feel bitterly about their grievances, remember earlier bruising events, and nurse deep hatreds for the 'atrocities' commit-ted by the other party. Negotiation as an alternative to violence is not always, or even necessarily, all 'sweetness and light'.

Even in the many negotiations where a degree of 'sweetness and light' is present, different solutions necessarily lie on the table. We negotiate because we disagree with each other's solution. We start with our non-agreed valuations before we reach 'an agreed valuation'. Negotiations towards an agreed valuation require the parties to move from the solutions they brought to the table. How is this movement managed? What brings agreement about? Here, the process highlighted in *Moral Sentiments* is easily recognisable from studying negotiators at work.

An 'agreed valuation' requires co-operation. Enmity hinders, but does not necessarily preclude, agreement. From two solutions to the same problem the parties can only agree to a single solution, normally different from the original two. One-way compromises are seldom acceptable. The movement of the parties from their original solutions expresses each party's contribution to the joint agreement. My approval of your modified opinions is to adopt them; to disapprove is to reject them.[7]

Differences of opinion are endemic in 'truck, bartering and exchange'. Negotiators are not price takers – if they were, they would not be negotiating. Emotions as to worth, merit and desert run high. Smith puts it well:

> But if you have either no fellow-feeling for the misfortunes I have met with, or none that bears any proportion to the grief which distracts me; or if you have no indignation at the injuries I have suffered, or none that bears any proportion to the resentment that transports me, we can no longer converse on these subjects. We become intolerable to one another. I can neither support your company, nor you mine. You are confounded by my violence and passion, and I am enraged at your cold insensibility and want of feeling.[8]

Walkouts, denigrating rhetoric, and angry threats cloud the air as negotiators let loose their passions that in the absence of empathy distort their perceptions. Your solution threatens my future; mine threatens yours.

The parties justify their stances in the negotiation debate. Movement in negotiation is far from a swiftly moving 'open cry' auction system. Negotiators make (long, and not always coherent) speeches, exchange questions and responses, and endure bitter exchanges threatening to spoil the chances for success. But new information that undermines the tenability of our stances may finally persuade us. So move we do, and with our mutual movement, tones and tempers change, sometimes dramatically, other times grudgingly, and usually accompanied by a sense of relief (even euphoria) as tensions ease and a common solution emerges. Capturing all that in a model of the process makes for cumbersome mathematics; hence valiant and ingenious attempts[9] to do so have been superseded by statements of Nash-type solutions.

The smithian negotiator becomes aware that only by 'lowering his passion to that pitch', which the other party 'is capable of going along with', can he hope for a 'concord of the affections' as a prelude to the harmony flowing from an 'agreed valuation'.[10] And what is true for one party is true also for the other. Interpolating from Smith, the angry negotiator 'must flatten, if I may be allowed to say so, the sharpness of his natural tone, in order to reduce it to the harmony and concord with the emotions of those who are about him.' What each feels is never exactly the same (they both view their own interests from different vantages), but by lowering expressions of their self-interests to make them more acceptable and to meet the other side's movement from whence they started the discourse, both sides review their passionate (often extreme) stances, looking at them in some measure with the eyes of the other party.

'The reflected passion ... is much weaker than the original one' and 'it necessarily abates the violence of what he felt' before the meeting.[11] Negotiators, in short, cannot get all they want and at some point realise the futility of their unmitigated selfishness.

In this manner, negotiators, suppressing their selfish inclination to demand everything for nothing or little in return, 'always endeavour to bring down [their] passions to that pitch, which the [other negotiator] may be expected to go along with'.[12] Traded concession-convergence, prompted by smithian conditional propositions, brings the negotiators towards 'agreed valuations', which 'are the most powerful remedies for restoring the mind to its tranquillity, if at any time, it has unfortunately lost it; as well as the best preservatives of that equal and happy temper, which is so necessary to self-satisfaction and enjoyment' and 'which is so common among men of the world.'[13] This is the 'negotiation dance', through which the parties approach each other's converging positions by trading reciprocal movement on the negotiable issues.

Two selfish persons in negotiation moderate their selfishness down to what is acceptable and, through conditional propositions they transmute their selfishness into an 'agreed valuation', which definitely is not an expression of their otherwise irreconcilable selfishness. They 'give to get' by reducing their demands and increasing their offers.

Think of the conditional proposition like the two elements, sodium and chlorine, which when separated are harmful to humans, but once linked to form ordinary table salt, are the foundation of life. Conditional propositions, likewise, consist of two elements, demands and offers, harmful when separated (because demands without offers are selfish and offers without demands submissively reward selfishness), but when linked conditionally – 'you can't expect to get one without the other' – they bring the negotiators to an 'agreed valuation'.

Linking conditions with offers defines the common propensity of truck, barter and exchange. That Smith taught the conditional proposition over two hundred years before it entered today's negotiation literature is remarkable, but not quite as remarkable as it lying ignored and unnoticed, a veritable sleeping beauty, for so long in *Wealth of Nations* (everybody, I assume, gets at least as far as Chapter 2!).

25
Of Distracting and Dismal Confusions

The butcher, the brewer, and the baker (a comment on an 18th-century diet?), have the contents of our dinners to hand but are not yet persuaded to hand them over:

> 'We address ourselves,' says Smith, 'not to their humanity but to their self-love, and never talk to them of our own necessities but of their advantages.'[1]

> 'When you apply to a brewer or butcher for beer or for beef you do not explain to him how much you stand in need of these, but how much it would be in [his] interest to allow you to have them for a certain price.'[2]

> Man ... works on the selflove of his fellows, by setting before them a sufficient temptation to get what he wants.'[3]

The consistent theme of these versions has nothing to do with single-mindedly selfishness. Quite the reverse, he refers to: '*their* advantages'; 'how much it would be in [*his*] interest'; and 'a sufficient temptation', and decries selfishly making an issue of what you want and why or how much you deserve it. For negotiators who populate markets today, their dinners and much else, depends on them learning the difference between the two approaches.

A common result of you acting selfishly and not addressing the other party's interests is their unwillingness to transact with you at all. Of course, your initial motivation is to seek (selfishly) your dinner, but doing without it as a result of a selfish disregard for their interests is not wise. The impartial spectator would disapprove of your selfish conduct until you curbed your 'selfish' ego and provided, via their interests, 'sufficient temptation' for them in return to provide your dinner.

Attempting *only* to serve yourself is bound to fail. The butcher, the brewer and the baker do not go to the trouble of preparing the beef, beer, and bread you want merely to satisfy their selfish egos. Nor do they give dinners away to whomsoever selfishly fawns for them. By contributing to your dinner in exchange for an 'agreed valuation', they acquire the wherewithal to conclude transactions with the proprietors of their other wants (they already have their dinners!). But they cannot get what they want from you without you getting your dinner. Addressing the interests or advantages of those who might make your dinner available is the universal method by which we acquire peacefully what we want from others.

Not everybody by any means has misunderstood what Smith was saying. Little gems of insight into his meaning appear in the most unpromising of sources:

> It has been customary to describe Political Economy as the dismal science, as the gospel of selfishness. In the hands of Ricardo and his disciples, Political Economy was certainly gloomy enough, and its gospel also too egotistically forbidding; but Smith's conception of economic science, including as it did the co-operative and sympathetic side of life, was eminently hopeful and enervating. His view of the industrial order was wide enough to give full play to that subtle psychological chemistry by which egoism is transmuted into altruism. In Smith's words: 'In civilised society man stands at all times in need of the cooperation and assistance of great multitudes, while his whole life is scarce sufficient to gain the friendship of a few persons.' In such a state, as Smith goes on to show, man can most satisfactorily connect himself with his fellows through the medium of the reciprocity of services – a process which invests self-interest with a social and ethical quality. From this social and ethical germ develops all the higher virtues of civilisation.[4]

Hector Macpherson's (1851–1924) unpretentious little book demonstrates a clearer understanding of Smith's works than has been exhibited by many distinguished authorities. The sentence: 'His view of the industrial order was wide enough to give full play to that subtle psychological chemistry by which egoism is transmuted into altruism', allied to the phrase, 'the reciprocity of services', cuts through the usual worthless babble about 'selfishness' and its associated ideas of 'economic man' (the one with the dismal personality).

Smith, writes Macpherson:

> knew that civilisation does not move along a straight line. Man is not swayed by one overmastering impulse, as assumed by the Ricardian school, that of seeking wealth. Man, especially primitive man, is prey to a thousand fears. At first he is more a superstitious than an industrious being. Out of this sprang religious wars. No sooner freed from this delusion than man falls victim to the economic delusion that wealth can be increased by conquest.[5]

This pure, unadulterated smithian analysis lies buried in Macpherson's obscure and unpretentious biography of Smith (he cites John Rae as his source[6]).

Economic science suffers, from what Macpherson called a 'distracting confusion', because it ignored how people actually satisfied their wants through reciprocal exchanges in real markets. Smith's insight is no manifesto to selfishness, nor a triumph of the one-sided pursuit of self-interest (or indeed, a paean to the 'granite of self-interest')! It is not necessary to wriggle to 'softer' interpretations of 'self-love' to defend Smith's insight.[7]

Those making the fundamental error see the smithian propensity only from a single person's initial viewpoint, forgetting that in all negotiated transactions there are at least two parties, not just one, and both of the parties has to consent to the solution if one is to be agreed. Those smithian authorities who did not test inductively his statements in the opening two chapters in *Wealth of Nations* (a 'very superficial and unnecessary chapter', indeed!) were handicapped from realising their full significance.

Scholarly literature on the economics of wage negotiation goes back to the 1930s,[8] using mathematical analysis to explain why parties alter their current stances (mainly from fear of coercive strikes).[9] Unfortunately, they did not test the arguments of their mathematical functions by observing the arguments of live negotiations.

26
Of Pins and Things

Smith is famous for his account of a pin factory. So famous, in fact, that the pin factory, the division of labour and the extent of the market are practically synonymous with his name. Let me lay this myth to rest.

Smith copied from Diderot's *Encyclopédie* the example of the pin factory, including the 18 operations that enabled ten persons to make 48,000 pins in a day, compared to one a day that might be made by one man undertaking all 18 operations.[1] He took the division of labour, including the limiting effects of the market from Hutcheson, who taught (1737–40) that 'the division of labour must be proportioned to the extent of commerce',[2] which is identical to Smith's assertion (1776) that the 'division of labour… must always be limited by the extent of the market.'[3] (See Appendix.)

Plato also refers to a division of labour in his *Republic*.[4] Closer to Smith's time, Sir William Petty had already outlined the division of labour in 1683[5] and, through the many references to it over the years in many books and pamphlets the concept of the division of labour was a familiar enough by the 1750s.

These facts were acknowledged by Smith when he wrote that the division of labour in a pin manufactory 'has been very often taken notice of' by others,[6] showing that he did not claim or imply that he noticed it first. Yet his clear statement denying his precedence has not prevented him from being lumbered for many years with an accolade he never sought (nor from being severely criticised as if he had made such an absurd claim on the division of labour).[7]

Professor Thorald Rogers, a late 19th century economist at Oxford University, asserted wrongly in 1888:

> One of the earliest phenomena in the progress of human societies is that which Adam Smith called the 'division of labour.' It appears that this great writer was the first person to call attention to the importance of this fact of life. At least I have not found that the French economists gave prominence to it.[8]

Unfortunately, though Roger's audience consisted of a dozen academic colleagues only[9] his book reached many thousands more and, under that and similar kinds of authority, incorrect attributions to Smith were repeated throughout the 20th century.

Did Smith visit a pin factory at all or did he merely copy somebody else's report? He did both. He reports unequivocally: 'I have seen a small manufactory of this kind where ten men only are employed, and where some of them consequently performed two of three distinct operations [of the eighteen]'[10] and he made a direct claim to personal observance when he asserted: 'I have seen several boys ... make, each of them, upwards of two thousand three hundred nails in a day.'[11]

Smith's account of the division of labour could not improve on Sir William Petty, cited above, who gave the example of the making of a watch. 'If one Man shall make the *Wheels*, another the *Spring*, another shall engrave the *Dial-Plate*, and another make the *Cases*, then the *Watch* will be better and cheaper, than if the whole Work be put upon any one Man.'[12]

The division of labour increases 'the productive powers of labour' through the increased dexterity of the workingman (practice improves performance). It also cuts down on time lost by switching from one operation to another and the great number of 'machines' invented to facilitate and abridge labour enables one man to do the work of many.[13] This last consequence can be misread. Smith was talking about simple aids and tools that made work less onerous, more specialised and not about the invention of complex powered machinery that replaced labour. That revolution in machine power technology came after Smith's time.

Examples of smithian division of labour are pre-measured 'jigs' to hold items in place for cutting, drilling or milling operations without having to re-measure and mark each piece again, or simple contrivances like the tying of string between a handle and a valve so that when the handle moved the valve opened and shut automatically.[14]

I am not comfortable with Rashid's criticism of Smith's focus on simple improvements in productivity from the re-organisation of labour instead of by the invention of (power driven) machinery that replaced rather than just augmented labour's contribution to output, and which put the 'entrepreneur and not the worker' at the 'centre of the stage'.[15] It is incontrovertibly true that 'the capitalist who is driven by the lure of profits to improve his machinery continually' played at the 'centre of the stage' in the next century, but the absence of acknowledgement of this unknowable fact should not be regarded as a deficiency in *Wealth of Nations*. When Smith was writing, capitalist innovations were still 'off-stage', without playing even bit parts, let alone them being stars of the show. If 'Smith's picture was misleading' it was only so because he did not enjoy Professor Rashid's hindsight. His account of the division of labour is primitive because the phenomenon in his time was primitive.

Smith believed that common workmen, not specialist designers, or 'philosophers', invented many of these simple productive aids,[16] thus qualifying his deep pessimism of how the division of labour makes common labourers 'as stupid and ignorant as it is possible for a human creature to become'.[17] 'Stupid and ignorant' some workers may have been, but as a group they also contributed intelligently to increasing productivity in workplaces dominated by simple tools to assist or augment but not replace labour, much like the bicycle did for travel. But he also conceded that 'many improvements have been made by the ingenuity of the makers of the machines,' which created a new business in machine improvements.[18] Without a doubt this development was the future; Smith did not anticipate its full ramifications, nor I suspect did precious few others.

Specialisation

The fabrication of machinery, therefore, in turn and in time, became a specialised profession and even philosophers sub-divided into 'tribes' or 'classes', just like 'every employment', with the same result: it created improvements in dexterity and the reduction of wasted unproductive time.[19] There was still a long way to go before social science, for example, was to divide into the intensely focussed specialist subjects, with which we are familiar today. In identifying these trends with the progress of society, he was, as a Moral Philosopher, acutely aware of the wide range of his subject's interests, from Natural Theology, through Ethics, Jurisprudence and Political Economy, and he might have wondered for how long these disciplines would remain comfortably within the scope of a single person. He ends his speculative piece with an unusual, for him, tantalising glimpse of what lay ahead:

> Each individual becomes more expert in his own peculiar branch, more work is done upon the whole, and the quantity of science is considerably increased by it.[20]

He had no doubts, however, about the impact of these trends upon society:

> It is the great multiplication of the productions of all the different arts, in consequence of the division of labour, which occasions, in a well governed society, that universal opulence which extends itself to the lower ranks of society.[21]

It is worth remembering on this, and other occasions, when he spoke of 'universal opulence' spreading to the lower ranks, he was not speaking about vast, sudden or rapid changes in their welfare. The changes would be small, but cumulative in an upward direction, marching behind the improving productivity of labour and contributing to the steady, 'very slow and gradual' consequence of general changes in the organisation of labour. More labour is hired for each expansion of the division of labour and where this takes formerly idle or casual labour into paid employment it spreads the crumbs of opulence to those bereft of steady income.

27
Of Common Coats and Opulence

It is easy to forget that Smith wrote about 18th-century independent arti-sans interacting with each other in ever more complex transactions to exchange increasing surpluses of their 'own output', for greater quantities of the surpluses of 'other workmen', or 'what comes to the same thing, for the price of a greater quantity of theirs'. With each supplying others 'abun-dantly' a 'general plenty diffuses itself through all the different ranks of society'.[1] He was not writing about labourers organised by the hundreds or thousands into 19th-century factories.

Smith uses the example of the production of the common labourer's coarse and rough woollen coat, to show how such an ordinary everyday item is a product of the labour of 'a great multitude of workmen.' Mandeville had a similar train of thought in his *Fable of the Bees* but did not develop it.[2] Smith's example shows the extraordinary complexity of the division of labour in commercial society, even one as primitive as that of mid-18th century Britain.[3] Today, our economies exhibit degrees of com-plexity many times greater than Smith's example. Think of what would be involved in describing the production of a microwave oven. A US graduate friend in the 1980s said that Professor Milton Friedman of Chicago used a common 'lead' pencil from his desk to exhibit Smith's example of a 'coarse and rough woollen coat'.

Beginning with the woollen coat itself, we have shepherds, sorters of the sheared wool, wool-combers or carders, dyers, scribblers, spinners, weavers, fullers, dressers, and many others, joining together in co-operating to com-plete the production of the coat. It does not stop there because the workmen are not in the same place as each other, or adjacent to workmen seeking woollen coats. Merchants have to transport the materials from the workmen who made the coats to others living in distant parts, and onwards to other workmen.

In some cases, shipping facilitated commerce, though accurate naviga-tion remained a problem up to the 1780s, until Cook's Pacific voyages proved that Harrison's chronometers measured longitude exactly, opening the world's seas to voyages navigated along Great Circles instead of shore-hugging or latitude-running dead reckoning. How many ship-builders, sailors, sail- and rope-makers were employed to bring the drugs for the dyers from 'remote corners of the world'?

Even the meanest tools of the workmen, let alone the sophisticated instruments of the watchmaker and ships' navigation officers, employed a large variety of skilled labour in their making. Setting aside the complicated machines of a ship, the fuller's mill and the weaver's loom, what about the simple metal shears the shepherd used to clip wool? Or the miners, builders of the blast furnace for smelting iron ore, fellers of timber, burners of the smelter's charcoal, brick-makers, brick-layers, furnace men, mill-wrights, forgers, and blacksmiths who produced them?

Taking into account the multitudes engaged in the production of a labourer's other clothes, and those other multitudes engaged in providing his household furniture, coarse linen shirts, shoes, bed, and the kitchen-grate where his food was prepared, the coals used for heat, which was dug from the bowels of the earth and brought to him, perhaps by sea voyage, followed by long journeys over land, and all the kitchen utensils, the furnishing of his table with knives and forks, earthen and pewter plates, and the production of his bread and beer, the glass windows which let in heat and keep out the wind and rain (with all the knowledge and art required for producing glass), together with all the tools of the workmen, it is evident that without the assistance of many thousands of people, the meanest person in a civilised country could not be provided with the basic items he and his family needed and without which they would live in even more dreadful poverty. Mandeville's point was only slightly different: the rich man's clothes and the fabulously extravagant dresses of rich women also produced work for poor labourers in scores of occupations.

Poverty is relative and Smith ends with a comparison. The common labourer is very poor compared to the extravagant luxury of the very rich, but the accommodation and expenses of the European prince does not exceed that of an industrious and frugal peasant to the same extent as the latter exceeds that of an African king, the 'absolute master of the lives and liberties of ten thousand naked savages.'[4]

Now, while Smith's choice of words grates on modern sensitivities (Lionel Robbins changed Smith's noun to avoid giving 'offence'),[5] it is worthwhile referring to earlier versions of his comparison of the common labourer in Scotland with the master of 'ten thousand naked savages.'

Smith held no illusions about the state of affairs in civilised countries. In his classroom he stated bluntly that the labour of the poor was sacrificed to 'maintaining the rich in ease and luxury' and that the landlord's idleness and luxury were maintained by the labour of his tenants and the industrious merchant. He went on:

> But every savage has the full enjoyment of the fruits of his own labours; there are no landlords, no usurers and no tax gatherers. We should expect therefore that the savage should be much better provided than the dependant poor man who labours both for himself and for others. But the case is far otherwise. The indigence of a savage is far greater than that of the meanest citizen of any thing that deserves the name of a civilised nation.[6]

Between his lectures and the *Wealth of Nations* thirteen years later he switched from comparing the relative poverty of a poor Scottish labourer with an 'Indian Prince' in North America to that of the poverty of an 'African king' (why he switched continents is not obvious). What was common to both examples was that the savage was free from 'landlords, usurers and tax gatherers' taking their share of his labour, which sounds great until you recall that his total wherewithal from the fruits of his labour was meagre in comparison to the common labourer's net income in Scotland. The difference in circumstance lay in the presence, or absence, of the division of labour. To be poor in Scotland was truly a burden, but to be 'rich' in the wilds of North America or Africa was an onerous burden indeed, without considering the utter destitution endured by the even poorer wretches lorded over by their richer 'kings'.

Smith did not imply that those at the bottom of the heap should be grateful for their lot on the grounds that they could be worse off (a kind of regional Panglossian complacency for their 'luck' in living in the 'best of all possible worlds'). To suggest as much parodies his intentions. Smith was comparing existing 18th-century societies, not doing PR for the 'best of all possible worlds'.

He refers to the 'rich and opulent merchant' living in far greater luxury, ease and plenty than his clerks to whom he gives a few directions, leaving them to conduct his business. His clerks too, lived in a state far superior to the artisans who finish the commodities created by the labourers, and who labour uncomfortably under cover from inclement weather to earn a livelihood. If we compare them not to the independent artisan they worked for, nor the merchant's clerks in whose name the products are purchased, let alone compare them with the rich merchant enjoying 'all the conveniences and delicacies of life', but compared them to the even poorer labourers below them we soon appreciate their relative affluence.

Poor men struggled with all the inconvenience of the soil and the seasons, including continual exposure to inclement weather and the most severe forms of labour at the same time. The labouring poor, who supported the whole of society and who furnished the means of convenience and ease for the richer classes, received a very small share of what they produced and were 'buried in obscurity' for their pains. But, compared to the savage, how was it that the poorest labourers in a civilised country accounted for such large shares of the conveniences of life, despite bearing on their shoulders the whole of the rest of the people? Smith's answer was that 'the division of labour amongst the different hands can alone account for this.'[7]

His conclusion had nothing to do with the inherent racial 'superiority' of Europeans over 'Indians' or Africans, or any such similar silly charge. His analysis pointed to the division of labour, and not racial inferiority, as the sole cause of the differences in their respective circumstances. It also linked a country's growth path to the slow and gradual expansion of markets to stimulate further divisions of labour, from which opulence spread to all sections of society.

The common labourer's woollen coat demonstrated the evolution of complex interlocking markets even for the least complex of products. Markets did not evolve by plan or design. They emerged from individuals responding to opportunities, perceived by them as local events, slowly linking them up in ever more complex relationships (production for 'distant sale'), each part dividing and sub-dividing as markets grew and drew vast numbers of people into providing co-operative assistance to each other. Each individual could believe he worked for himself, yet, in fact, he worked for numerous, mostly anonymous, others, i.e., his customers and his customers' customers.

28

Alienation: Rhetoric or Substance?

It is well to remember the advantages of gaining steady employment for those who had no, or limited, means of acquiring their subsistence; what those with low wages lost in low living standards was compensated for in the predictability that regular, wages provided for their families. The State gradually became a major source of regular paid employment, blurring the line between real jobs and sinecures, and the professional classes (including Adam Smith and Robert Burns), sought Customs posts for the security they brought to those with sufficient interest to get them. By the late 18th century the State had far more patronage than ever before to dispense in paid employment and sinecures out of its greater tax harvests, matched only by the greater expenditures passing through the sticky hands of 'retainers' for rewards. Nobody accused the 18th-century State of spending wisely, efficiently or honestly.

Because permanent full-time work was rare, those without interest made do with casual, seasonal and itinerant employment, often in more than one trade, as was the norm before the factory system. Until then, labourers took what work they could find. The 'dark satanic mills' were still 60 or more years away in the distant future.

Critics of market mechanisms point to their manifest weaknesses as they emerged out of the harsh realities of the old, largely agricultural order (much the same comments were made about the weaknesses of markets following the collapse of the Soviet Union and the slow transition to market capitalism). The 'de-humanisation' of work theme, awaited somebody to articulate it. Smith did,[1] as had Adam Ferguson, nine years earlier.[2] Both saw de-humanisation as a consequence of the division of labour, potentially signalling a heavy human cost for the immense gains in productivity in the commercial age, unless, as Smith recommended, its effects were ameliorated by government action in education. Incidentally, Karl Marx, ignorant of *Jurisprudence*, incorrectly referred to Ferguson as Smith's 'teacher' and his 'master', and described Smith as being a 'pupil' of Ferguson, even accusing him of 'reproducing [Ferguson's] work'![3]

Smith believed that agricultural labourers were more skilled than artisans. Bashing metal hardly varied, he believed (he knew more about farming than metal or woodwork), but ploughing with horses or oxen required much judgement and discretion on the part of common ploughmen, generally regarded as a model of 'stupidity and ignorance' for their defects in manners, uncouth accents and limited vocabularies. Yet their understanding of the varied tasks on a farm was generally superior to the town labourer 'whose attention from morning to night is commonly occupied in performing one or two very simple operations.'[4]

To spend a lifetime performing a few simple operations reduces the occasions to invent expedients for removing difficulties that seldom if ever occur. Labourers who lose these habits generally 'become as stupid and ignorant as it is possible for a human creature to become.' Hirschman suggests Smith 'celebrates' the division of labour in Book I only to 'castigate' it in Book V.[5] Did Smith lose the plot? Not entirely, because there is a plausible explanation for his different treatments in Books I and V.

Agricultural workers, who fed the whole population, accounted for about half the available workforce in Britain. The other half either starved for want of the wherewithal to buy food from the agricultural sector, or they found work in the non-agricultural sector. But without the division of labour there would not have been enough work for them and not enough income to buy their subsistence. In short, if the division of labour were curtailed, society faced an economic calamity, hardly likely to cure anybody's uncouth ignorance or understanding.

Smith continues in a famous and much quoted passage to describe 'alienation':

> The torpor of his mind renders him, not only incapable of relishing or bearing a part in any rational conversation, but of conceiving any generous, noble, or tender sentiment, and consequently of forming any just judgment concerning many even of the ordinary duties of private life. Of the great and extensive interests of his country, he is altogether incapable of judging; and unless very particular pains have been taken to render him otherwise, he is equally incapable of defending his country in war. The uniformity of his stationary life naturally corrupts the courage of his mind, and makes him regard with abhorrence the irregular, uncertain, and adventurous life of a soldier. It corrupts even the activity of his body, and renders him incapable of exerting his strength with vigour and perseverance, in any other employment that that to which he has been bred. His dexterity at his own particular trade seems in this manner, to be acquired at the expense of his intellectual, social, and martial values. But in every improved and civilised society this is the state into which the labouring poor, that is, the great body of the people, must necessarily fall, unless government takes some pains to prevent it.[6]

To be sure, it is a damning indictment of the side effects of the division of labour. Smith contrasted societies preceding the improvement of manufactures and the extension of foreign commerce, focusing on the effects of the division of labour on a country's martial prowess (as did Ferguson).[7] And, not for the last time, Smith makes it clear that he thinks it is the government that should 'take some pains to prevent' alienation. Some 'watchman state' where a government should have responsibility for preventing workmen being 'incapable of exerting' their strength and intellectual powers in what must have been hundreds of thousands of locations in the country!

But everybody cannot go to Glasgow University! They can go to school, however, and learn at an early age to 'read, write, and account', which for a 'very small' expense the public can 'facilitate, can encourage, and can even impose upon almost the whole body of the people'.[8] Elementary education and physical exercise imposed by the government, not by markets (though nothing prevented them being provided by markets and utility, as always determining delivery) were his remedies for the defects of alienation.

Smith, a philosopher, visited small manufactures but never worked in one and neither did Marx, nor had either of them experienced the anxieties of a labouring man with an uncertain future without a source of income. Smith spent his uncertain future after Oxford in the tranquil comfort of his mother's house in Kirkcaldy. He viewed common labour from the privileged and materially comfortable vantage of an educated professional, not from the hopeless and imposed idleness of an uneducated labourer bereft of employment, no matter how menial, or how hungry he was. That there is dignity in even low paid work that supports a labourer's family, often escapes the appreciative notice of many easily disturbed, but comfortably off intellectuals.

Professor McCulloch, editor of 19th-century editions of *Wealth of Nations*, disagreed thoroughly with Smith's observations on the relative intelligence of agricultural and town workers. He went so far as to suggest, implausibly, that the absence of mental stimulation of those 'who are constantly engaged in burnishing a pin' forces them to cultivate their mental powers, not to decline into imbecility. By working with numbers of others (and the numbers were getting larger with the growth of large scale capitalist enterprises in the 19th century) workers had 'constant opportunities of discussing every topic of interest or importance' that gradually trained them into habits of thinking and, from the 'collision of conflicting opinions', sharpened their intellects![9]

He made trenchant comments on the famous 'alienation' passage quoted above, regarded Smith's exposition as 'unfounded as well as can be imagined', and argued that the facts were 'completely the reverse', particularly his reference to the decline of the martial prowess of labourers. He quotes, in his rebuttal, the success of General Elliot's light horse during the seven years' war (1756–63), all of which men were recruited from the tailors of London.[10]

I think it safe to assume that Smith's comments on the decline of the labourers' mental faculties from the division of labour were rhetorical pillars in support of his case for setting up schools to teach the basics to children, rather than a serious policy to avert something they were supposed to be in danger of suffering from throughout their adult lives. Smith's rhetoric ran ahead of his case.

This is not to deny the unwholesome nature of factory life in the 19th century – though the implication that life for the poor before the factory system was a golden age of summer picnics, maypole dancing and sweetness and light, from which joys they were snatched and turned into brain-dead simpletons, cannot be taken seriously.

Smith's examples of the division of labour (the pin factory and the common labourers' coat) show that he considered the phenomenon was as much a division of labour in making specific products as it was a division of labour between enterprises of different sectors. His belief that market linkages between sectors were the engines for opulence across the whole of society brought him close to anticipating input-output analysis.

29
What Industrial Revolution?

Often declared as an apostle of capitalism, Smith showed no sign that he was aware (and nor I believe were his contemporaries) of the transformation of his fourth stage of commerce into a new, unanticipated, capitalist fifth stage, the first green shoots of which were then appearing timidly in England, less so in Scotland. In the next century the consequences of this phenomenon became known as the 'Industrial Revolution', which revolutionised the world of commerce as Smith envisaged it. James Watt, who worked away quietly in Glasgow University's instrument workshop from 1756 to 1765, a few yards from Smith's lecture rooms, had no notions of where his fastidious instrument repairing and innovative tinkering would lead him in coming decades.[1]

When did the fifth 'capitalist' stage begin? This is a controversy over dates. Walt Rostow, with improbable exactitude, picked out the precise year for the start of Britain's 'take off' into industrialism. He chose 1783,[2] seven years before Smith died and seven years after *Wealth of Nations* was published.

The coincidental symmetry opened an academic debate over whether Smith noticed, or should have noticed, that something of major significance was afoot and, if he didn't notice what was going on, what did this say of his powers of observation? It is, however, a debate of more importance to the hijackers of Smith's legacy than its defenders. Smith's reputation can survive acknowledgement that he missed the coming industrial revolution and capitalism of the 19th century, but those who claim he was the 'apostle' or 'high priest' of capitalism cannot but be embarrassed by a lack of evidence that he was aware of what he was alleged to be preaching.

Ashton, even more rashly that Rostow, actually fixed the exact day(!) on which the industrial revolution began. He chose 26 December 1760,[3] when they lit the first furnace at the Carron Ironworks, near Falkirk. Smith in nearby Glasgow, though he knew Dr John Roebuck, the firm's main projector, fairly well did not make anything of this allegedly momentous event.[4]

Notably, 1760 is twenty three years earlier than England's 'take off' into industrialism, according to Rostow, suggesting that this momentous change began in Scotland and not its southern neighbour, no doubt gratifying to we Scots but less convincing if you prefer evidence.

Some say Smith did not fail to 'anticipate' the industrial revolution but showed 'remarkable insight' into what was going on around him.[5] Others say that he ignored what was happening ('innovations', 'inventive genius' and 'business spirit') and this was a major 'error of judgement' on his part.[6] Such assessments enjoy the luxury of hindsight, enabling them to berate Smith's supposedly erroneous judgement half a century before the event, though they obviously only learned about the industrial revolution themselves well over a century after it. Hindsight is not sufficient qualification to criticise Smith's absence of foresight.

Kindleberger versus Hartwell

Debate about Smith's lack of prescience of the industrial revolution and capitalism is largely about evidence. We can only demonstrate his awareness by traces of it in his books or correspondence. If his alleged awareness left no such traces we conclude he was not aware.

His critics are reduced to assessing what he *ought* to have known, bearing in mind that dedicated modern researchers, with access to myriad 18th-century newspapers, books, pamphlets, patents, parliamentary reports, private correspondence, diaries and other sources of the period found in vast libraries of neatly catalogued source materials and via the Internet (including from antiquarian booksellers of unrivalled sophistication), have an incomparable advantage over what was available to Smith. It should also be noted, but often is not, that Smith wrote *Wealth of Nations* largely either while travelling in France or in his mother's house at Kirkcaldy, and not in a university library.

Professor Kindleberger examined the argument that Smith was aware of the forthcoming industrial revolution by reference to his sources in *Wealth of Nations* and concluded that 'most of the books Smith relies on, moreover, are fairly old, published in the first quarter of the eighteenth century, and the bulk of his detailed illustrations relate to this period as well'.[7] He noted, as an American, how Smith had a 'superb record' for prescience in respect of the rebellion in the American colonies, but he had absolutely no record of prescience of the coming industrial revolution, allegedly happening right under his nose. Smith's analytical insight obviously stopped well short of foresight.

R. M. Hartwell, a leading British authority on the history of the industrial revolution, critiqued Kindleberger's data and claimed that 'Adam Smith was aware of the economic changes occurring during his lifetime, which coincide with the background and beginnings of the industrial revolution.'[8]

Hartwell focused on Kindleberger's assertion about the references in *Wealth of Nations*. However, Hartwell quietly switched from proving Smith's 'awareness of the industrial revolution' to his showing Smith's awareness of 'eighteenth century growth', an entirely different focus.[9] Obviously, 18th-century economic growth was evident to Smith; that, after all, was what *Wealth of Nations* is about, and he made economic growth, an indicator of the success of commercial society, the main focus of his analysis. Nobody at the time explained economic growth in terms of the 'industrial revolution', or 'capitalism'.

Kindleberger asserted that Smith relied mostly on books published in the first quarter of the 18th century. Hartwell challenged his assertion. If he had succeeded, then Kindleberger's claim would lose credibility. First though, Hartwell shifted the goal posts again (typical of fractious academic discourse) by switching from books quoted in *Wealth of Nations* to the books in Smith's library and found that the 'majority date from after 1750'.[10] Smith drew on books beyond those listed in a catalogue of his private library (he had also donated his collection of moral philosophy books to Glasgow University in 1764).[11] By restricting the references to his separate private library (based on Bonar's catalogue)[12] and by excluding the classics to which Smith avidly referred, Hartwell 'massaged' the evidence to get his result.

Next, he returned to Kindleberger's actual assertion, having helped his sample by first 'excluding the classics', reporting that 'a fairly complete examination of the authors referred to' in *Moral Sentiments* and *Wealth of Nations*, show 'only about a quarter of them were published before 1750, and more than half were published for the first time after 1750'.[13]

Examining *Moral Sentiments* and *Wealth of Nations*, the former has references to books published before 1750 to books after 1750 in the ratio of about 5:1, and, after excluding the classics, this ratio drops only to 3:1. This is a clear majority of pre-1750 books, suggesting that *Moral Sentiments* (published in 1759) was based mainly on books published before 1750. A clear win for Kindleberger.

Taking *Wealth of Nations*, on the other hand, the ratio of pre- to post-1750 book references is 7:5, (another win for Kindleberger) and, excluding the classics, the ratio is 5:6, a marginal success for Hartwell. Both scholars, I should remark, on this disputatious occasion were impeccably well mannered; sadly, in my experience, an exception in academic disputes.

However, just because a book was published after 1750 does not convey anything about Smith's alleged degree of awareness of the industrial revolution or capitalism. Most, if not all of the books Smith refers to in *Wealth of Nations* were not relevant to any aspect of the industrial revolution; for example, Hutcheson's book published in 1755 was posthumous (he died in 1746; and his book was completed in 1742), while others were about foreign countries, including those on India, China, Patagonia and North

America, and Cook's voyages to the Pacific, all a long way geographically and economically from the first green shoots of the industrial revolution in Britain. There is absolutely no significance that his 3,000-volume library contained 'many published in the seventies and eighties', because Smith referenced a mere handful of these in the editions of *Wealth of Nations* he edited up to 1790.

Smith's alleged awareness of the industrial revolution showed few traces, if any, in his published Works, and this left 'awareness by association' as a possible source of evidence, though, it must be said, it is pathetic evidence at best. Hartwell attempted to prove his case by reference to Smith's social activities and travels! First, he refers to Smith's well-known affection for clubbing, at least while a professor at Glasgow (1751–64) and intermittently during later years in Edinburgh and London.

After his return from France in 1766 he retired to Kirkcaldy for six years to write *Wealth of Nations* and he was almost entirely unsociable. His dearest friend, David Hume, wrote to him in 1769, begging him to come to Edinburgh for company and even challenging him, in near desperation, to meet him on Inch-Keith island in the Forth and agree not to leave until 'we were fully agreed on all points of controversy.'[14] From 1773 to 1777 Smith was in London. He became a Fellow of the Royal Society and, in 1783 he was a founding Fellow of the Royal Society of Edinburgh. Hartwell quotes Smith's tour of famous Parisian salons in 1764–6 but, in his post-1776 years, sociability of this kind and scale were distant memories. He seems to have switched off his public interest in contemporary affairs and tended to be circumspect about anything controversial except with his closest friends.

Hartwell listed Glasgow, Oxford, Edinburgh, London, Paris and Toulouse that Smith visited – and the minor ones of Geneva, Bordeaux and Montpelier, not forgetting Kirkcaldy. He does not provide evidence that these visits contributed anything to Smith's awareness of the industrial revolution or capitalism, or that either phenomena 'took off' in the cities he might have passed through or read about. He left Oxford in 1746 never to return, he visited Paris, Geneva, Toulouse, Bordeaux and Montpelier in 1764–6 never to return, and in his last years he only visited Edinburgh, Glasgow and London. The evidence does not justify Hartwell's claims.

Smith certainly knew individuals who were merchants or manufacturers and corresponded with them over the years. His correspondence with Edmund Burke reveals a dispute between Mr Champions (1743–91) and Mr Wedgewood (1730–95) over patents for China pottery;[15] with John Glassford (1715–83), the richest tobacco merchant and shipper, mentioning two of Smith's cousins, one involved in a broad tape weaving 'factory' founded in 1732, and the other seeking a career in merchant shipping;[16] William Pulteney (1729–1805), mentioning difficulties in business and banking;[17] John Roebuck [1718–94],[18] founder of the Carron Iron

Company, mainly about the war in America; and of course many letters to and from William Strahan and Thomas Cadell, printers and publishers, mainly about new editions of his books. In no sense do any of his extant letters show that Smith was aware of the great changes just beyond the horizon.

30
Significance of Smith's 'Unawareness'?

Why is it important to prove that Smith was aware of the impending industrial revolution? Because the fact that he was not aware rankles those who believe *Wealth of Nations* is a treatise on the economics of capitalism. That he was not aware, and there is little to no evidence that he was aware of anything remotely akin to an industrial revolution, throws into doubt claims that he was a progenitor of the economics of capitalism.

Believers in the prevailing orthodoxy convince themselves that he had been aware of the impending growth of large scale manufacturing, driven by powered machinery and owned by large private capitals, all closely associated with the new capitalism and constituting, presumably, not a new fifth stage added to Smith's four stages, but, in a complete fiction, that Smith really meant by his fourth Age of Commerce the then unknown phenomena of capitalism! Belief is the mother of their 'facts' – he *ought* to have been aware, therefore he *must* have been aware. That he was not aware creates a problem for those who believe he wrote a treatise on capitalism, but not for those who treat *Wealth of Nations* as an account of mid-18th-century commercial society.

W. Cunningham, interestingly in the part of his book entitled 'Laissez Faire', makes pertinent points that put the earliest years of the industrial revolution (which he locates as from 1770 to 1850) into proper perspective:

> There have been many different forms of industrial invention. Sometimes there have been the introduction of new processes, as in the important series of experiments by which the problem of smelting and working iron, with fuel obtained from coal, was finally solved; ... Other improvements have consisted in the employment of new implements, by which the skilled labourer is assisted to do his work more quickly or better; one example has been noticed in the flying shuttle, and the substitution of the spinning-wheel for the whorl and spindle was another. But such a change is hardly to be described as the introduction of machinery. A machine as commonly understood, does not assist a man

to do his work, it does the work itself, under human guidance; its characteristic feature is that it is an application of power, and not of human exertion. ... The invention of new processes and new implements has not such a necessary and direct result on the employment and remuneration of labour as occurs with the introduction of machines. So far as the wealth of the realm is concerned, the development of the coal and iron trades was of extraordinary importance, but the substitution of mechanical inventions for hand labour in the textile trades brought about a revolution in social life throughout the country.[1]

As Cunningham makes clear, it was the introduction of machinery that rendered it necessary to concentrate labourers in factories, where the machines were power driven, and not leave them dispersed in the countryside. This was an entirely different mode of production from the 'cottage industry' familiar to Smith. For most of Smith's life, cottage industry was the norm, with labourers working manually driven machines as artisans or for piece wages for merchants in rooms that were part of their houses. Factories in the 19th century severed the connection between rural occupations and cottage employments, up to then closely entwined.

Smith's manufacturers were 'small, independent masters, rarely employing more than twenty men and girls, with most of the work done by family or apprentices.'[2] The economics of these places pepper the pages of *Wealth of Nations*, and the evident benefits of loosening the grip of corporate laws and practices enthused Smith in his relentless drive against the mercantile system.[3] By contrasting the commercial bustle of non-incorporated towns like Birmingham (where fortunes were made in buckles, buttons and candlesticks) with older corporate towns like Sheffield (where traditional, established products predominated), Smith's convictions were confirmed. Incidents of 'factories' larger in scale than the cottage system (e.g., Taylor's Birmingham 'toy' factory, 1759; Roebuck's Carron Iron, 1760; Boulton's Soho factory, 1765, for example) with their divisions of labour and simple machines, using known technologies and labour practices, were signs of a scaling up of commercial production to serve rising prosperity promoted by larger markets; they did not portend the industrial revolution.

Moneyed men in the 18th century were merchants rather than manufacturers; moneyed men in the 19th century were employers of labour in machine power driven factories rather than merchants. For the labourers, cottage industry enabled them to fall back on supplementary income from rural occupations in economic slowdowns; in the factories they were vulnerable to the fluctuations of trade and were cut off from rural fallbacks. It was a totally different world from the one Smith lived in. He was dead by the time evidence for the new age accumulated and became incontestable.

If he thought about the evolution of age of commerce, he looked no further than to national agricultural improvement, led by the 'middling orders' of small-scale farmers, both in Britain and the American colonies. He thought America had a promising future and that they would do exceptionally well over the next one hundred years.

This does not constitute evidence that Smith favoured a form of 'agrarian capitalism', unless you re-define 'capitalism' merely to be producers selling in markets, which dilutes capitalism as a phenomenon to cover the Roman Empire and probably earlier still. It also ignores his four Stages and his Age of Commerce, creating a muddle by inventing 'capitalism' centuries before it appeared in the 19th century. Though independent yeoman farming was a dynamic economic force in the 18th century, including in the American colonies, Smith considered that large landlords, living off agricultural rents, were a spent force.

Smith's conception of modern society was the restoration of a previously existing commercial fourth stage that had been interrupted and reversed by the fall of the Roman Empire. Smith wrote about the fourth age of commerce (producers responding to markets) and did not see it as a completely new age in human progress. He believed that the age of commerce was already three thousand or more years old and he believed that the expanding commerce visible in Europe was its recovery from a feudal interregnum.

But even here, in European territory with which he was familiar, he knew nothing of the Eastern 'temple economies' and the economic structures of antiquity, painstakingly detailed by Professor Silver.[4] Nor did he have access to modern research on the roles played by commerce (and the temple economies) in India;[5] and foreign trade in Arabia and Persia (he was, however, familiar with Marco Polo's account of his visit to China – 'Marco Polo, who visited it more than five hundred years ago, describes 'one of the most fertile, best cultivated, most industrious, and most populous countries in the world').[6]

He barely looked beyond the 1770s, except, notably, in his comments on the future of the American colonies as an agricultural and commercial power, which he considered would likely be richer than Britain in wealth and population by the 1870s, but without anticipating how new technology would transform them into a major industrial power.[7] Anybody looking to *Wealth of Nations* for a handbook of American capitalism is looking in the wrong place and at the wrong author.

Smithian opulence was not just having a sufficiency of food. It meant having manufactured products (clothes, domestic utensils, furniture, bedding, carpets, curtains, stoves, trinkets, baubles, and artefacts of all kinds) and these required a substantial and sustained growth in the activities of merchants and manufacturers.

Wealth of Nations devotes many pages to the removal of impediments to allow the productive forces of commerce to do their work. For Smith that was a big enough, long-term agenda that faced many obstacles, political, social, historical and constitutional, without introducing fanciful speculation about future revolutionary changes in technology and social organisation of which he had not an inkling, clue or suspicion. Moreover, for the last 14 years of his life he ceased to be involved in the search, as he was rather 'busy' searching for contraband, not for 'capitalism'.

31
Why Smith 'Retired'

It is easy to miss the fact that by 1777 Smith had 'retired' from active research and serious academic work. In 1780 Smith explained his retirement in a letter:

> Upon my return to Britain [1766] I retired to a small Town in Scotland the place of my nativity, where I continued to live for six years in great tranquillity, and almost complete retirement. ... In the Spring of 1773 a proposal, which many of my friends thought very advantageous was made to me to go abroad a second time. The discussion of this proposal obliged me to go to London ... For four years after this London was my principal residence, where I finished and published my Book. I had returned to my old retirement at Kirkcaldy ... when by the interest of the Duke of Buccleugh, I was appointed to my present Office; which though it requires a good deal of attendance is both easy and honourable.[1]

If Smith had gone abroad in 1773 he might not have finished *Wealth of Nations*! As it was he took the post as Commissioner of Customs in Edinburgh in 1778, effectively retired, and did not finish *Jurisprudence*.

The reasons for his failure to publish his long promised work on *Jurisprudence* have been the subject of speculation. It had nothing to do with his 'indolence' or his being 'too busy' with his duties as a Commissioner of Customs in Edinburgh. It had everything to do with the political and personal embarrassment at the success of the American War of Independence. Smith lived in a Constitutional Monarchy. He was a much-respected authority on political economy and he had the ear of King's Ministers in British Governments. That ought to have been a clue to why he went silent for 14 years until his death.

Cast your mind back to Smith's 1763–4 lectures on constitutional monarchy and the six characteristics of the democratic foundations of British democracy (Chapter 15). Now note how these principles were among those incorporated into the Constitution of the United States. They were not born of the accretion of centuries of constitutional development within a changing British monarchy; they were carried into effect by force of arms against the same British monarchy, long lauded by Smith for its democratic credentials and for its anticipated demise into impotent symbolism. The North Americans leapt from being British colonies governed by the King's representatives into a full-blown new sovereign state, more advanced in democratic principles and their application than the motherland.

Smith cast the likely tensions, should there be a parliamentary alliance between the mother country and her colonies (the solution to the war that he preferred), as arising from a union between 'the monarchical and democratic parts of the constitution.'[2] He conceded that 'difficulties and great difficulties might occur in its execution' but stated firmly that none of them were 'insurmountable' and, significantly for where the real problem might lay, he alludes not to the 'nature of things' in such a union, but from the 'prejudices and opinions of the people on this and the other side of the Atlantic'.[3] In other words, the real problem lay in the politics and personalities of the respective elites in Britain and its colonies, particularly within the British monarchy for which the idea of letting a democracy into a union of parliaments was anathema, especially one that would 'take over' the government of both parts of the union within a hundred years and 'remove' the 'seat of the empire', from London to a place like New York.[4]

It is not difficult to see Smith's problem. How could he publish *Jurisprudence* and not cause great offence to the King and the King's Ministers? To endorse the colonists' version of the six democratic principles in the US Constitution would give succour to the victorious enemies of the King; to decry the US Constitution would deny everything he had lectured and written about the democratic credentials of British liberty. How would he explain his proposal for a union of monarchy and democracy following the defeat of the King's army and navy: with relief or regret? What form would a comparison of the two constitutions take: friendly or hostile?

Jurisprudence could not ignore the US Constitution, and Smith had no honourable way to obfuscate the issues. His sympathies for the application and development of the six principles of constitutional liberty as expressed by the American ex-colonists are apparent in *Wealth of Nations* and in his related correspondence on the American War. There would also be abundant reports on his many private conversations in his social hours on the conduct and fortunes of the War and its post-war evolution.

By the time of the French King's execution, followed by the excesses of the Terror in 1793–4, an elaboration on his democratic six principles in a recently published *Jurisprudence* would have been too provocative for the safety of his friends' and for his own posthumous reputation. As it was, after his death, some of his social conversations appeared to have been noted by the authorities in their interviews in 1793–4 with his friends, particularly Dugald Stewart.[5]

To discuss the American experience and how it related to the evolution of British justice and liberty potentially posed severe political problems for Smith. His need not to alarm a fearful, and perhaps vengeful, establishment with an endorsement (for he could in good conscience do naught else) of the democratic virtues of the new American constitution, with its separation of powers, adult male franchise, and republican principles, leaned heavily in favour of him choosing not to finish *Jurisprudence*. Hence, he didn't.

He did not need to become a Commissioner of Customs (1778) for the income it provided (he had his life pension from the Duke of Buccleugh, and indeed offered to give it up in view of his appointment).[6] So, if it was not for the money then what else? As far as can be seen, he did not search after the King's Honours.

He knew the consequences (indeed, he relied upon them) of such an appointment for his unfinished *Jurisprudence*, and his expression of regret in a letter to Andreas Holt in 1780 may be read as a version of his alibi:

> The only thing I regret in it is the interruptions to my literary pursuits, which the duties of my office necessarily occasion. Several Works which I have projected are likely to go on much more slowly than the otherwise would have done.[7]

He also described his duties as a Commissioner:

> I am occupied four days in every Week at the Custom House; during which it is impossible to sit down seriously to any other business: during the other three days, I am liable to be frequently interrupted by the extraordinary duties of my office, as well as by my own private affairs, and the common duties of society.[8]

Fully aware of the consequences, he chose deliberately to frustrate any hope of his completion of *Jurisprudence*, despite his (faded) commitment to his private, and juvenile, dreams of Newtonian glory. Avoiding confrontation between his beliefs and the comforts of his mother's final years was so ingrained in his personal habits, that discreetly suppressing publication of his democratic quasi-republican beliefs to avoid exciting the fears and insecurities of the upper reaches of the British Establishment was for him a typically prudent decision.

His young friend, Dugald Stewart, chose discretion over reckless promotion of Smith's six principles, and in this he followed his mentor's example by downplaying their practical significance, stating that 'The improvements they [the political economists] recommend are to be effected by means too gradual and slow in their operation, to warm the imaginations of any but of the speculative few; and in proportion as they are adopted, they consolidate the political fabric, and enlarge the basis upon which it rests.'[9] He added a curious foot- and an end-note to the original text, reflecting the official pressure exerted on him while preparing his paper for publication. The footnote reported that 'in printing the following section' he had decided to 'confine myself to a much more general view of the subject than I once intended.'[10] End note 'G' is tantalising for what it implies but does not elaborate upon:

> By way of explanation of what is hinted at in the foot-note … I think it proper for me to *now* add, that at the period when this memoir was read before the Royal Society of Edinburgh, it was not unusual, even among men of some talents and information, to confound, studiously, the speculative doctrines of Political Economy, with those discussions concerning the first principles of Government which happened unfortunately at that time to agitate the public mind. The doctrine of a Free Trade was itself represented as of a revolutionary tendency; and some who had formerly prided themselves on their intimacy with Mr Smith, and on their zeal for the propagation of his liberal system, began to call in question the expediency of subjecting the disputations of philosophers, the arcane of State Policy, and the unfathomable wisdom of the Feudal Ages.[11] [emphasis in the original]

The problems that Smith anticipated if he were to publish *Jurisprudence* were very real and were felt by his associates. Stewart's attempt to assure the authorities that political economy was a long-term gradualist process of no threat to the established order was occasioned by the coincidence of his RSE memorial to Smith with the start of the Edinburgh Sedition Trials, in which 'exciting disaffection to the government' was treated as a crime, punishable by transportation.

Stewart's Note G reveals the official view that advocating Free Trade, as Smith most certainly did in *Wealth of Nations*, could become confused with the 'first principles of government' and 'agitate the public mind'. How might Smith's *Jurisprudence* have been regarded, with its history of the 'first principles of government', its paean to democracy over the tyranny of (absolute) monarchy, and its principles of liberty by men who would sit in judgement of his reputation and with the physical safety of his friends and sympathisers in their hands? Lord Justice-Clerk Braxfield (Robert MacQueen),[12] presiding judge at the Edinburgh Sedition Trials and known, unpopularly, as the 'hanging judge', was not given to indulging defendants with the benefit of doubt when he had made up his mind from the start as to their guilt.

No wonder some of those 'who had formerly prided themselves on their intimacy with Mr Smith, and on their zeal for the propagation of his liberal system, began to question the expediency' of remaining associated with his Works or his memory and slunk away, to the sarcastic disgust of Stewart.

Implicitly, Stewart denied any intent by Smith to cause disturbances among the uneducated mobs that his interrogators feared were about to descend on them and their ilk.[13] The authorities thought there might be a case against Stewart based on his praise of the author of *Wealth of Nations* and, perhaps, hearsay reports of Smith's social conversations. But what they did not have was the manuscript of *Jurisprudence*.

Absent the damning evidence of *Jurisprudence*, nobody could make mischief with Smith's reputation. He was unaware that students had copied and preserved their notes of his jurisprudence lectures. But by lying undiscovered for 100 years, their eventual re-appearance did his reputation no harm.

Smith anticipated correctly that trying to distinguish between lukewarmly supporting change in the American colonies (for that is the drift of his remarks about them) and an elite's suspicions, from the 'incontrovertible' evidence in a published *Jurisprudence*, that he encouraged radical political change in Britain, was not worth the risk.

Following the American Revolution (1776–83) and the French Terror (1793), to be seen to be challenging monarchical rule by men unimpressed with the subtleties of good sense, was an unattractive but, fortunately, an avoidable challenge. He anticipated the danger he was in and chose silence. Those unfortunates, less prudent in expressing their views in public, suffered up to 14 years transportation to New South Wales.[14]

32
On Laissez Faire

The case against the presumption that Smith subscribed to 'laissez faire' principles on the lonely grounds that he never used these words, is not the only nor the strongest evidence. Fortunately, the case is much stronger.

First though, I have two observations. The French words laissez faire mean to 'let things go their own way' or 'to leave alone'.[1] In effect, say some economists, because Smith's prescriptions in his political economy more of less meant 'leave alone', why make a fuss when people associate laissez faire with his name? This line of argument is bolstered by an instance of Smith supposedly using the equivalent words in English:

> Projectors disturb nature in the course of her operations in human affairs; and it requires no more than to *let her alone*, and give her fair play in the pursuit of her ends, that she may establish her own designs.[2]

The words '*let her alone*' are clear enough but strangely, Smith does not use the phrase elsewhere as a laissez faire maxim. And note the 'her' refers to Nature and it is Nature that is to be left alone in 'her operations in human affairs' and not that of humans in pursuit of their interests. This passage obviously refers to a larger smithian theme (not reported by Stewart in his selected extracts from the 1755 'paper' – see Appendix) on Natural Liberty and Nature's 'providential intentions', including the 'propagation' of the species'. The quotation that Dugald Stewart drew to our attention was singularly unhelpful in illuminating questions about Smith and laissez faire in commercial societies.

Smith opened his Lectures on Rhetoric with a clue to his non-use of '*laissez faire*'. Perspicuity of style requires, he wrote, that the words used:

> should be natives if I may [say] so of the language we speak in. Foreigners though they may signify the same thing never convey the idea with such strength as those we are acquainted with and whose origin we can trace.[3]

Replacing the words 'let her alone' with 'laissez faire', might work in the 1755 passage, but this leaves open the many opportunities he had, despite his advice on style, to use laissez faire elsewhere. The fact is he didn't.

One occasion where he did argue strongly for removing laws from interfering in a market, is the special case of mishandling a 'dearth of corn', which could lead to a famine.[4] His criticism was directed against mercantile legislative interventions in local scarcities of corn by which politicians respond to disorderly expressions of the popular will and the misguided clamour against corn merchants. By making the scarcities much worse they can turn them into famines. Summarising a long and detailed argument on the history of the corn trade, its dearth and famines in Europe, Smith exclaims:

> That security which the laws in Great Britain give to every man that he shall enjoy the fruits of his own labour, is alone sufficient to make any country flourish, notwithstanding these and twenty other absurd regulations of commerce ... The natural effort of every individual to better his own condition, when suffered to exert itself with freedom and security, is so powerful a principle, that it is alone, and without any assistance, not only capable of carrying on the society to wealth and prosperity, but of surmounting a hundred impertinent obstructions with which the folly of human laws too often encumbers its operations; though the effect of these obstructions is always more or less either to encroach upon its freedom, or to diminish its security.[5]

In this case, because Smith considered that a monopoly of corn supply was impossible in a dispersed market (surely, an empirical question?) and therefor the prevention of famine would be better facilitated by free trade in corn and not by 'the violence of law' (or the mob). His concern was famine prevention, not a theory of laissez faire.

In another singular case, Smith discusses the theories of the French Physiocrats, which 'represents the produce of the land as the sole source of the revenue and wealth of a country', which he adds, 'has so far as I know, never been adopted by any nation, and it at present exists only in the speculations of a few men of great learning and ingenuity in France.'[6]

In surveying the practical consequences of such theories he alludes to the inevitable endeavours by which agriculture would be encouraged and manufacturers discouraged. These policies distort the 'share of capital in society that would naturally go to' industrial uses and 'forces from a particular species of industry some of the share capital which would otherwise be employed in it.' This would 'retard, instead of accelerating, the progress of the society towards real wealth and greatness, and diminishes, instead of increasing, the real value of the annual produce of its land and labour.'[7]

This assessment leads to his statement in favour of no restraints, and no encouragement, on the independent judgement of people about how to use their capital. Before, we jump to conclusion that we have found Smith's predilection for laissez faire, bear in mind that he is arguing against the Physiocratic notion that agriculture alone is the source of true wealth – all the rest is 'sterile' – and therefore the Physiocrats were disposed to promote agriculture at the expense, if need be, of the 'sterile' occupations. The capital Smith is referring to is that used by artisan labour and their simple manual tools. He states, unequivocally, in conditions of natural liberty, that:

Everyman, as long as he does not violate the laws of justice, is left perfectly free to pursue his own interest his own way, and to bring both his industry and capital into competition with those of any other man, or order of men. The sovereign is completely discharged from a duty, in the attempting to perform which he must always be exposed to innumerable delusions, and for the proper performance of which no human wisdom or knowledge could ever be sufficient; the duty of super-intending the industry of private people, and of directing it towards employments most suitable to the interest of the society.[8]

For the avoidance of doubt, I should remind you that when Smith is referring to 'industry' in this context he is referring to the 'industrious-ness' of people, mainly small employers of the artisan class, and not owners of capitalistic industries. He is also referring to policies aimed by a government at promoting favoured activities at the expense of those in manufacturing believed, incorrectly, to be 'sterile', i.e., non-productive, in Smith's sense. He was not advocating general laissez faire, a distinction not always appreciated by those making use of these quotations without regard for the meaning of these words in the 18th century and their meaning later.

Shortly after starting to write *Wealth of Nations*, Smith met several French economists during his tutorship tour with the Duke of Buccleugh in 1764–6, and he was familiar with their books and with the use and meaning a few of them might have placed on laissez faire in conversation. (While Smith's spoken French apparently left a lot to be desired, he was a proficient reader and writer of French, Italian and German – and, of course, spoken and written Latin, and ancient Greek.)[9]

Clearly, French words come from France, but there is a mystery about these particular words and how they were transposed from ordinary French usage into words packed with sinister meanings when used as a maxim, usually, and strangely, printed in italics and also hyphenated when they appear in English sentences.[10] Despite avid hunts for the origins of laissez faire as a maxim, the paucity of evidence is remarkable.

MacGregor's *The Laissez-faire Doctrine*, summarises the evidence.[11] The French *Journal Œconomique* published an anonymous letter saying: 'it is reported of Colbert that, when he convened several deputies of commerce at his house, and asked what he could do for the benefit of trade, the most sensible and plainest spoken among them replied in one [phrase], "*laissez nous faire*". Have we ever sufficiently reflected on the good sense of that short answer?'

That letter is now ascribed to the Marquis D'Argenson (1694–1757), written seventy years after the 'plain spoken' merchant, a M. le Gendre, according to MacGregor, responded to Colbert's question in Lyons in 1680.[12] Another merchant, Jean Vincent, Seigneur de Gournay, coined the phrase '*laissez-faire et laissez-passer*'. Apparently, both merchants were reacting against a common enough feature of the French economy in the 17th–18th centuries (and we may note, still a diluted feature of modern France in the 21st century), that of intense government regulation of every detail and the 'dictatorial' organisation of industry and trade, involving a 'poor manufacturer who could not read and an inspector who could not manufacture.'[13]

Smith's strictures against interference by government, local guilds and corporations had similar origins in his antipathy to interference in the freedom of merchants and manufacturers to depose their stock in pursuit of advantages as they saw fit. As we shall see, Smith and the Physiocrat's common cause against mercantile interference had little to do with the meaning attributed to laissez faire a century later.

Laissez faire in these early years was more an oral mantra than a written one and the oft obscure and rare sightings of its use contributes to the mess made of its provenance. The Physiocrats did not take up Laissez faire as a maxim and it 'lapsed into the half-world of popular usage'.[14] Francois Quesnay used 'complete freedom of trade' and not laissez faire in his *Thirty General Maxims of Economic Government,*[15] and by doing so missed an ideal opportunity, should he have wanted it, to root the phrase in *La Tableau Economique* (1758/67), his most famous contribution to economics.[16]

Apart from Bentham's use of the maxim in a letter in 1808, the field is empty until John Stuart Mill resurrected it from obscurity in 1848. Even as late as 1846, the House of Commons, as reported in 1,500 pages of *Hansard*, conducted a long and tumultuous debate on the repeal of the Corn Laws without anybody mentioning laissez faire once.[17] Yet if ever an issue was a litmus test of the depth of feeling of those in favour of free markets, the debate on the Corn Laws was certainly the one where cries for laissez faire, should it have been a maxim known to and used by its proponents or disregarded contemptuously by its opponents, would have been heard, not just once but many times.

The silence can only embarrass those who promote the view that laissez faire is connected with Adam Smith's legacy. This was an invention of mid-19th century exponents, mixed with some out of context remarks from *Wealth of Nations*, and for which it has taken not inconsiderable detective work to find hints of its origins in a conversation in 1690, some isolated instances of its use in the 1750s and practically nothing else until 1848. Only flaky attribution associates laissez faire with Smith.[18]

He declined to use the expression, partly because of his deliberate preference for more accurate phrases in English to convey what he meant, but also, I suggest because he did not believe that a general policy of laissez faire was practical or advisable, and I shall show that in significant policy areas in *Wealth of Nations* he wrote intentionally and with forethought in breach of laissez faire prescriptions.

He wrote in favour of natural liberty in the street markets of towns and villages and he railed against regulations and interference from local guilds (tightly knit local employers, mainly artisans), corporations (town councils) and parliamentary statutes that were the legacy of the mercantile system. These were his prescriptions for his world of commercial small-scale markets and not for an entirely different, capitalist, world seventy to a hundred years in the future.

His critique of specific interventions in liberty did not endorse a doctrine of general laissez faire. It was sensible not to encourage governments and their inspectors to tell merchants and manufacturers how to address their own interests, but should merchants and manufacturers (of whom he was deeply suspicious as a group) be left completely alone to do whatever they wanted with their capital? Their monopolising proclivities told against such a policy, as did their irritating and harmful actions against the interests of others, including their records of blinding legislators with plausible pleas for Acts of Parliament to rig markets in their favour at the expense of the interests of their customers and competitors.

Merchants and manufacturers by their successful exclusion of parliamentary intervention against employers' combinations to lower wages or resist increases, and their success in marshalling the extremities of the law against employee combinations, had forsaken any trust that they would manage themselves without disgracing their stewardship in a regime of laissez faire. All this was before the behaviour of their successors, the capitalists in the 19th century, with their trenchant resistance to modest parliamentary legislation on hours of work, safety and the exploitative employment of women and children.

The laissez faire maxim was an example of snappy repartee for a special instance (against Colbert's regulations, inspectors and controls) and not a serious general smithian policy for all markets at all times and in every situation.

33
The Wonderful World of Adam Smith?

Like many students in the 1960s, I read Robert Heilbroner's *Worldly Philosophers*.[1] He covered a lot of ground in his entertaining and authoritative style and he filled in the background to many of the names (Smith, Malthus, Ricardo, Marx, Mill, and Marshall) mentioned *en passant* by our lecturers. Examiners, however, did not require us to know anything about the careers, circumstances or contributions of the great economists (regrettably, then as now, economics was taught largely without the history of its ideas), but Heilbroner's biographies overcame the universal imperative of students to avoid reading the non-examinable. For that I remain impressed, and grateful.

However, I devote space to Heilbroner's work because, while his *Worldly Philosophers* has had little impact on the modern economics profession,[2] it has been widely read by students and the general public (its 7th edition was published in 2000),[3] and a companion volume, *Teachings from Worldly Philosophers*, was published in 1997.[4] Blackstone issued a set of audiotapes and described *Worldly Philosophers* as the 'most widely read text on the history of economic thought ever written'. Heilbroner's impact on popular assessments of Adam Smith makes him worthy of attention. I address my critique to his readers more than to my academic colleagues, many of whom, incidentally and unfortunately, repeat similar themes to Heilbroner's, despite historians of economics not being impressed by his ideas.

Smith would have approved of Heilbroner's perspicuity of style, his painting his subjects in colour and his use of memorable anecdotes to illuminate his version of the lives of 'great economic thinkers.' I do not believe, however, that he would have approved of Heilbroner presenting him as an 'other worldly' philosopher divorced from reality, a sort of fantasist of fanatical laissez faire prescriptions, who exposed his victims to the merciless abominations of 19th century Victorian capitalists (who 'bedded, boarded and exploited' little children in the cotton mills),[5] and who were even worse in real life than their caricatures claimed them to be.

Heilbroner took Smith's narrative of the market operating under the explicit, and oft repeated, condition of perfect liberty and justice, dropped these conditions without acknowledging what he had done, and presented what was left as an account of how actual markets worked according to Smith's 'laws'. He then asked: 'does the world really work this way?' But, unlike Smith who spent many scores of pages in *Wealth of Nations* explaining why and how the world did not work this way, Heilbroner makes the astonishing statement that 'to a very real degree it did in the days of Adam Smith'.[6] True, only if Heilbroner accepts that Smith was referring to market stalls selling vegetables, buttons, baubles and such like, and not to Victorian capitalists, or to their successors in today's markets! With his canard behind him, Heilbroner explores the differences between markets in the 20th century and their alleged smithian predecessor in the 18th evolving towards Smith's vision of 'Valhalla' – a witticism, like sarcasm, best ignored.[7]

Heilbroner's assessment of the laissez faire proposition concludes that 'if one left the market mechanism alone and allowed it and the great social laws to work themselves out, it was inevitable that progress would result.'[8] The validity of Heilbroner's conclusion depends on how 'alone' we left the market mechanism. Totally and absolutely, or to the qualified extent that Smith suggested it might best be left alone, always provided we lived in perfect liberty and in the absence of monopoly and foreign trade protection (and threats of the depredations by our neighbours)?

By the 19th century, new style monopolists and powerful, new capitalistic interests intervened, based on unforeseen revolutionary new technologies, with close affinities and access to legislators with their very anti-smithian imperialistic ambitions. These changes swept Smith's street markets off their pinnacle at the top of the value chain.

Heilbroner lumbers Smith with guilt by association because 'rising capitalists ... found in Smith's Treatise [*Wealth of Nations*] the perfect theoretical justification for their own opposition to factor legislation' to 'remedy the scandalous conditions of the times.'[9] But by the time this was happening, Smith was long since dead.

Industrialists would not have found much in *Wealth of Nations* to construe as his support for their blocking of legislation against employing children in factories and coalmines! His opposition to parliament's creation of legal monopolies, foreign trade protection and ancient restrictive employment practices (seven year apprenticeships, etc.,), did not signify his opposition to any and all legislative intervention; nowhere did he endorse a blanket policy of laissez faire. Anybody using Smith's name in support of such nefarious policies relies on public credulity and not on *Wealth of Nations*.

Heilbroner gives no evidence to support his assertion that 'Smith's theory does unquestionably lead to a doctrine of *laissez-faire*'. It most certainly does not! Why did Smith fail to advocate laissez faire prescriptions in *Wealth of Nations* despite his knowing Dr. Quesnay and his *tableau économique* (1767)?[10]

In contradiction to the bulk of his essay, Heilbroner announces that 'even today – in blithe disregard of his actual philosophy – Smith is regarded as a *conservative* economist, whereas in fact, he was more avowedly hostile to the *motives* of businessmen than most New Deal economists.'[11] 'Blithe disregard', indeed! How stark does a contradiction have to be before we perceive that there is something worthy of further investigation?

Having disregarded Smith's philosophy in *Wealth of Nations*, Heilbroner, with just three pages to go, should have been impressed enough by the arresting fact that Smith was a trenchant critic of businessmen for him to consider rewriting his essay. Heilbroner, perhaps, was carried away by his rhetoric in what was a well written, but inaccurate, essay.

34
In the Absence of Perfect Liberty

Perfect liberty and justice, however, did not exist in the actual markets known to Smith, making expectations of perfect factor mobility idealistic, not realistic; they remained his theoretical constructs. Smith's narrative is a benchmark for, not a description of, the real world. Smith elaborates on variations between perfect and real world markets, and I shall untangle the narrative in what follows as a prelude to commenting on the laissez faire problem in economics – that there are two distinct interpretations of what it means as a policy prescription, neither of which accords with Smith's views. Together they explain why he did not refer to laissez faire, nor subscribe, implicitly or otherwise, to prescriptions associated with it.

Take the zero-sum wage bargain, which in perfect liberty and justice is settled by supply and demand, but in interventionist regimes is settled by open conflict between masters and workmen. If there are too many labourers looking for work, their competition drives the wage rate down; if there are too many masters looking for labourers, their competition pulls the wage rate up. Beyond this mechanism, attempts at intervention cannot help labourers or masters to opulence. If the economy grows, the demand for labour intensifies and this accords with the happiest state of the labourers and their families. More children survive into adulthood, parents enjoy higher living standards than their grandparents, and all the great orders of society share in the general opulence (though not to the same extent!).

The second interpretation adds people to the first. 'In the great chessboard of human society, every single piece has a principle of motion of its own,'[1] a problem we don't have when we model physical (including astronomical) forces. In political economy everything is simple until you include people. They just do not behave according to the dictates of the theorist.

To account for the behaviour of people in labour markets, Smith set aside the imperatives of 'perfect liberty and justice', and studied and wrote extensively about the real world. These data showed that both sides played the wage determination game differently. Aware as they were of the imperatives of competition, labourers and masters applied principles of motion of their own, altogether different from the scripts written for them in the theories: masters and workmen tried on occasion to form 'combinations' to eliminate competition that worked against them.

Smith credits labourers as a group combining to raise, and masters combining to reduce, wages. Labourers could only exert pressure on masters if they collectively agreed (combined) to refuse to work (strike) until they are paid higher wages and thus, by combining into something like a union, prevent competition among them that would result in their accepting the lower rate offered by masters. Likewise, masters exerted social pressure on any master tempted to employ anybody at a higher wage, thus preventing competition between the masters resulting in them paying what was demanded by labourers. The same purpose is served when labourers combine to prevent a wage reduction and masters combine to enforce one.

Realistically, Smith notes that it is not difficult to foresee the outcome of such disputes 'upon all ordinary occasions' – masters enforced compliance because they were fewer in number and could combine more easily and maintain their solidarity. Besides, the law was on their side – and so were the local magistrates who enforced it. The law treats combinations of master and workmen differently: 'it prohibits those of workmen' to raise wages, but there are 'no acts of parliament against [masters] combining to lower' them. Masters can 'hold out much longer', for a 'year or two', whereas 'many workmen could not subsist for a week'.[2]

Smith's interest in the real world was not distant because he makes the point, possibly from being privy to private discussions between masters with whom he had extensive social contact, that combinations of masters are rarely heard of outside the circle of masters involved, while those of workmen are frequently reported, adding:

> But whoever imagines, upon this account, that masters rarely combine, is as ignorant of the world as of the subject. Masters are always and everywhere in a sort of tacit, but constant and uniform combination, not to raise wages of labour above their actual rate. To violate this combination is everywhere a most unpopular action, and a sort of reproach to a master among his neighbours and equals. We seldom, indeed, hear of this combination, because it is the usual, and one may say, natural state of things which nobody ever hears of.[3]

It is worse for the labourers when masters combine to lower the going wage. He intones, surely from 'inside' information, that such combinations of masters 'are always conducted with the utmost silence and secrecy, till the moment of execution.' When the workmen submit without resistance there is not much of a problem. But combinations to cut wages can provoke a 'contrary defensive combination' by workmen combining 'of their own accord to raise the price of their labour.'[4]

The trap for workmen in forming combinations is easy to spot. They had to bring the contest to a speedy decision because they could not hold out for long. Thus:

> They have always recourse to the loudest clamour, and sometimes to the most shocking violence and outrage. They are desperate and act with the folly and extravagance of desperate men, who must either starve, or frighten their masters into an immediate compliance with their demands.[5]

Masters clamoured for action against the labourers, and the magistrate and the courts reacted with such severity that workmen 'very seldom derive any advantage from the violence of those tumultuous combinations' and they 'generally end in nothing, but the punishment or ruin of the ringleaders.'[6] For example, the public whipping through the streets of James Granger, a leader of the 1787 weavers' strike[7] – '*pour décourager les autres*'.

Whereas attempts to intervene by reducing competition in the wage market – the unambiguous aim of both parties – ended badly for the workmen and led to Smith's overall pessimism as to the efficacy of labourers' combinations, the same cannot be said of how masters, merchants and manufacturers, dealers and traders intervened in markets to the severe disadvantage of their customers. Largely, they got off Scot-free. It is doubtful that Smith, if the issue had come up, would have opposed the repeal of the Combination Acts. He shows no sympathy for their bias in favour of masters, but shows sympathy for labourers caught up their one-sided consequences.

35
Monopolists in Product Markets

Monopolies by individuals, trading companies, or by secret arrangements between groups of suppliers are by far the biggest interference in market prices. Themes on the iniquities of monopoly recur all through *Wealth of Nations*. Monopolies were anti-competitive and, therefore, targets for Smith's ire. He seldom let up on them, but he made certain significant exceptions on pragmatic grounds, compromising his commitment to free competition in favour of the important practical political advantages they created in the real world (the Navigation Acts for example). These are interesting examples of Smith's breaches of laissez faire prescriptions.

Monopolists kept their markets under-stocked below the level of effectual demand to sell their products above their natural prices and thereby raise profits above their natural rates. It's as if a strawberry seller could keep the market permanently under stocked in so that he could set strawberry prices higher than they would be in a well-stocked market full of competitors. This would create the price gap between the monopoly price, the highest that can be got, and the free competition ('natural') price, which is the lowest that can be extracted from competitive sellers and still allow them to remain in business at some acceptable (lower) revenue level. Monopolists squeeze buyers and make excess profits; competitive sellers squeeze each other's prices to the lowest they can afford without having to quit their business.[1]

High monopoly prices reward the avarice of monopolists; low competitive prices punish the impotence of competitors. The former benefits the producers' share of revenues, the latter benefits the consumers' share of annual output. For this reason there is always a predictable inclination among competitive producers to create monopoly privileges and to resist new entrants. And it does not require high intelligence to note that if you are the single supplier of a product in a market, no matter how humble your product, it pays you to supply less than the effective demand. For example, if the strawberry seller knew that fifty people wanted his strawberries, he knows that to supply enough for thirty allows him to charge higher prices to the keenest of the customers frantically clamouring for his strawberries.

Smith comments, sardonically, on the different presentations made by 'our merchants and master-manufacturers' on the ill effects of high prices compared to the 'bad effects of high profits'. They 'are silent with regard to the pernicious effects of their own gains. They complain only of those of other people.'[2]

From the 'discovery' of the benefits of restricting supply, it is a short step to combine with others to restrict a town's suppliers to licensed members of a traders' or producers' guild, and to refuse licences to new entrants. Smith was perfectly informed on these matters, not least because Glasgow University had afforded accommodation to young James Watt when the Glasgow trade corporations in 1756 had refused him permission to set up an instrument workshop in the town (the University grounds were outside the town's jurisdiction).[3] Restrictions against new entrants were pernicious; they inhibited the growth of commerce.

Monopoly protects itself by licences, Royal Charters, statutes, regulations, local ordinances and import duties. These entrenchments endure for centuries, unless swept away by government. No wonder Smith felt that the prospect of international free trade being restored to Britain to be as 'absurd' as it was 'Utopian'.[4] Smith resolutely opposed these specific interventions by government in the economy and not any and all interventions. Some interventions he supported wholeheartedly.

To secure higher profits, stockowners reduce costs by innovation, protect their trade secrets, conceal their windfall gains, and remain secretive about local singularities of situation (special soils, local waters, special timbers, sources of minerals and such like).[5] European countries, with vested interests in overseas exploration, went to great lengths to conceal maps of distant lands and their coastlines (ships' captains ordered all personal logs and dairies to be handed in before landfall on their return from voyages); rich vineyards in France hid their wealth by living in shabby buildings, keeping their rents down; and wise innovators who reduced costs refrained from boasting of their success to rivals.

Monopoly pricing supported by laws occasioned greater inequalities than would occur under perfect liberty. The exclusive privileges of corporations restrained competition by only allowing members 'freedom' to trade. Apprenticeships of up to seven years had to be served in the town where they intended to conduct future business and had the effect of restraining competition to a much smaller number of artisans than otherwise – plus, the law restricted to two the number of apprentices a master may employ.[6] (Interestingly, early universities adopted seven-year degrees from the practice of seven-year apprenticeships.)

Because towns were governed by traders and artificers, 'it was the manifest interest of every particular class of them, to prevent the market from being over-stocked, as they commonly express it, with their own particular species of industry; which is in reality to keep it always under-stocked.' The necessity of securing these privileges for their own trade induced them to secure the same for other trades and, with the proviso that each recognised trade would buy only from other recognised trades, they consented, in effect, to pay dearer for what they wanted in order to receive more than they would have received if markets were open to outsiders.[7]

By these means they also raised their prices in the nearby country, to the disadvantage of country consumers. Stock and labour were attracted to the town, seeking the most 'advantageous employment',[8] but the town's restrictions inhibited such growth, and slowed the spread of commerce and opulence.

Imposing high duties upon foreign manufactures and goods imported by foreign merchants served the same purpose of raising their monopoly prices in the absence of free competition. From the 'clamour and sophistry of merchants and manufacturers' others are easily persuaded that the private interest of a part, and a subordinate part of society, is the general interest of the whole.'[9] Smith reinforces his message that he was not speaking up to protect a future new class of capitalists:

> People of the same trade seldom meet together, even for merriment and diversion, but the conversation ends in a conspiracy against the publick, or in some contrivance to raise prices.[10]

He also denied that corporations were needed for 'better governance' and argued (expressing a surprisingly modern marketing concept) that the 'real and effectual discipline' over a workman was not his guild 'but that of his customers.'[11]

36
Against the Public Interest

Smith's litany against the imperfections introduced into markets by merchants and manufacturers included reviewing their probity when addressing others, particularly legislators, in support of their interests.

As during their whole lives they are engaged in plans and projects, they have frequently more acuteness of understanding than the greater part of country gentlemen. As their thoughts, however, are commonly exercised rather about the interest of their own branch of business, than about that of society, their judgement, even when given with the greatest candour (which it has not been upon every occasion) is much more to be depended upon with regard to the former of these two objects, than with regard to the latter. Their superiority over the country gentleman is, not so much in their knowledge of the publick interest, as in their having a better knowledge of their own interest than he has of his. ... The interest of the dealers, however, in any particular branch of trade or manufacturers, is always in some respects different from, and even opposite to, that of the publick. To widen the market, and to narrow the competition, is always in the interest of the dealers.[1]

He could not be clearer. Merchants, manufacturers, and dealers, lack candour (lying by omission), act against the public interest, reduce competition whenever they can, and undermine perfect liberty and justice. Smith was not divorced from the real world. In fact, his close connections with, and shrewd observations of, real players in real markets fully inform his narrative. His shots hit their targets; he demonstrated mastery of his subject, and he had strong convictions on where public support for or against the interests of master manufacturers ought to lie:

To widen the market may frequently be agreeable enough to the interest of the publick; but to narrow the competition must always be against it, and can serve only to enable the dealers, by raising their profits above what they naturally would be, to levy, for their own benefit, an absurd tax upon the rest of their fellow citizens. The proposal of any new law or regulation of commerce which comes from this order, ought always to be listened to with great precaution, and ought never to be adopted till after having been long and carefully examined, not only with the most scrupulous, but with the most suspicious attention. It comes from an order of men, whose interest is never the same with that of the publick, who have generally an interest to deceive and even to oppress the publick, and who accordingly have, upon many occasions, both deceived and oppressed it.[2]

As a simple test of where Smith might have stood on 19th century legislation to do with factories, hours of work and the employment of children in coalmines, he makes it clear that what would be in the public interest likely would be against the private interests of dealers, and, if the dealers campaigned against such legislation, there was no room for credulity in judging the merits of their proposals. Smith urged the public to pay careful attention before adopting their recommendations.

Did it not occur to those reading these passages, that the misappropriation of Smith's legacy by unscrupulous toadies for the defence of the interests of cotton mill owners in debates on the Factory Acts throughout the 19th century might be worthy, at least, of their suspicion? Smith's presumption was that dealers acted contrary to the interests of the general public. Can there be any doubt as to which side Smith was on? Heilbroner wrote that 'rising industrialists found [in *Wealth of Nations*] the perfect theoretical justification they needed to block the first government attempts to remedy the scandalous conditions of the times'. Assuming this was a fact – somebody articulated a case for their nefarious ends and quoted Smith in support – in what way was this Smith's fault and to what extent did their claims merit credibility? Where, for basics, in *Wealth of Nations* did the spokesmen for industrialists find the 'perfect theoretical justification' for their outrageous claims? This is a claim worth challenging by reference to what Smith did write rather than a placid acceptance of the mischievous rants of those demanding laissez faire for their businesses?[3]

The spirit of monopoly, ubiquitous in commercial society, could only become entrenched if merchants and manufacturers were left alone to strive might and main to drive competitors out of business, using fair means and foul, while spouting laissez faire platitudes, which was why Smith had no truck with anything that encouraged their pernicious anticompetitive doctrines.

Society, says Smith, should not facilitate the wishes of merchants and manufacturers by entrenching monopolies in law and reducing competition in practice. In the treatment of monopolies, laissez faire is never a good policy and, unsurprisingly, nor is leaving players in competitive situations exposed to temptations to create monopolies! Those linking Smith's name to laissez faire are mistaken.

The only force strong enough to combat monopoly and sustain competition was government, which created real problems for Smith because 18th-century 'State failure' for him was no less serious than 'market failure'.

The men who ran the State – and Smith knew many of them – seldom earned his approbation for their policies, and though they always received his respect by virtue of their rank, he recognised their susceptibilities to the cant of those bent on securing monopolistic protection.

37
The Impartial Competitor

Nathan Rosenberg peoples his essay with 'capitalists' in place of 'merchants and manufacturers' – brevity over verbosity is admirable, except where it sacrifices accuracy.[1] He commented:

> A businessman who had been taught to regard Adam Smith as a capitalist apologist might well be excused for wondering what sort of strange capitalist apologetics this is, and if this is what we are likely to get from our friends, just what may we expect from our enemies?[2]

Rosenberg is right that a 'businessman' should be excused errors imparted by his teachers; but any teacher who taught him that Adam Smith was 'a capitalist apologist' surely should not be so easily excused!

Rosenberg complains that when Smith turns his attention from poor labourers to the 'economic behaviour of capitalists' his 'attitude shifts from compassion and understanding to one of compulsive and cantankerous criticism and suspicion'.[3] No wonder, for Smith regarded merchants and manufacturers as bent on subverting their progressive role into a determined campaign to undo the competitive dynamic that made them useful to society.

It was from the anonymity of impartial competition, not from their inclinations or intentions, that merchants and manufacturers were driven to serve nature's purpose. On the contrary, by subverting competition with monopoly, merchants and manufacturers reduced society's potential capacity to grow at a level consistent with natural liberty and justice and slowed down the spread of opulence to the poor. And this subversion was not driven by the folly and dictates of government but came from within the heart of the commercial system itself.

Smith took into account the consequential prolongation of the misery and poverty of the great bulk of the people caused by the nefarious behaviours of merchants and manufacturers, who, pursuing high profits through monopoly, necessarily strove against the interests of society, unless curtailed by the imperatives of impartial competition. In a system of liberty and justice, businessmen were free only to compete, not free to monopolise.

Smith favoured what he called 'the liberal reward of labour' because he believed higher wages 'increased the industry of the common people.' Moreover, they improved the bodily strength of the labourer and the 'comfortable hope of bettering his condition, and of ending his days perhaps in ease and plenty, animates him to exert his strength to the utmost. Where wages are high, accordingly, we shall always find the workmen more active, diligent, and expeditious, than where they are low...' He observed that while some labourers respond to high wages with idleness (called today a 'backward bending supply curve of labour') by substituting extra hours of leisure for fewer hours of higher paid work, the real danger is that workmen when liberally paid were 'apt to overwork themselves'.[4]

When two contrary but equally plausible predictions are possible from the same change in the wage rate, a debate ensues, one arguing that it is better to keep the poor so busy with low wages that they must remain industrious to acquire the necessities of life and the other that it is better to pay them liberal wages to induce them to work harder. Rosenberg cites Arthur Young's view (1771) that 'every one but an idiot knows that the lower classes must be kept poor or they never will be industrious',[5] and Sir William Temple's view (1758) that the only way to keep industrial labourers 'temperate and industrious, is to lay them under the necessity of labouring all the time they can spare from meals and sleep, in order to procure the necessities of life.'[6] These views, dominant in Smith's time, ran directly counter to his recommendations.

Echoes of similarly hotly contested, though empirically testable, propositions were heard throughout the centuries since 1776, covering daily hours of work, safety, hygiene, child labour, minimum wage legislation, holidays, sick pay, pensions and compensation for accidents, industrial injuries and other basic human rights. I think it safe to hazard a guess as to which great order in society Smith's sympathies might have inclined him towards.

His preference for higher over lower wages was also in line with a central tenet of his philosophy. Along with the propensity to truck, barter, and exchange, he picks out:

> The uniform, constant, and uninterrupted effort of every man to better his condition, the principle from which publick and national, as well as private opulence is originally derived, is frequently powerful enough to maintain natural progress of things towards improvement, in spite of the extravagance of government, and of the greatest errors of administration. Like the unknown principle of animal life, it frequently restores health and vigour to the constitution, in spite, not only of the disease, but of the absurd prescriptions of the doctor.[7]

This principle is not a sign of a seditious selfishness merely for more wealth. It manifests itself in everyday normal events. If you are sitting in a draught you move your seat or shut the window; if you are damp you dry yourself; if you have a stone in your shoe, you take it out; if there is anything you can easily do to ease your labours you will do it; and if you can make yourself more comfortable you will do so. Trying to better your condition is so common you do not think anything of it. And why should you when the:

> desire of bettering our condition ... though generally calm and dispassionate, comes with us from the womb, and never leaves us till we go into the grave. In the whole interval that separates those two moments, there is scarce perhaps a single instant in which any man is so perfectly and completely satisfied with his situation, as to be without any wish of alteration or improvement of any kind.[8]

Increasing your wages gives you more options than you have on low wages (you have absolutely no options, of course, on no wages). Across the society of the labouring poor, Smith believed that higher real wages raised them from the hopelessness of abject poverty towards the 'happiest and most comfortable' of conditions that were to be found in the progressive state.[9]

The interests of the landed proprietors, who contributed about 50 per cent of national income in the 1770s[10] and whose 'revenue costs them neither labour nor care, but comes to them, as it were, of its own accord, and independent of any plan or project of their own',[11] were unlikely to mislead the public in respect of legislation. They were too indolent or ignorant to fleece the public with biased legislation (though they were not indifferent to the repeal of the Corn Laws in the next century).

The second great order – those who lived by wages – like the landed proprietors, is closely bound up with the fate of society with the major difference that, while landlords are incomparably better off than waged workers in periods of rising prosperity, nobody 'suffers so cruelly' than the labourers in periods of decline.

> But though the interest of the labourer is strictly connected with that of society, he is incapable either of comprehending that interest, or of understanding its connection with his own. His condition leaves him no time to receive the necessary information, and his education and habits are commonly such as to render him unfit to judge even though he was fully informed. In the publick deliberations, therefore, his voice is little heard and less regarded, except upon some particular occasions, when his clamour is animated, set on, and supported by his employers, not for his, but their own particular purposes.[12]

To what extent the seemingly modest proposals of Smith for the education of the children of the labouring poor would have gradually altered this situation is impossible to say, assuming they had been implemented, which they were not. Leaving the great mass of people uneducated and incapable of realising their interests was believed to be in the interests of the majority of the third great order in society, that of the master manufacturers, or those that 'live by profit.' They did not need to do anything positive to realise this particular interest – they just had to do nothing strenuous towards educating anybody's, other than their own, male children. Girls were largely ignored, even in middle class families, as unworthy of education except in their acceptance of domesticity and in learning impeccable manners.

Masters employ their stock for profit and put into motion the useful labour of society. Unlike the landlords' rent and the labourers' wages, profits do not rise and fall with prosperity. Profits are naturally low in rich and high in poor countries and are 'always highest in the countries which are going fastest to ruin.'[13] This differentiates the interests of the owners of stock from the interests of landlords and labourers. Their thoughts are exercised constantly with the interests of their own branch of trade, and not that of society and their judgements when given with candour (which is not always the case) are more likely to be accurate with respect to the interests of their own business than with society's. Their superiority over the country gentleman comes not from their knowledge of the public interest, so much as them having a better knowledge of their own interests than he has of his.[14]

In short, the employer of stock was not to be trusted when expounding on the public interest. He was more likely to be spouting in favour of what will benefit him and not about what might benefit society. Profit seeking owners of stock should always be 'listened to with great precaution' and nothing they propose should be adopted 'till after having been long and carefully examined, not only with the most scrupulous, but with the most suspicious attention.'[15]

38
The Mercantile System

Wealth of Nations contains a long polemic in the whole of Book IV against what Smith called the *mercantile system*,[1] a deformed variation of the commercial system characterised by state intervention in political economy, ostensibly to enrich the people, but really to enrich the State (i.e., the sovereign). Smith is more circumspect however; he says 'It proposes to enrich both the people and the sovereign.'[2]

Some suggest that the mercantile system, as presented by Smith, was not a real doctrine guiding the policies of the British State, but was, instead, a convenient straw man set up for an easy knock down.[3] However, if we treat mercantile propositions as corruptions of perfect liberty and justice, we get sufficient benefit to warrant a brief discussion of his actual recommendations to remove specified, but not all, State interventions in markets.

Mercantile doctrine begins from the observation that sovereign states fight foreign wars and need the wherewithal to do so. Allegedly, they do this best by accumulating gold and silver in peacetime and spending bullion on their armies in wartime. This led to the spurious policy (futile too, for it only promoted lucrative smuggling trades) of prohibiting the export of gold or silver. To this policy, a balance of trade embellishment was added: export more than you import, because by curbing imports using taxes (tariffs) and prohibitions, and by allowing gold and silver bullion from foreigners to flow into the country to pay for their trade deficits, rather than out of the country to pay for ours, the State grew strong enough militarily to thwart attempts by envious neighbours to encroach on our territory. The mercantile system, in these terms, was a neat but fallacious policy for credulous governments inclined to warfare as an instrument of State policy.

Interestingly, Smith drew attention to the nefarious practice of merchants convincing parliament to enact the necessary laws, thereby revealing his understanding of the true nature of interventions in compromising perfect liberty and justice.

> They were addressed by merchants to parliaments, and to the councils of princes, to nobles, and to country gentlemen; by those who were

supposed to understand trade, to those who were conscious to themselves that they knew nothing about the matter. That foreign trade enriched the country, experience demonstrated to the nobles and gentlemen, as well as to the merchants; but how, or in what manner, none of them well knew. The merchants knew perfectly in what manner it enriched themselves. It was their business to know it. But to know in what manner it enriched the country, was no part of their business. This subject never came into their consideration, but when they had occasion to apply to their country for some change in the laws relating to foreign trade. It then became necessary to say something about the beneficial effects of foreign trade, and the manner in which those effects were obstructed by the laws as they then stood.[4]

Smith was well aware of the tendencies of lobbyists, through special pleading, to compromise perfect liberty and undo the benefits of free international trade. All examples in his narrative, as they apply to international trade, focus on the interventions of governments acting on the prejudiced advice of self-interested private parties. To the extent that private interests loaded their advice in their favour, it was unlikely to be in the public interest. Smith wrote many pages detailing the history of past errors in the advice given to governments, pointing out the foolhardy nature of such advice and his suspicions of the advisors' motives.

Smith wanted the State to stop intervening in business decisions, but his wish was predicated firmly on, first, a substantial agenda of State sponsored corrections, by reforms and repeals, to erroneous past interventions, and second, he wanted the legislators to exercise a suspicious vigilance to prevent past abuses recurring or new ones appearing. As has been said before, the price of eternal vigilance is boredom, an inevitable consequence of the need to fight the same battles over and over again.

A militant policy of laissez faire would not prevent these abuses recurring. Merchants and manufacturers, and their workforces, if persuaded to share their interests, could not be trusted to self-police their behaviour. Only the impartial anonymity of competition prevents monopoly, and then only if sustained by a government completely deaf to special pleading and as determined to prevent them gaining even a foothold by never conceding to them a respite from competition.

Mercantile theorists identified wealth with gold and silver. Wealth lies in what money can purchase (if it is available) and, ultimately, money is valuable only for the products it purchases.[5] Just as a country, with the wherewithal to purchase all of the wine it wants, so too it can purchase all of the gold or silver it wants whenever it requires any. There is no need to hoard it.

Freedom of international trade 'without any attention of government', will always supply what a country needs.[6] By wrapping their private interests in persuasive political rhetoric (coloured with images of strong boxes brimming over with the king's gold and silver), merchants bluffed governments into making laws to interfere in markets to give them a monopoly.

> By restraining, either by high duties, or by absolute prohibitions, the importation of such goods from foreign countries as can be produced at home, the monopoly of the home market is more or less secured to the domestick industry employed in producing them.[7]

Typically, Smith goes immediately into detailed examples, demonstrating that he had an acute sense of what happened in the real world.

39

The 'Invisible Hand'

Home-market monopolies undoubtedly encourage those industries sheltering behind them, increasing the employment and stock they draw upon,
but 'whether it tends either to increase the general industry of society, or to
give it the most advantageous direction, is not, perhaps, altogether so
evident.' The quantity of industry in society cannot expand beyond what
its capital can maintain; all that can happen is part of it may be diverted
from where it otherwise would have gone, without the certainty that the
artificial direction it takes is likely to be more advantageous to society than
that into which it would have gone of its own accord.[1]

This is an empirical question turning on the extent to which home
investment in a particular industry under monopolistic protection adds to
national output more than it would do if it followed a non-protected inclination that allowed other, neglected, industries to flourish. Smith implies
an advantageous outcome is unlikely, and follows with a chain of reasoning leading to his third, and final, reference in his Works to an 'invisible
hand'.

The metaphor has a curious history. In current economic doctrine the
'invisible hand' is regarded as quintessentially smithian and it is given
today the cardinal status of the main plank in his political economy. So
much so, that the 'invisible hand' has become one of his most quoted
statements and, upon which, a whole raft of meanings are attached. It is
now regarded erroneously as the smithian paradigm for market economies,
a wholly exaggerated promotion from an isolated metaphor into the very
essence of Smith's economics. Yet he mentioned it only three times in all
of his published works[2] (and one of his three mentions had to do with
pagan superstition and had nothing to do with economics).

For the most part of the 19th century, the invisible hand was not even
mentioned as a uniquely smithian doctrine at all; only in the 20th century
did it attain iconic status, but then more students than ever were studying
economics and more lecturers than ever were teaching it. In terms of his
legacy, it is as if someone rummaging among his possessions had found a

button in a discarded coat pocket and told the world that it should be trea-
sured as a unique smithian heirloom with special significance.

There are reasons to doubt that Smith regarded the 'invisible hand'
metaphor as something special. The absence of multiple references to it is
only one of them. Among other stronger reasons are the diverse contexts in
which he used it. In *Wealth of Nations* he almost mocks (even sneers at) the
unconscious actions of 'wholesale merchants', who seek their own security
by selling their goods in the home market in preference to selling them
abroad and by doing so give their greatest support for domestic industry,
which was not part of their intention.[3] Look, he says, as sub-text, how silly
these 'clever', self opinionated but naïve, men are for being unaware of
their (unintentional) role as the involuntary servants of society's ends.

His reference in *Moral Sentiments* is more venomous than sarcastic,
and rails at the 'proud and unfeeling' rich who, in spite of their 'natural
selfishness and rapacity' in pursuit of their 'own vain and insatiable
desires', advance 'the interest of the society, and afford the means for the
multiplication of the species.'[4] The high and mighty, so-called wise and
wonderful, great order of merchants and manufacturers, despite themselves
and their odious behaviour come good despite themselves in the end!
Moreover:

> In ease of body and peace of mind, all the different ranks of life are
> nearly upon a level, and the beggar who suns himself by the side of the
> highway, possesses the security that kings are fighting for.[5]

None of this says anything about a general, let alone defining, trend
in commercial society. He used the same metaphor to portray the unconscious contribution of the late feudal lords to their own eventual dissolution into landed tenancies, and to portray the unconscious contribution
of merchants to national advantage despite their motives. The same merchants, and their associated manufacturers, were capable of pursuing their
own monopolising interests to the severe disadvantage of society's general
interest in maximising growth in national income and in the spread of
opulence. No invisible hand operates here to advance society's interests
despite actions taken in response to the intentions emanating from the
dark minds of greedy monopolists.

Wilful disregard for society's interests is all too common in commercial
society from all the great orders (including, the very common poor when
led by populists who would destroy opulence with their wild agendas)
and steely intervention by legislators may be opportune to reverse what
has already been agreed, or accepted, and to prevent what will likely
happen in the absence of intervention. Markets are not immune to the
corrupting influence of monopolising anti-competitive players, against
which the metaphor of the invisible hand is just that, an allusion serving

another purpose in Smith's prose and, a weak, because non-existent, counter against these forces. Relying on the invisible hand to produce visible results may prove a triumph of hope over experience and as illusory as the proverbial leopard changing its spots.

Only markets kept free (by rules, not laissez faire) in the world can stand against monopolising influences; only actions that have unintentional consequences can shift the balance between the great orders or achieve beneficial outcomes for society. Competitive economics does not include establishing monopolising variants; protection does not create free trade; and the invisible hand, like the wrath of the god, Jupiter, is an unreliable guardian of the impartial integrity of markets.

When 20th century legacy teachers elevate the scarce mentioned invisible hand into *the* very essence of the smithian market, they give it a semi-religious and spiritual status, wholly unintended by Smith. Modern 'true believers' lost in awe of the 'holy' mystique of markets miss his irony. Some critics even see the metaphor of the invisible hand as an expression of Smith's alleged religious convictions![6]

To cap it all, the 'invisible hand' was not an original metaphor of Adam Smith's. Emma Rothschild[7], in her masterly account of Smith's 'invisible hand', reminds us of Shakespeare's lines from the 'Scottish' play:

> Come, seeling night,
> Scarf up the tender eye of pitiful day,
> And with thy bloody and invisible hand,
> Cancel and tear to pieces that great bond
> Which keeps me pale![8]

Shakespeare's Macbeth calls for the invisible hand of darkness to hide his murder of Banquo; Smith's unintended 'legatees' use their exaggerated claims of the invisible hand to hide their obfuscation of Smith's intended meaning.

Starting in Newtonian fashion – stating a clear principle assumed to be proven – Smith develops his argument. In this case, Smith asserts that every individual continually exerts himself to find the most advantageous employment for his stock for himself and not for society, but despite his narrow focus, studying only his own advantage, 'naturally, or rather necessarily,' leads him to prefer the employment most advantageous for society.

Smith sets out to prove a proposition, probably relevant for a simple commercial society with little foreign trade, that every individual endeavours to employ his stock as near home as he can and, in consequence, he is led to support domestic over foreign industry, because he has greater trust in people he can see and has greater comfort from his familiarity with local laws.[9]

The state of Scotland's roads played a large part in discouraging foreign trade ventures, except those close to ports. Compared to the same capital placed abroad, revenue and employment go to a greater number of the inhabitants in the home country. Given his profit motive, he places capital in those industries that produce the greatest profit.

But the annual revenue of every society is 'always precisely equal to the exchangeable value of the whole annual produce of its industry'. And as every individual endeavours to employ his capital in this manner, every industry produces as much revenue as it can. Thus, Smith sets up the conditions for his spirited conclusion that the individual:

> neither intends to promote the publick interest, nor knows how much he is promoting it. By preferring the support of domestick to that of foreign industry, he intends only his own security; and by directing that industry in such a manner as its produce may be of the greatest value, he intends only his own gain, and he is in this, as in many other cases, led by an invisible hand to promote an end which was no part of his intention. Nor is it always the worse for society that it was no part of it. By pursuing his own interest he frequently promotes that of the society more effectually than when he really intends to promote it. I have never known much good done by those who affected to trade for the publick good. It is an affectation, indeed not very common among merchants and very few words need to be employed from dissuading them from it.[10]

All Smith's clear reasoning in the above, and in many similar cases, is predicated on the absence of any and all monopoly arrangements, tolerated or protected by laws, which is not the same as a blank cheque, crossed with the words 'laissez faire', and handed to owners of capital to do with it whatsoever they like.

40
The Ends of Monopoly?

Those claiming the authority of Smith in support of laissez faire, aligned a man of high moral reputation in the 18th century to a reactionary obstruction of modest reforms to the appalling practices of 19th-century owners of the 'dark satanic mills', who, with legal impunity, arrogantly enforced upon working men, women and children, shameful injury and injustice in pursuit of their self interests. The proselytisers for laissez faire for themselves, clamoured indecently to prevent their victims applying the same right of laissez faire when they struggled to resist by brave, but pathetic, combinations against the worst exhibitions of the vileness of their 'betters'. The word 'goose', but not 'gander', springs to mind.

One of the inevitable consequences of instituting a laissez faire freedom would be the tendency for stockowners to attempt to manage their circumstances and to create monopolies to reduce competition. While Smith railed against statesmen, councils and senates for attempting 'to direct private people in what manner to employ their capitals' he was savvy enough to warn against giving a monopoly of the home market to private individuals, which 'must in almost all cases, be a useless or a hurtful regulation'; useless if domestic produce was as cheap as foreign produce, and hurtful if it was not.[1]

There is no point in attempting to make things that you can buy cheaper than you can make them. If you do, you sell your more expensive output to acquire less of the output of other industries (another hint of input-output analysis?). Remember, behind the price of anything, the factors of production, land, labour and stock, embodied in the product, exchanges for the land, labour and stock of other products you wish to buy. Therefore, if the product you want is cheaper to buy than to make, in effect you exchange more of your land, labour and stock to make it than you would need to buy it. This exchange diverts scarce factors that could be used to produce products that exchange more profitably. The remedy is obvious: buy that which is cheaper to buy than what it costs to make it yourself.

Incidentally, as a reminder of the boundaries of Smith's age of commerce, his examples here are for clothes, shoes and a farmer's produce. On the national scale, Smith asserted that the prudent conduct of a private family 'can scarce be folly in that of a great kingdom'[2] and if foreigners can supply us with a commodity cheaper than we can make it, better buy it off them with some lesser part of the commodities we can make advantageously and have more advantageous output leftover to buy other outputs. This strategy can only enhance, not diminish, a country's industry – a lesson not yet learned by modern protectionists.

The contrary strategy of creating monopolies for merchants and manufacturers in the home market diminishes a country's output by possibly diverting it into less productive industries and away from those in which the country has some advantage. Smith cites his famous example of the 'manifest absurdity' of growing grapes in Scotland to make good wine at a cost of thirty times the expense of purchasing it from Bordeaux and Burgundy.[3]

Those who attempted, and attempt still, with some success it must be admitted, to graft a laissez faire interpretation onto *Wealth of Nations* harm market economies, especially when shorn of adherence to the smithian principles of natural liberty and justice. Innocent people reaped what was sowed in the unspeakable horrors of the communist anti-capitalist experiments in the 20th century, and might again in whatever fate awaits the victims of juvenile 'anti-globalisation' in the century to come.

41
Smithian Markets

The markets Smith wrote about were not the abstract markets his distant successors analysed at the end of the 19th century and bled to death mathematically in the 20th. And it is more than a difference between description and analysis; Smith addressed completely different phenomena, in a different age and for a different purpose. Smithian markets were located in time and space, and were real events, not equations. Smith walked through these markets in Kirkcaldy, Glasgow and Edinburgh; he touched their produce and spoke to the sellers, even acted occasionally in the role of a (frugal) buyer.

Ferdinand Braudel, in his magisterial *Wheels of Commerce*, captures the lively, bustling images of smithian markets, reeking in their smells, colours, noises and crowds, albeit from a French perspective ('mule loads of frogs,' etc.,):

with all the bustle and mess, the cries, strong smells and fresh produce ... a few trestles, a canopy to keep off the rain; stallholders, each with a numbered place, duly allotted in advance, registered and to be paid for as authorities and landlords decreed; a crowd of buyers and a multitude of petty traders – a varied and active proletariat; pea-shellers, who had a reputation for being inveterate gossips; frog-skinners (the frogs came in mule load from Geneva or Paris), porters, sweepers, carters, unlicensed pedlars of both sexes, fussy controllers, who passed on their derisory offices from father to son; second-hand dealers, peasants and peasant women recognisable by their dress, as were respectable townswomen looking for a bargain, servant girls who had worked out, so their employers complained, how to make something out of the shopping money; bakers selling coarse bread on the market-place, butchers whose displays of meat encumbered the streets and squares, wholesalers ('grossers') selling fish, butter and cheese in large quantities; tax-collectors. And everywhere of course were piles of produce, slabs of butter, heaps of vegetables, pyramids of cheeses, fruit, wet fish, game, meat which the butcher cut up on the spot, unsold books whose pages were used to wrap up purchases. From the countryside there are came straw, hay wood, wood, wool, hemp, flax and even fabrics woven on village looms.[1]

After the collapse of Rome, smithian markets re-emerged from the 12th to the 15th century, growing and replicating their distributive functions in thousands of locations across Europe. Braudel shows that between 1500 and 1640 there were over 800 regular markets in England and Wales close to localities of about 1,000 people, each serving local populations of about 7,000.[2]

In the region around the town of Caen, northern France, there were 197 fairs lasting from one to three days (15 days in Caen itself), or 223 fair days a year, and, in addition there were 85 markets in the region each week, accounting for 4,420 market days a year.[3] If these figures were replicated across all of France, it would amount to a prodigious presence of local markets and fairs in the economy, and of the social phenomena of 'truck, bartering and exchange' between producers and consumers.

Remnants of these old style markets remain today, though now they are somewhat subdued, relatively hygienic (and as officiously controlled – even in the 'car boot' or 'yard sales' of recent years). The Third world teems with them, replicating with their anarchistic truck, barter, and exchange the theatre of markets the world over from time immemorial. In Edinburgh, the old markets are more ghost haunted than remnants, their names evocative of a long gone past: Haymarket, Grassmarket, Fleshmarket Close, Cowgate, Market Street, etc. This was Smith's world. He heard, smelt, touched and traded in it.

The old markets were policed after a fashion, always spilling over their physical constraints. Their activities grew in the untidy progression of an erratic cavalcade of petty entrepreneurs, not in pursuit of a government's grand design, but in response to the dispersed local stimuli of opportunity for local people to make their living in 'truck, barter and exchange', the neglected phenomena of modern economics.

Braudel records the march to modernity through the proliferation of smithian markets in towns and villages, as they grew more prosperous and became more populous. No open space was too large for long, as market stalls and customers spilled over into nearby streets, spreading their noise, filth, smells and colours into every corner, around which crowds in the disorderly pursuit of their business and entertainment, jostled and exchanged polite endearments and foulmouthed curses and oaths in abundance.[4] With growth came specialisation. Middlemen replaced the producers who had been in face-to-face contact with their customers. The trickle down effect of opulence took time to spread, but spread it did, throughout the late 19th century, as links between producers' intermediaries and consumers grew in complexity.

42
Commercial Revival

In Smith's Scotland, the transformation of revived commerce took many forms. Professor Devine traced the transformation in his fine study of the Scottish merchant class.[1] Incomers, mostly petty, a few grand, quietly and gradually eroded the protectionism and restrictive practices of the merchant classes in the 16th and 17th centuries, and the officious grip of the burgesses and their monopolies on trade slipped in favour of 'unfreemen' and 'unfree towns and villages'. Non-burgesses gained rights to trade on payment of small sums, and new members joined the guilds on similar terms, after only three, not seven, year apprenticeships, supplemented by a steady accession of outsiders by marriage into established families, by looser rules of apprenticeship and by purchasing their rank.[2]

Devine concludes that these trends in the inability to enforce discipline on trading by non-members (formerly punished by heavy fines), were 'a clear acknowledgement of the futility of attempting to impose traditional monopolies in a period of vigorous commercial activity'.[3] With growing opulence fuelled by good harvests, characteristic mainly for 1640–1750, the unquestioned social superiority of the trading burgesses in previous centuries slowly gave way to a town burgess being an, albeit superior, social symbol rather than an indicator of economic status. Smith, a non-trader of course, was elected a burgess of Glasgow, a purely social honour by 1755.

Devine provides useful statistics from the historical records of the trends amongst those who bought and sold. While incomplete, they give a flavour of what happened. The unofficial non-guild run sector grew in the late 17th century and the authorities gradually acquiesced to the trading of the 'small shopkeeper, pedlar, hawker and packman' selling retail in the towns and distributing goods purchased from wholesalers to customers in the country. Edinburgh council minutes noted in 1692 that 'a great many women, servants and others who turning wearie of their services, have, out of a principle of avarice and laziness, taken up little shops which is evidently hurtful to the trading burgesses who bear the public burdens of the place.'[4] Buying and selling no doubt had attractions over a servant's long

173

hours at the beck and call of the mistress of the house and subject to her husband's harassment.

Registered burgesses were officially authorised to 'buy and sell'. A minority of them (about 20 per cent), the 'merchant adventurers' and the wealthiest of the group, engaged in foreign trade as well as local. The official merchants were stratified by the value of the 'stock' they were worth. In Aberdeen, in the 1690s, out of 239 merchant burgesses, only 27 'possessed stock valued at ... £530' and above. At the bottom of the rankings, 62 merchants had stock valued at up to £27 (some of them must have had very small valuations indeed) and a middling group had stock 'assessed at between £27 and £260'. In Edinburgh, a richer town than Aberdeen relatively speaking, only 2 were worth less than £27, the middling group of 51 were worth up to £530, and a top 10 were worth between £1,590 and £2,688.[5]

These not overly large sums and the nature of the merchants' stock itself showed the precariousness of their chosen trade. Those who entered at the bottom of the ladder were scarce able to survive, let alone to reach opulence in a generation. Those further up were vulnerable to the shifting fortunes of anything dependent on foreign trade, as Devine points out in the 'spectacular bankruptcies' that 'punctuated' the boom years of Scottish North American and Caribbean trading.[6]

A few very rich merchants or 'great landlords', who accumulated relatively rich savings of £4,000, could invest in the purchase of landed properties, but most investments of this kind were relatively modest.[7] More common were loans from successful merchants of between £8 and £100 to various individuals who sought to enhance their small businesses or keep them going. Those who invested in trades such as sugar, wool, glass, soap, paper, leather, lead, pins, rope, linen, sailcloth, gunpowder, salt, hardware, and spirits, might make loans of less than £500 each, useful but petty amounts compared to the capitals mobilised in the 19th century.[8]

The percentage of merchants active in the late 17th to mid-18th centuries was not large. Devine cites Professor Smout's assessment that Glasgow's community of merchants numbered 400–500 out of a population of 12,000, or about 4 per cent. Aberdeen's community numbered 239.[9] Their opulence probably made up for their lack of numbers but it is still a narrow presence to build a case for the existence of a capitalist class of entrepreneurs. These were market merchants buying and selling goods farmed locally, manufactured in small workshops by artisans, or shipped from abroad. As merchants they were significant contributors to the growing commercial economy. But by no stretch of the imagination can Smith's 'merchants and manufacturers' be interpreted as identical or similar to what modern economists recognise as capitalists, 'proto' or otherwise.

In Birmingham, its petty manufacturers, called 'Toy makers' from being the makers of domestic trivia that were not quite necessities and were a long way short of luxuries. These were consumed by the middling orders of merchants, manufacturers, landed gentry, artisans and labourers in commercial upswings (and, of course, what Smith called, disparagingly, 'Aldermen's wives' and ministers and magistrates).

Looking further south to a more advanced commercial society (still dominated by agriculture) in England, a local directory described the Toy Makers' products:

> Divided into several branches as the Gold and Silver Toy makers, who make Trinkets, Seals, Tweezer and Toothpick cases, Smelling Bottles, Snuff Boxes, and Filligree Work, such as Toilets, Tea Chests, Inkstands,. &c &c. The Tortoishell Toy maker, makes a beautiful variety of the above and other Articles; as does also the Steel; who make Cork screws, Buckles, Draw and other Boxes: Snuffers, Watch Chains, Stay Hooks, Sugar knippers &c. and almost all these are likewise in various metals.[10]

Uglow notes that Matthew Boulton's father was a successful Birmingham Toy Maker and young Boulton, long before he teamed with James Watt to manufacture powerful engines, began his manufacturing life learning and applying the 'japanning' technique to cover metalware with layers of varnish, including pictures.[11] Smith described the manufactories of Birmingham as meeting the demands of 'fashion and fancy' and paying wages higher than in more traditional trades[12] because their customers were willing to pay more for petty 'luxuries' from their increasing opulence.

Smith accounts for sources for the growth of manufactures in commercial society. One was from the import of foreign manufactured products in exchange for 'rude produce', leading in time to import substitution; the other was from natural growth by 'the natural refinement of those household and coarser manufactures', which even the 'poorest and rudest countries' must produce locally.

A fertile country, he mused, relatively landlocked with no easy access to foreign trade, produces an abundance of cheap agricultural produce, encouraging skilled workmen, attracted by the low cost of living compared to other places, to settle in the community; there they work up the materials from the land in exchange for surplus food, increasing the value of the food producers' surplus; the cultivators, receiving better prices for their surpluses are able to purchase more of the manufactured goods 'they have occasion for' and they are encouraged to improve their land to secure larger surpluses from its increased fertility.

Manufacturers, improving the quality of their produce, first supply their neighbourhood and, if successful, more distant places. Whereas the cultivators' rude produce and the manufacturers' coarse products could not sustain a distant market, improved manufactured products can justify the expense of sending them greater distances. While local corn could not be transported economically, surplus improved quality local cloth can be, its small bulk representing a higher value in surplus food. Smith identifies the English cities of Leeds, Halifax, Sheffield, Birmingham and Wolverhampton as examples where manufacturing has 'grown up naturally', adding that 'such manufactures are the offspring of agriculture'.[13] Exporting good quality manufactures to Europe paid for the import of fine wines from France and Portugal, closing the circle of British farmers, manufacturers, and merchants importing from French farmers, viticulturists, and merchants.

This smithian view is different in content from those presented in standard textbooks. His Scottish perspective is small-scale commerce, close to the land, with small scale manufactures subordinate to agriculture. French, English and Scottish industry predominantly was still at the artisan stage in the mid-18th century, with England slightly more advanced, but not by enough yet to presage a major shift in production techniques from handcrafted manufactured items to power-driven machined products of the factory age. Those searching for capitalist industry in 18th century Europe, who do so with marxian (or laissez faire!) tinted magnifying glasses,[14] are stronger on assertion that on evidence.

Walsh and Gram, for example, quote the assessments of historians that France, unlike, allegedly England – but not Scotland – was a backward country in the march of its economic system to capitalism ('which did not yet exist on a large scale in French industry')[15] in 1789. Quoting George Rude, they undermine their own neo-marxian case that 18th century political economy was about capitalist forms of exploitation rather than Smith's commercial age:

> There was no factory system or industrial 'belt', though enterprising textile manufacturers had set up establishments that, on occasion, employed up to 400 or 500 or even 800 workpeople under one roof. Apart from the multifarious petty trades plied in the markets ... the prevailing mode of production was still that of the traditional workshop in which the journeyman, though his prospects of promotion were becoming more and more remote, still shared the work and the gossip, and often the board and lodging, of his master.[16]

This corresponds to other assessments of the extent of capitalist industry in England and Scotland as late as 1821:

> At the foundation of the Edinburgh School of Arts in 1821 [progenitor of Heriot-Watt University], the factory system had made limited impact outside the Lancashire cotton areas; the typical workman was a craftsman working on his own or in a small enterprise. It was in a watch and

clockmakers, not a factory, that Leonard Horner [brother of Francis Horner] outlined to Robert Bryson his ideas for educating Edinburgh mechanics.[17]

If you begin with a problematic premise, your conclusions are vulnerable to evidence.

43
Of the Virtues of Frugality

Smith exalted the virtue of 'frugality' as the maxim of the commercial age. Those who sought to grow their businesses could do so only by the gradual accretion of what they could save from the revenue earned from their relatively meagre stock. There was almost no active market in shareholder funds. What the merchant or manufacturer saved he invested in his own ventures or loaned it to somebody else in their business. How else would they grow it?

> Whatever part of his stock a man employs as a capital, he always expects his to be replaced to him with a profit. He employs it, therefore, in maintaining productive hands only; after having served in the function of a capital to him, it constitutes a revenue to them.[1]

Having sold the product of their labour and made a profit from the revenue above his outlay, the owner of capital can increase his meagre stock, from which he can repeat the process of steady accumulation, unless, Smith notes, he diverts part of his stock into 'unproductive' use. 'Capitals', Smith warns, 'are increased by parsimony, and diminished by prodigality and misconduct.'[2] Not only the 'great landlord or the rich merchant, but even the common workman, if his wages are considerable, may maintain a menial servant'.[3] All such expenditure on servants is unproductive in Smith's narrow growth terms, and he did not approve of it.

Frugality funded savings out of revenue; prodigality squandered revenue in unproductive trifles and the 'wages of idleness'. Revenue transformed into capital creates a 'perpetual fund' to maintain productive hands 'for all time to come'. Revenue diverted from productive capital into consumption was also a social 'crime': 'If the prodigality of some was not compensated by the frugality of others, the conduct of every prodigal, by feeding the idle with the bread of the industrious, tends not only to beggar himself, but to impoverish his country.'[4] This makes 'every prodigal ... a publick enemy, and every frugal man a publick benefactor.'[5] It is the same with every 'inju-

178

dicious and unsuccessful project in agriculture, mines, fisheries, trade, or manufactures' which 'tends in the same manner to diminish the funds destined for the maintenance of productive labour.'[6]

However, without consumers actively spending out of revenue, the frugal merchant, manufacturer and farmer had no source of revenue from which they could be frugal! Clothes without buttons and shoes, breeches and stockings without buckles and pins, present a sorry sight of frugal rectitude.

Can we dispute that the focus of Smith's many references to frugality were heavily laden with carefully composed images of the skimping merchant, many of whom made an extra farthing here and there by their deviousness and not a little cheeky charm, and that they had a tendency to cheat where they could get away with it? The psychology of the merchant in commercial society was paucity through frugality.

Smith's horizons in his treatment of economic growth are bounded by the limitations of the economy he studied. But his model is clear enough. The annual produce each year creates a small surplus over its costs and in the disposition of that surplus growth could take place in the following year, but would not if revenue is expended on 'non-productive' (i.e., non growth inducing) consumption. The choice between prodigality and frugality was dispersed among thousands of players, each facing the temptation to consume non-productively or to apply their surplus to the employment of productive (i.e., growth inducing) labour.

There was also the prospect that even those making the latter, frugal choice would do so in an injudicious manner – a failed project – which has the same effect as if they had consumed it like a prodigal. Hence, if the owners of surplus revenue over last year's costs, consumed too large a proportion of it on non-growth consumption, growth would not continue; if they spent too much on failed projects, growth would not continue; and only if the proportion allocated to growth inducing activity in successful projects was above a minimum proportion would growth next year be obtained.[7] And any growth obtained was likely to be small each year, though compound interest operates at even minute levels of growth to raise national income in time (dividing 70 by the annual growth rate gives the doubling time in years).

Merchants were a mixed blessing in Smith's commercial age. Those with options of mobility were suspected of a lack of patriotism and for having detrimental effects on capital accumulation. Where a merchant located and conducted his business was a matter of indifference to him and it took a 'very trifling disgust' to provoke 'him to remove his capital, and together with all the industry which it supports, from one country to another'. His capital did not belong to any particular country unless 'it has been spread as it were over the face of that country, either in buildings, or in the lasting improvement of lands.'[8]

Investing moveable capital in the 'face of a country' immobilised it in the medium term from intemperate and hasty crossing of borders. It took time for a merchant to sell his land or buildings and realise his investments into cash. On these lines, Smith was adamant that it was the capital invested in the improvement of agriculture which was 'the most durable, and cannot be destroyed but by those more violent convulsions occasioned by the depredations of hostile and barbarous nations continued for a century or two together.'[9]

Smith's commendation of agricultural improvements, especially by small landed proprieters, indicated a significant economic bias, not always noted. He was more favourably disposed to the productivity enhancements of good tenant and 'yeoman' farmers than he was to the investment activities of merchants and manufacturers.[10]

Compared to his assessments of the motivations of manufacturers, particularly in respect of their pernicious resort to monopoly, Smith was positively disposed towards the 'middling order' of small (but not too small) farmers, whose many virtues he praised throughout *Wealth of Nations*, and from which order he was a member through his maternal grandfather:

> A small proprietor, however, who knows every part of his little territory, who views it with all the affection which property, especially small property, naturally inspires, and who upon that account takes pleasure not only in cultivating but adorning it, is generally of all improvers the most industrious, the most intelligent, and the most successful.[11]

44
On Market Interference

One way to clarify what seems to be a set of contradictory stances by Smith on market interference (his support on some occasions for preventing interference and his recommendations on others for encouraging it) is to examine briefly his stance on some 18th-century issues. These are best considered in the context of his critique of restraints on competition, though it also encompassed equity and fairness.

Smith alludes to the policy in Europe of restraining competition in certain employments, which he put down to the 'exclusive privileges of corporations' in towns. To be employed in these trades it was necessary to have served an apprenticeship under a properly qualified master, who was allowed to have a specified number of apprentices (often as few as two). The apprentice had to serve his master a specified number of years (usually seven). Both requirements restrained the number of persons who entered a trade.

Smith provides an interesting tit bit: the incorporations of trades were 'antiently [sic] called universities' and the ancient universities copied the even more ancient seven-year term of apprenticeship to become a 'master' tradesman as the appropriate duration of study for a master of arts degree before the graduate could have scholars or apprentices 'study under him'.[1] The Elizabethan Statute of Apprenticeship (1562) prohibited any person (except discharged soldiers and seamen) of exercising any trade or craft unless he had previously served an apprenticeship of seven years, aligning the law with the practice of the trade corporations.

Among the rules, as 'foolish as can be imagined', was the prohibition on coach makers making coach wheels, or having anybody make them for him unless they were master wheel-rights, as defined in the Statute. The Statute applied to market towns but not to country villages in England, and excluded trades that were not exercised at the time of its enactment (1562), enabling the manufactures of Manchester, Birmingham and Wolverhampton to escape its provisions, a factor not without significance for the late 18th and early 19th century growth of powered industry in these towns.

Smith sets out his case against restrictive apprenticeships:

> The property which every man has in his own labour, as it is the original foundation of all other property, so it is the most sacred and inviolable. The patrimony of a poor man lies in his strength and dexterity of his hands; and to hinder him from employing this strength and dexterity in what manner he thinks proper without injury to his neighbour, is a plain violation of this most sacred property. It is a manifest encroachment upon the just liberty both of the workman, and of those who might be disposed to employ him. As it hinders the one from working at what he thinks proper, so it hinders the others from employing whom they think proper. To judge whether he is fit to be employed, may surely be trusted to the discretion of the employers whose interest it so much concerns. The affected anxiety of the law-giver lest they should employ an improper person, is evidently as impertinent as it is oppressive.[2]

From this principle based on the rights of labourers he tackled the likely objections of defenders of long and restrictive apprenticeships, covering topics that were to become familiar in the public debates that occurred during attempts to repeal the Statute of Apprentices in 1814. He did not think seven-year apprenticeships were a guarantee against shoddy workmanship, which was 'generally the effect of fraud, and not inability'. He added his approval of legislation to provide quality assurance in 'sterling silver marks upon plate, and the stamps upon linen and woollen cloth',[3] which was a significant extension of the State's role in markets because manufacturers could not be trusted to guarantee the quality of their products, and the discipline of the consumer was too dispersed and ineffective to constrain the rogues among them.

Apprentices were 'likely to be idle' while journeymen working 'by the piece' were 'likely to be industrious'. This phenomenon was caused by an apprentice's aversion to labour 'when for a long time he receives no benefit from it' (whatever he produced was owned entirely by the master who sold and kept the income), whereas the journeyman enjoyed the income from his work.

There was also no benefit from the long duration of apprenticeship because it was unnecessary. 'The arts, which are much superior to the common trades, such as those of making clocks, and watches, contain no mystery as to require a long course of instruction' and 'cannot well require more than a lesson of a few weeks: perhaps those of a few days might be sufficient.'[4]

Who would be losers if the Statute were repealed? Masters, of course. They would lose the wages they pocketed by not paying apprentices for the seven years of unnecessary instruction in their trade 'secrets'. The years of unpaid labour, in effect, are the price the apprentices pay to join a restrictive club of quasi-monopolists who charged more than what would be the competitive price for their products. Existing apprentices from the old regime, would lose too because in trades easily learned they would experience more competition and lower profits when they became masters. 'But', said Smith, 'the publick would be the gainer, the work of all artificers coming in this way much cheaper to market.'[5]

Social justice leavens his approach to legislation that intervenes in markets and belies his false reputation for laissez faire. This theme is a separate argument to those based on the economic consequences of such interventions and their restraints on perfect liberty. He summarised his preferences for certain classes of interventions by distinguishing between those who gained and those who lost from interventionist legislation. Clearly, he was not indifferent to the distinction; if anything that distinction alone determined his likely preferences:

> Whenever the legislature attempts to regulate the differences between masters and their workmen, its counsellors are always the masters. When the regulation, therefore is in favour of the workmen, it is always just and equitable; but it is sometimes otherwise when in favour of the masters.[6]

To ensure that this generalisation is supportable by his readers in particular cases, he refers to the law obliging masters to pay their workmen in money and not in kind as 'quiet just and equitable' and, therefore, explicitly indicating that some interventions by the State in the private bargains of masters and workmen and the monitoring of conformity by masters with the law were appropriate. Smith regarded their justness as self-evident.

And in case his partiality for the interests of the labouring poor over the masters was missed, he gave an example of an intervention that was not 'quite just and equitable'. He felt the law fell short of treating workmen and masters equitably in its treatment of allowing, without punishment, masters to form combinations to reduce the wages of workmen, while 'the law would punish [workmen] very severely' if they combined to resist such proposals. In doing so he made it clear he felt the combination laws were unjust, observing that: 'if [the law] dealt impartially, it would treat masters in the same manner.'[7]

The banning of all combinations, either of masters or workmen, would still treat workmen more harshly, because masters 'commonly enter into a private bond or agreement' to promote their combinations in relative secrecy to hide their behaviour more discreetly in their private dining rooms away from the public gaze, while workmen were compelled by a lack of facilities to meet en mass in public places, in full view of the masters' and the magistrates' informers.

The Law of Settlements, or poor law, was Smith's other target. Just as the Apprenticeship laws obstructed labour from entering any profession it was capable of becoming qualified to perform, and the Masters' Guilds and Corporations prevented stock from moving between occupations, the poor law provisions stopped unemployed common labourers from moving between nearby areas in search of work. Even if they found work they were driven away by regulations prohibiting residence outside the parish they were already resident in.[8]

The intention of the Act originally was to raise funds for maintaining the poor in each parish for residents in that parish only. In time, restricting the admission of new residents became an end in itself, and without their certificates of residence they could not look for or, if successful, take up employment. Smith was concerned with the absurdities of the regulations and their obstruction to the free movement of labour (a necessary feature of an expanding economy), such as the requirement to reside in a new parish for 40 'undisturbed' days. Later, the qualifying residence count could only begin after publication of the notice of residence in the parish church after divine service on a Sunday – an onerous barrier to becoming resident if the churchwardens were also dispensers of poor relief and not minded to increase the supplicants. Because they needed a certificate from the parish they were in, it was extremely difficult to get one for presenting to another parish.

The editors (1976) of *Wealth of Nations* add a note[9] to the effect that Smith's focus on the absurdities of the regulations of the poor law may have exaggerated the extent of its applications in practice, at least by the time Smith was writing. But as a clear example of the inequities of legislation that interfere negatively in markets, his discussion on the Act of Settlement in the full flower of its absurdities is unmatched. The power of commercial growth in practice to begin to break down statutory regulations, as was happening with the Apprenticeship, Corporation and Settlement laws by the mid-18th century, did not remove the need to criticise their merits.

45

Famous Exceptions to Free Trade

Just as Smith was reticent to employ the words laissez faire, he also did not use the words laissez passer ('let it pass'), because he was not in favour of unrestricted free international trade, though Smith was quoted with greater authority on free international trade than he was on laissez faire.[1] It comes as a minor shock to some people (it did to me when Professor Andrew Skinner drew my attention to it in 1975 – I was researching the economics of defence) to discover that Smith, contrary to his reputation, adamantly advocated two major breaches of free international trade.

The first major breach was when a particular industry is necessary for defence. Britain's defence in the 18th century depended upon the number of sailors and shipping it could muster for wars against its main rivals (the Dutch, French, Russia, Spanish and Portuguese navies, later joined by the US Navy), any combination of which could severely damage British interests in international trade. The Acts of Navigation, originally enacted under Oliver Cromwell and elaborated upon by Charles II and his successors, gave British ships with British crews, a monopoly of British trade. Subsidiary regulations prohibited for strategic reasons the colonies exporting ships' accessories (masts, spars, rudders and sails) and naval supplies, and prohibited their conveying ordinary commercial exports to anywhere other than via Britain first.

Smith discusses their details and concludes that the acts of navigation are 'not favourable to foreign commerce, or to the growth of opulence which can arise from it.'[2] If this were a purely commercial prohibition to protect commercial interests by government fiat, he would have launched his familiar critique (what an excellent examination question that would make!). But it was not an example of 'the wretched spirit of monopoly'[3] as he makes clear:

> As defence, however, is of much more importance than opulence, the act of navigation is, perhaps, the wisest of all commercial regulations of England.[4]

Of significance for us, Smith's prescription amounts to another endorsement of the principle that certain interventions by the State, in this case
for 'reasons of State' (a familiar principle from mercantile thought!), are
acceptable on a case-by-case basis. He sets aside the self-interest argument
that owners of stock in shipping and its workmen (the sailors), and all merchants and manufacturers who supplied them, commercially benefited in
the same manner as if a pure monopoly was imposed by supine governments in thrall to private interest groups. In wars, the owners of the factors
employed in shipping put at risk their capital bound up in their merchant
ships and cargoes, and the lives of seamen (who might be 'pressed' into the
Royal Navy).

This breach in his anti-monopoly critique was acceptable only from the
perspective of defence of Britain against the depredations of neighbours.
Smith could hardly argue otherwise and retain credibility with the people
he sought to influence in Britain in the real world of 18th century Europe.

By the late 18th century, the Royal Navy employed over 200,000 people
in its warships and dockyards, as seamen and marines, crews of its supply
vessels, artisans and labourers, ordnance depots, sail lofts, rope stores,
global stations, supplies and central administration. It was probably the
largest industrial organisation in the world at the time and it was no mean
factor in Britain's impregnability from foreign rivals. As defence is a small
part of a commercial society's annual output, Smith's acceptance of the
Navigation Acts opened doors to claims by other merchants and manufacturers that this or that sector was 'strategic' and eligible, therefore, for
similar protective treatment. *Wealth of Nations* did not end the free trade
versus protection argument – it boosted it.

Smith's second major breach of free trade covers the imposition of a
domestic tax upon certain items of home produce. It is reasonable, said
Smith, to impose the same tax on the imports of produce taxed domesti-
cally because without it this would discriminate against home produce.
This was quite different from conceding a monopoly to home producers by
a tax on imports but not on domestic produce.

Imposing taxes on foreign imports stops the 'clamorous complaints of
our merchants and manufacturers',[5] who also find arguments for extending
like-for-like taxes to other imports. Smith rejected such arguments as
'absurd'.[6] He also notes that nations seldom fail to retaliate ('revenge' he
calls it) against foreign high duties and prohibitions imposed in their countries and suggests that in the French case the Minister was 'imposed upon
by the sophistry of merchants and manufacturers who are always demanding a monopoly against their countrymen.'[7] He regarded the advantages
and disadvantages of trade policy as an empirical question and not one of
absolute principle.

Where high duties and prohibitions bolster a trade in particular manufactures for any reason and, as a result, it employs a large number of hands

behind the protective barriers, a sensible change in policy to abolish foreign duties should not be rushed:

> Humanity may in this case require that the freedom of trade should be restored only by slow gradations, with a good deal of reserve and circumspection otherwise cheaper foreign goods of the same kind might be poured in so fast into the home market, as to deprive all at once thousands of our people of their ordinary employment and means of subsistence.[8]

Smith was also conscious of the side effects of economic prescriptions and anxious that they should be acknowledged and treated, especially where they affected low-income common labourers. He was not a laissez faire ideologue immune to the common decencies, but a man cognisant of the high responsibilities of anyone who gives principled advice, which, if heeded by governments, was likely to affect the lives and subsistence of others. No wooden pieces on society's chess board here!

Smith's absolute disdain for monopoly cannot be doubted but neither can his regard for the 'wider picture' of the great issues of State. He was confident that leaving things alone could produce eventually the optimum results in practice, depending on the context, and where it could not, or did not, he was as confident that it was necessary for the State, funded by public revenues, to intervene.

46
Of Strawberries and Buttons

Smith's political economy is a study in contrast. A natural mechanism, operating under impartial competition and the total absence of monopoly, in the long run produces opulence beneficial to all mankind.[1] In contrast, imperfect people populate a real world, where private monopolistic interests interfere in the natural order to produce above-optimal results for themselves and sub-optimal results for customers. Essentially, the contrast between what an economy could be and what it was in practice, informed his critique of a commercial society lumbered with the policy distortions of mercantile politics and the spirit of monopoly.

Monopolists score low marks on any scale measuring their concern for others. As assuredly, mercantile interests (incidentally, their intellectual descendants are still with us) score low on their concern for the damage their policies inflict on a nation's potential for general, as opposed to their own, opulence. Mercantile interests, and legislators doing their bidding (and, of course, when the direction of bidding is in the reverse direction), cross the fuzzy line separating the judicious protection of the public good from the cloying habits of unnecessary interference. In between regrettable monopoly and irresponsible laissez faire, a smithian balance should obtain. He was prejudiced in favour of liberty, supported by a reluctance, but not prohibition, to contemplate State interference should market failure make it necessary. The choice between liberty and regulation was not easy, considering that market and state failure were equally burdensome on wealth creation and liberty.

A third, heterogeneous, group, oblivious of the distinction between theoretical harmony and imperfect reality, quote selectively from Smith's rhetoric in pursuit of their special cases. Viner's world-weary sarcasm bites: 'an economist must have peculiar theories indeed who cannot quote from [*Wealth of Nations*] to support his special purposes.'[2]

Smith on natural and market prices

Smith faced facts about the real world. Men conducted themselves in all parts of it in different ways and manners because different circumstances prevailed locally (a theme developed by his former student, Professor John Millar, in his *Origin of the Distinction of Ranks*).[3] A wide range of behaviours was the norm, but local circumstances altered cases, none more so than in commerce. Smith resolved the apparent economic anomalies (different prices applying in different areas for the same produce) by invoking concepts of 'natural' and 'market' prices to explain their local variations, though in doing so he caused minor expository muddles.[4]

I go through Smith's market model in a rather basic manner despite the good advice of a colleague, who questioned my approach on the sound grounds that Smith's clumsy construction would irritate today's professional economists. I agree that a competent first year economics' student could derive the essence of a smithian market model in half a dozen lines of simple notation, supported by a half page of text, but I have persisted with my original decision because it is beneficial to be reminded painfully of just how primitive was his model. Smith's account of the market is precisely that of a simple street market in a fixed locality. It was hardly the elegant market theory taught today. Plainly others understood the mechanics of markets before Smith, but we should not judge his account by modern neo-classical standards, or by what economists wrote many years after him.

Smith had a cost of production approach to prices, as did the classical economists.[5] The three main incomes from rents, wages, and profits were regulated partly by the general circumstances of each society, its riches or poverty, its advancing, stationary, or declining condition, and partly by the nature of each employment. The 'neighbourhood' featured prominently in smithian markets because neither regional nor national influences on prices were as important as they were to become later, because transport between regions of goods for distant sale was precarious, difficult and selective.

Circumstances in a neighbourhood, and the general condition and fertility of local land, regulated agricultural rent. The absence of certain artisans in a particular neighbourhood precluded markets for their output, though they might be active in a flourishing market fifty miles away. Smithian markets were local not national, exemplified starkly by the contrasting lack of opulence in the Highlands compared to the Lowlands of Scotland, and the contrast between Scotland's relatively backward commercial life compared to the south of England.

A brief look at his prices model shows its suitability for, because it was derived from, small-scale transactions in street markets, fairs, souks and bazaars, the world over. If you keep in mind a street market, with a number of competing sellers of, say, fruit and vegetables or buttons and buckles, you'll get the picture. By modern standards, his economics were simplistic. Gavin Reid synthesised Smith's analysis of natural and market prices using modern techniques (lightly touched with simple mathematical notation), and readers who find his exposition a trifle wordy should consult it.[6] The basic point about 18th-century markets is their demonstration of the responses to local price signals.

For my example, I choose a mythical strawberry seller. The example, not in *Wealth of Nations*, is a small personal tribute to Adam Smith, who was fond of strawberries and enjoyed having a plate of them for his breakfast each morning.[7]

Thousands of real buyers and sellers made their economic decisions in real street markets and, for practical men and women, buying and selling was not difficult, provided they had money to buy or something to sell. When it is near the end of the market day, for example, and a seller still has, say, strawberries left, she cuts her prices to sell the remainder before close of business. Otherwise she has to dump them. Fruit perishes whereas buttons do not, but she is in the strawberry, not the buttons business.

Conversely, if within a few hours she sells half of her strawberries, she raises her prices, hoping to sell the remainder at a higher price while she has some left. Smith's model does no more than describe the unsophisticated reactions of sellers to changes in supply and demand.

Why then did Smith complicate a simple supply and demand model with 'natural' and 'market' prices? Because he was interested in the different people who co-operated to produce things for sale, and identified what they contributed to production and how, further back in the supply chain, co-operators reacted to changes in prices for their contributions. He grafted factor contributions onto a simple supply and demand model for market stalls in a market space.

Prices of strawberries are determined by the costs contributed by the three main co-operators in their production. First, rent is paid to the owner of the land on which tenants plant their strawberry beds. Rents in Smith's time were major sources of income to landowners; agricultural incomes then being nearer to half of the annual income of British society than today's distant three per cent. Landlords ensured they got their (large) share of these revenues.

Second, gardeners earn wages for tending the plants, picking strawberries and carrying them to a street market in a nearby town. Wages are labour costs. Third, the tenant earns his share from the returns on his 'stock' (an 18th century word for 'capital', used interchangeably in *Wealth of Nations*). Out of his stock he invests in fertiliser and useful hand tools, etc., and in preparing his strawberries for sale. As owner of the stock, he has to earn greater revenues than his original investment because he and his family need subsistence, and he also needs new stock for next season's strawberry market. His subsistence and stock are paid for from his revenues and he must make the minimum profits to cover these, otherwise he must change trades.

Smith's 'Natural' price is simply the price sufficient to pay 'according to their natural rates', the landlord's rent, the wages of the labourers and the profits on his 'stock'.[8] Potential customers do not see it this way; they know nothing of landlord's rent, labourer' wages or the stockholder's expectations for his family's subsistence, or what he needs to prepare his plants for next season. In fact, customers are truly indifferent to a seller's circumstances. They need to know only one thing: the price on the piles of strawberries.

What happens when there are too few buyers willing to buy strawberries? Smith called any price differing from the price that met the expectations of the parties co-operating in production, the 'market price'. His friend, David Hume, wrote, saying, 'If you were here at my fireside, I should dispute some of your Principles. I cannot think, that the Rent of Farms makes any part of the Price of the Produce, but that the Price is determined altogether by the Quantity and the Demand'.[9] He implied that Smith should put aside his 'natural' and 'market' price distinctions. This might have made Smith's market mechanism clearer, but only at the price of obscuring his interest in analysing what lay behind the behaviours of the contributors to production as they reacted to price changes of the products.

'Perfect liberty' allows the unfettered movement of owners of land, labour and stock to move in and out of any line of business, depending on whether they recouped their costs and made their expected profits or suffered unexpected losses. The stockholder did not have to sell his output at a loss, neither did landlords have to supply land below their rental aspirations, nor did labourers have to work for wages below their family's subsistence. In conditions of natural liberty, owners of the 'factors' of production ceased to co-operate at will, whatever the inconveniences of their decisions for other players.

Smith said people with cash in hand and willing and able to buy constituted 'effectual demand' (nowadays, 'effective demand'), distinguishing effectual from wishful demand from those who wanted the products but were not willing, or not able, to pay sufficient cash for them. By the simple expedient of sticking to Hume's notion of demand and supply – quantities demanded, backed by cash, and quantities supplied, in the expectation of recovering their costs – it is easy to see what happens when demand is greater or lower than supply.

When demand was greater, competition among potential buyers raised the price, and when demand was lower, competition among sellers lowered it. Of course, a temporary lull in demand could mislead the seller into dropping his price unnecessarily, or he could misread a short spate in demand and raise his price rashly. Any errors meant he sold at too low a price, while his rivals continued selling at higher prices, earning expected profits, or he sold nothing at too high a price and did not earn what he needed for landlord's rent and labourers' wages. If they got these adjustments right more times than wrong, sellers would remain in business; if they judged them wrongly too often, they would not. There is nothing personal in the way that smithian markets punish misreading of their price signals.

Market prices depend on the discrepancy between demand and supply, and from other influences like the consumers' wealth and their proclivity for 'wanton luxury', their degree of animation to conclude deals, and the importance to them of acquiring the products.[10] Smith had his finger on the pulse of buyers busily haggling, sometimes tentatively and sometimes tenaciously, with market traders. Notably, he recognised that it was not just pure price that determined demand; other factors, including the extent to which these factors animated the eagerness of the potential consumers, influenced different consumers differently.

In effect, sellers judged all the hidden influences on consumer demand, and all the known influences on supply, simply by observing the changing (or unchanging) quantity on sale at different times. Potential consumers judged the net effects of the influences on their demand, and the hidden influences on producers willing to supply, from the changing (or unchanging) prices of different times. Amounts for sale and their prices summarised the private assessments of a vast amount of information in the minds of the suppliers and consumers without anybody conducting complex calculations or in-depth interviews.

Consumers and producers made separate decisions that brought demand and supply into balance, if only momentarily. Regular adjustments caused repeated market clearing choices, demonstrating, truly, that a smithian street market was an efficient mechanism whatever the circumstances, intentions, predilections, thoughts or dreams of the participants (though all these influences played their parts in the repeated rounds leading to outcomes).

If supply exceeded demand, prices fell and the contributors necessary for the supply of the product faced receiving less than they expected for their contributions. The contributors reacted predictably.[11] Unable to obtain his full rent, the landlord withdrew part of his land from the tenant, forcing him to economise on land, while the landlord put it to other uses with other tenants, or left it fallow; labourers, unable to receive their full wages, withdrew some of their labour and sought part time work elsewhere (which they could do in 18th-century labour markets); and the tenant withdrew some of his stock from, in my example, strawberry production, and placed it elsewhere – perhaps into buttons. The overall result: the actual supply of strawberries reduced towards the demand for strawberries. For simplicity, Smith compressed these adjustments into an instantaneous event that in real, not theoretical, markets took time to work through.

The exact opposite happened when supply was insufficient for demand. Prices rose and the contributors could receive more than they expected, with predictable results. The landlord increased the land he committed to his tenants' strawberry fields; labourers increased their supply of labour by withdrawing it from elsewhere; and the tenant increased the stock he committed to strawberry production. The supply of strawberries increased in due course towards the demand for them.[12]

When 'perfect liberty' existed, factors such as land, labour and stock were perfectly mobile, preventing prices from changing other than for short periods.[13] Factor flight reduced output and buyers' competition raised prices. Similarly in reverse, if market prices rose, factor inflows increased output and seller's competition reduced prices. All prices for all products, in his narrative, gravitated continually towards equilibrium prices that balanced supply with demand.[14]

Essentially, that is the core of the model in *Wealth of Nations*. Because most economists are not familiar with the works of Smith's contemporaries (for example, Sir James Steuart)[15] they have taken on trust third party testimonials of the originality of parts of *Wealth of Nations*. They assume, incorrectly that Smith originated the analysis of the simple market mechanism, a claim not made by Smith but imputed to him by others.

47

Cheerful and Hearty Economics

There are two more things we should review from Smith's narrative. First, what determines the shares of the revenues paid to rent, profit and wages? This looks fearfully uninteresting – a result of my posing it in economic terms. But it is central to his narrative: the parties bargain for their shares in unequal contests.

Landlords have a private monopoly of land (from the age of agriculture) and take the lion's share of the output produced on, or collected from, it by the tenant.[1] In the arts and manufactures sector master artisans, who hire labourers, provide the materials for their work and pay them wages. The master deducts from the sales revenue his share as replacement of his stock used in production (tools, wood, iron, etc.,) and his profit.[2] Thus, the landlord, the labourer and the master divided the entire revenue between themselves. It is a cost of production theory of price.

The second question is: what determines the degree of commitment of the owners to the factors of land, labour and stock to apply them in, say, strawberries, as opposed to some other product?

Landlords, as monopolists, charged rent and judged what 'the farmer can afford to pay'.[3] What landlords considered their tenants could afford seldom indulged their incapacities. In conditions of perfect liberty land-lords could only attract tenants if the tenants could maintain their sub-sistence, replace their stock and make a profit from the sale of their output. If they could not pay rent under current market prices they quit their tenancy. If market prices were rising, rents increased. Landlords did not contribute to higher or lower prices; they gained or lost as a consequence of market demand and supply.

The wage of the labourer depends upon the contract made with the master. Their interests were not the same (zero sum bargaining): the labourer desired more pay from the master and the master desired to pay less.[4] The usual outcome was the compliance of the labourer with the wage offer of the master, because masters legally could agree among themselves in a neighbourhood not to exceed a certain wage rate more easily than the workmen could agree (illegally) among themselves not to work for a wage below a demanded minimum.

What then determined the wage rate? There was a minimum theoretical level below which wages could not fall indefinitely. The labourer's wage must 'at least be sufficient to maintain him'. And he must have more than this 'to bring up a family' otherwise 'the race of workmen could not last beyond the first generation'.[5] As it was, by modern standards, there were horrendous rates of child mortality.

Circumstances could give the advantage to labourers, such as when demand for labour continually increased year by year and competition among masters bid up wages, and the secret agreements of masters to keep wages from rising, faltered or failed.[6] Thus, when a 'landlord, annuitant or monied man' had revenue greater than needed for his family's maintenance, he employed new or additional menial servants; when independent workmen, weavers or shoe-makers (the archetypical smithian masters) were likewise better off, they employed more labourers out of the surplus so as to profit from selling their output.[7]

Critically, the increase in demand for labour increases from the growth in revenue and stock in every country, and *cannot possibly increase without it.*[8] Wage labour must await economic growth to improve its share of wages and employment. And this leads to two of Smith's famous statements:

> It is not the actual greatness of national wealth, but its continual increase, which occasions a rise in the wages of labour. It is not, accordingly, in the richest countries, but in the most thriving, or in those which are growing rich the fastest, that the wages of labour are highest.[9]

and

> It is in the progressive state, while the society is advancing to the further acquisition, rather than when it has acquired its full complement of riches, that the condition of the labouring poor, of the great body of the people, seems to be happiest and the most comfortable. It is hard in the stationary, and miserable in the declining state. The progressive state is in reality the cheerful and the hearty state to all the different orders of the society. The stationary is dull; the declining, melancholy.[10]

Higher wages for common labourers were conducive of their better health and to encouraging enthusiastic attitudes to work, both outcomes likely to make labourers more favourable to their industry and discipline, whereas low wages led to sickness, lassitude and indiscipline.

What drove the third great order, that of the master, the owner of stock, to vary his contribution to the preparation and production of output? It had to be related to, but not necessarily be solely determined by, his profits from committing his stock to ventures. For one thing, in the absence of profitable ventures he lived off his stock for as long as he could and for as long as it lasted, and he then reverted to being a labourer for somebody else.

Increasing the amount of stock tended to lower profits because stock-owners who bid up the wages of labourers to work on their stock, reduced their profits.[11] Variations in profits or wages in different occupations in the same location would tend to zero because where differences were evident 'many people would crowd into the advantageous, or desert the disadvantageous, employment until the variations were eliminated'. This would be the case where 'things were left to follow their natural course and where there was perfect liberty' because 'everyman's interest would prompt him to seek the advantageous, and to shun the disadvantageous employment.'[12]

48

Accumulation and Employment of Stock

Smith's exposition of circulating and fixed capitals is standard, non-controversial and uncomplicated, as befits simple accounting for small businesses with few sources of borrowing, other than in small amounts. The accumulation of stock is a pre-condition for the division of labour and remains a pre-condition for continuing new sub-divisions of labour as stock continues to accumulate.[1] Hence, Smith's interest in economic growth and the forces that promoted it.

Stock divides into two parts: that part called capital, from which the master expected his revenue or profit, and that part which provided for his current consumption. Revenue spent in consumption did not replace itself, as it was a withdrawal from the productive sector (an original case of you 'can't eat your cake and have it'). To provide revenue he employed his capital in 'raising, manufacturing, or purchasing goods and selling them again with profit'. These were his 'circulating capitals'. He also improved the land and purchased 'useful machines and instruments of trade'. These were his 'fixed capitals.'[2]

Merchants required circulating capital, mainly to buy goods at lower prices than the prices for which they sold them; iron-works required large fixed capitals in the heavy machinery they used. Artificers and small manufacturers required varying amounts of fixed capital (needles, lasts, weaving machines, and such like) but mostly they required circulating capital – for workmen's wages and materials – to be repaid from profit on the sale of output.[3]

The general stock of society divided into three portions. First, the portion reserved for consumption, which generated no revenue or profit: some consumed immediately (food), and some over a period (clothes, houses, furniture, etc.).[4] These expenditures added nothing to growth of the consumer's stock.

Second, the portion called fixed capital, which generated revenue or profit without 'changing masters', and included useful machines and instruments of trade; buildings such as shops, warehouses, workhouses, farm buildings, stables, and granaries; capital devoted to improvements to the land by 'reducing it into the condition most proper for tillage and culture'; and that which today we call 'human capital', in the form of the 'acquired and useful abilities of the inhabitants or members of the society' gained by 'the acquirer during his education, study or apprenticeship'.[5]

Third, the portion called circulating capital, which generated revenue or profit by changing masters. It consisted of money used to buy the stock of provisions for sale in the possession of the 'butcher, the grazier, the farmer, the corn-merchant, the brewer, &c.'; the materials, 'whether altogether rude, or more of less manufactured' but remaining in the hands of the 'growers, the manufacturers, the mercers and drapers, the timber-merchants, the carpenters and joiners, the bricklayers, &c.'; and, finally work 'made up and completed' and 'still in the hands of the merchant or manufacturer', and frequently found in the shops of the smith, the cabinet-maker, the goldsmith, the jeweller, the china-merchant, &c.'[6]

From Smith's discussion of the people who used stock or capital in his time, it is clear that he was thinking of small, dispersed cottage-style workshops. The likes of Josiah Wedgewood (1730–95) were unusual until the 19th century. His large-scale versions of manufactories, located in one place, took advantage of ambitious divisions of labour using existing, not new, technology or steam power. Smith's people were not typical 19th-century capitalists, owning large, power-driven factories, employing thousands of workers.

Working butchers, graziers, farmers, corn-merchants, blacksmiths, jewellers, cabinet-makers, mercers, drapers, joiners, and brewers, etc., were not representative of the leaders of the industrial revolution! Nor were farm implements, machines and instruments of trade, such as needles, lasts, weaving machines, and such like, which had been around for a long time, products of a technological power driven revolution. Profitable buildings, such as shops, warehouses, workhouses, farm buildings, stables, and granaries serving a commercial society were a long way from being confused with large-scale capitalist factories.

Farmers predominate in his panorama (not surprising as agriculture dominated the economy well into the next century) and when they were busy they were 'reducing [land] into the condition most proper for tillage and culture', using the instruments of trade, mainly handheld tools and harnesses, reins, ploughs, wagons, carts, horseshoes and such like, needed for managing 'horse power', of the animal not the mechanical kind.

Into this environment, and assuming perfect liberty and justice, Smith asserts a general principle that 'in all countries where there is tolerable security, every man of common understanding will endeavour to employ whatever stock he can command in procuring either present enjoyment or future profit' and 'a man must be perfectly crazy' who does not employ all the stock which he commands, whether it be his own or borrowed of other people, in immediate enjoyment, or in fixed or circulating capital. He would always prefer to put his stock to work.[7] His faith in the fact that enough people were perfectly sane and not crazy, shines through his political economy and is summed up in his assertions about what motivates hundreds of thousands of people, minding their own businesses without the dictates of governments or the exhortations of philosophers.

49
On Doing More Harm than Good

By way of warning, Smith pointed to the deleterious effects on society of depending on 'revenue', i.e., the rich spending their stock on a society of 'idle' servants or anybody else who consumed but did not create a 'revenue' for them, instead of employing industrious labourers who did create such revenues. In some cases, these consumers of revenue were truly idle, in the common meaning of the term, but it is wrong to interpret Smith's 'unproductive' labour as necessarily always 'idle' and 'useless'. The criterion at the base of Smith's concepts of productive and unproductive labour is whether the labour added to future revenue or merely spent current revenue, i.e., was it '*re*-productive'?[1]

His concept of productive and unproductive labour incorporates the useless wastrels that populate any society; it also includes some of the necessary and useful spenders, but not creators, of revenue. The essential point is whether labour re-produces its consumption of revenue or not, though it is clear that he felt society should limit its expenditures on useful consumers to gain maximum net revenue, and thereby higher annual growth, from a given annual outlay. Walter Eltis correctly interpreted this (often missed) significant smithian point in a modern discourse on high public expenditures in 1976.[2]

Spending from revenue reduces the exchangeable value of the annual produce of the land by failing to improve it; investing revenue in employing productive labourers increases annual produce by putting them to productive work. 'Capitals', he adds, 'are increased by parsimony, and diminished by prodigality and misconduct.'[3] A person can save from his revenue to add to his capital and may either employ additional productive hands, or lend to another to enable him to do so. By lending he increases his revenue from the interest he earns on his loans:

> Parsimony, and not industry, is the immediate cause of the increase in capital. Industry, indeed, provides the subject which parsimony accumu-

lates. But whatever industry might acquire, if parsimony did not save and store up, the capital would never be greater.[4]

Sources of capital did not include the regular issue of shares to make a market in them, a phenomena known but not widely used because, with few exceptions (canal building for example), business opportunities requiring access to large capitals were relatively few for most of the 18th century. The organic growth of capital came from parsimonious savings and small scale borrowing from the savings of others at the expense of self-indulgent consumption. It was small scale, because capital requirements were small scale, as befitted a small-scale enterprise economy near the beginning of its hardly started capital growth path.

Smith was suspicious of 'joint stock companies', a commercial organisation well known in the 18th century, and one destined to be the foundation of capitalism in the 19th–20th centuries.[5] Yet shareholder capital, synonymous with modern capitalism, grew out of the joint stock company. Now, this was strange behaviour from the so-called 'high priest' of capitalism!

His initial concerns were the great trading companies in foreign lands, some well established, others exploiting newly fancied opportunities. The main instrument for exploiting the 'regulated companies' derived from precedents set by the old corporations of trades in the cities, inheriting from them their restricted memberships, monopoly practices and burdensome regulations acting against the interests of their customers.[6] They aimed to 'raise the rate of their own profit as high as they can; to keep the market, both for the goods which they export, and for those which they import, as much understocked as they can: which can be done only by restraining the competition, or by discouraging new adventurers from entering into the trade.'[7] In short, the joint stock trading companies attracted Smith's ire because they were, or wanted to be, monopolists.

He cites Sir Josiah Child on why joint stock companies were better than regulated companies:

The directors of a joint stock company ... having only their share in the profits which are made upon the common stock committed to their management, have no trade of their own, of which the interest can be separated from that of the general trade of the company. Their private interest is connected with the prosperity of the general trade of the company; and with the maintenance of the forts and garrisons, which are necessary for their defence. They are more likely, therefore, to have that continual and careful attention which that maintenance necessarily requires. Secondly, The directors of a joint stock company have always the management of a large capital, the joint stock of the company, a part of which they may frequently employ, with propriety, in building, repairing, and maintaining such necessary forts and garrisons.[8]

Child's happy antidote to the failings of regulated companies came under Smith's searching scrutiny: how had it worked in the practice of the great trading companies, particularly the East India Company?

Smith compared joint stock companies with the more common private 'copartneries', where partners may only dispose of their shares to another partner. Joint stock company shareholders could sell their shares to anybody willing to buy them at an agreed price or one set by a 'stock market' (the term is still with us). Partners were bound for the debts of a partnership to the full extent of their private fortunes, whereas shareholders in incorporated joint stock companies were only bound to the extent of their shares.

Joint stock companies were managed by a Court of Directors, subject to a general court of proprietors (shareholders), who 'seldom understand anything of the business of the company' and 'receive contentedly such half yearly or yearly dividend, as the directors think proper to make to them.'[9] It was the ease with which people could become shareholders and their 'total exemption from trouble and risk, beyond a limited sum', which encouraged many of them to become 'adventurers in joint stock companies', rather than hazard their fortunes in any private copartnery. This enabled joint stock companies to draw upon significant sums of capital. Smith's predictable assessment applies his standard self-interest theme:

> The directors of such companies, however, being managers rather of other people's money than their own, it cannot well be expected, that they should watch over it with the same anxious vigilance with which the partners in a private copartnery frequently watch over their own. Like the stewards of a rich man, they are apt to consider attention to small matters as not for their master's honour, and very easily give themselves a dispensation from having it. Negligence and profusion, therefore, must always prevail, more or less, in the management of the affairs of such a company. It is upon this account that joint stock companies for foreign trade have seldom been able to maintain competition against private adventurers. They have, accordingly, very seldom succeeded without an exclusive privilege; and frequently have not succeeded with one. Without an exclusive privilege they have commonly mismanaged the trade. With an exclusive privileged they have both mismanaged and confined it.[10]

Wealth of Nations devotes twelve pages to criticising overseas trading companies operating as joint stock companies, pulling no punches and leaving no doubt that these arrangements were designed to 'support negligence,

profusion and malversation of their own servants, whose disorderly conduct seldom allows' the company, despite its monopoly, to do any better,
and often it does much worse, than what would be achieved for shareholders by free trade.[11]

With this background, Smith saw only one kind of business where a joint
stock company arrangement would successfully carry on business, without
monopoly privileges, namely, in 'which all the operations are capable of
being reduced to what it called a Routine, or to such uniformity of method
as admits of little or no variation'. He offered four possibilities for a successful joint stock company: in the banking trade, in insurance, making and
maintaining a 'navigable cut or canal' and of bringing a water supply to a
city.[12]

In addition, it was necessary to establish 'with the clearest evidence' that
the undertaking was of much greater utility than allocating the capital to
'common trades' and that it 'requires a greater capital than can easily be
collected into a private copartnery'. Smith emphasised that apart from his
four examples he 'had not been able to recollect' any others where the circumstances were 'requisite for rendering the establishment of a joint stock
company.'[13] He concluded, warning that:

> the joint stock companies, which are established for the public spirited
> purpose of promoting some particular manufacture, over and above
> managing their own affairs ill, to the diminution of the general stock of
> society, can in other respects scarce ever fail to do more harm than
> good.[14]

Only in one short discussion on the Hudson Bay Company (Canada) does
Smith concede that a joint stock company would do as well as a copartnery. The Hudson Company's unique locality in the far north of Canada,
the bleakest imaginable environment in that 'miserable, though extensive
country', meant it required modest capital only, and in these unique
circumstances a 'joint stock company, consisting of a small number of proprietors [shareholders], with a moderate capital, approaches very nearly to
the nature of a private copartnery, and may be capable of nearly the same
degree of vigilance and attention.'[15]

Bearing in mind that Smith compared a joint stock company with the
older copartnery form of organisation, it suggests that smaller scale joint
stock companies, with relatively moderate capital, in principle could function with 'vigilance and attention' for their shareholders. Unfortunately
for proponents of him being the 'High Priest of Capitalism',[16] he surmised
this was possible only in the single instance of the Hudson Bay Company,
for which there was never likely to be any serious imitators. The fact
that he missed an opportunity realise the great future awaiting joint
stock companies with the advent of capitalism in the 19th century, only

underlines that Smith looked backwards from his century and not for-
wards towards ours.

His bile against joint stock companies, however, was highly influenced
by the quasi-criminal debacles experienced by the South Sea Company and,
even more so, by the East India Company ('how unjustly, how capriciously,
how cruelly they have commonly exercised [powers to make war], is too
well known from recent experience').[17]

50
Doom and Gloom?

A singular approach to Adam Smith's legacy uniquely illustrates how it has become contaminated by political controversies about capitalism. The approach presents a distinctive and pessimistic interpretation of an aspect of Smith's work by extending it from the period for which it was written to (still pending) problems associated with a period at some distance in the future, for which Smith had nothing to say.

Besides his popular writings, Professor Heilbroner published many academic papers, among which is 'Paradox of Progress'.[1] Heilbroner presents a 'gloomy' interpretation of Wealth of Nations. He discusses its 'darker side', its 'grim finale', and a 'perverse state of affairs' leading to a 'general poverty' and a 'Malthusian precariousness',[2] allegedly a consequence of Smith's growth model for commercial society (as if models determine the future!).

First, we must distinguish between the theoretical consequences of a primitive growth model, written over 200 years ago, and the real world consequences for the real world commercial society, out of which grew modern capitalism and its unimaginable technological progress. Smith's attempt to model growth did not have the advantages of 200 years of scholarly work on growth models, which are meat and drink to graduates today. Hence, Smith's theoretical model had no predictive value of the future at all. Like his labour theory of value, the terminal logic of his growth model is an historical curiosity. For an authoritative and influential account of Smith's growth model, see Eltis, 1984.

Of course, by associating Smith's growth model with the evolution of capitalism, Heilbroner made a straw man suitable for a political critique but, because Smith's growth model had nothing to do with the evolution of capitalism from the next century, it should be disconnected and Heilbroner's critique should be left to stand on its own merits

At worst, Smith's model was wrong, simply because neither he nor it could anticipate all the factors that actually happened in the economy to make irrelevant its gloomy conclusions about what might happen if a society were ever to reach a stage where there was no more room or incentive for further economic growth. For all intents and purposes, therefore, the eventual demise of a simple commercial society in Smith's model is non-operational. The post-smithian future, as we know, from the development of a capitalist system of production (the Fifth Age?) and a vastly expanded, and still expanding, boundary of its full compliment of riches, by-passed the gloomy termination of Smith's age of commerce in his simple growth model.

A short summary follows (with my explanatory comments in brackets) of Professor Adolf Lowe's fine exposition of the smithian model of the economy[3] (upon which Heilbroner based his essay).

Growing output arises from extending the division of labour, which in turn raises the demand for labour (more individual operations means more employees have to be hired) and raises money wages (it costs more to hire extra people). Increasing productivity from the division of labour reduces prices (a greater quantity produced lowers unit costs of output), which in turn, raises the real wage (money wages buy more lower priced output). Prosperity enables more children of the labouring poor to survive (lower priced, higher quantities of better food and warmer clothing are purchased), enhancing the supply of labour through the generations (as more children survive to adulthood they join an expanding workforce). As wages rise, profits fall (higher costs of labour, lower prices of output), curbing the accumulation of stock (lower rates of return) and slowing growth. In time all the quantity of stock that can be employed in the different trades is fully committed (all profitable projects are completed) and no more labour can be employed (no capital to employ them profitably), causing wages to fall under the competition of unemployed, uneducated and morally crippled labourers (from alienation and intense division of labour) searching for work. Wages fall to subsistence and below; starvation and child mortality increase and population falls; national output declines. The commercial age becomes a disaster, and Smith's 'model of progress' leads to 'both social and economic failure'.

Heilbroner finds a paradox in Smith: growing commercial societies raise the wages of labour and, the faster the growth, the higher the money wage and the higher the 'real wage' – what the wages of the increasingly 'alienated' labourers will buy – and, inevitably, it all ends in tears. Wages and profits are driven downwards by the termination of growth when a 'country has acquired that full complement of riches which the nature of its soil and climate, and its situation with respect to other countries allowed it to acquire; and which could, therefore, advance no further.'[4] Neither Smith nor Heilbroner define the 'full complement of riches', but it must be, in theory, a plausible undated state of any future economy, though not within the time horizons of Smith or his critics, either then or today.

Stationary situations and knife-edge instability are a weakness of all theoretical economic growth models for societies well short of the happy state of opulence towards which they are supposedly headed. No country stood in the sunshine of natural liberty and justice. Those which Smith identified as being close to stationary (China) or going backwards (Bengal) had not 'arrived at this degree of opulence' – they had become stationary, or were in decline, long before reaching opulence for reasons other than the endogenous dynamics of the model. They were subjected to exogenous shocks, such as a politically inspired neglect of foreign commerce, or the imposition of laws governing trade, or the result of a century of plunder by foreign adventurers (Bengal particularly), which, to put it mildly, were strong disincentives to commerce.[5] Hence, stagnation, or worse, reverting to decline, is possible in any economy if they pursue incorrect policies; progress is not guaranteed.

Assuming, for the sake of argument, that society overcame all obstacles to natural liberty and justice and acquired the absolutely full natural compliment of its riches, consistent with its location, climate and soil, then Smith admits (he could do little else if the defined terms materialised) that it would inaugurate a general stagnation, causing a general poverty, and ignorant labourers would suffer the full and final consequences of the intensified division of labour.

What is missing in Heilbroner, and in all predictions of the future, are considerations of the 'x' factor, i.e., knowledge, unknowable in advance, of those factors of technological change, scientific discoveries, or innovation that alter future growth paths. In the case of Malthus and his predictions, two hundred years of history has not been kind to them; the predictions of the Club of Rome lost credibility after only twenty years, when the dated horizon of their predictions of society's collapse passed with no sign of the predicted events.[6]

Countries like China and Bengal, given their 'soil, climate, and situation', could grow towards opulence by overcoming the institutional barriers causing them to stagnate, but, and this is a cause for real gloom, by succeeding in their goal of breaking out of stagnation, theoretically they would only delay, but not eliminate, the inevitable terminus of their growth paths and the eventual impoverishment of their people. So if an economy stalls for any reason and hits a stagnation barrier and then succeeds in overcoming institutional barriers to growth, it hits the final barrier anyway, only later. The lives of our grandchildren (or if not them, then their great-grandchildren's) are doomed to be blighted, irreversibly and forever at some time in the future, if not beforehand. Bleak prospects, indeed!

As if unsure that Smith's honest doom-laden paragraphs in *Wealth of Nations* are too good to be true for a critic of capitalism, Heilbroner asks three questions: is Smith's paradox 'ultimately [of] major importance' (no, it isn't!); is 'the coincidence with moral decay and economic decline … not merely one more example of the endless anomalies and perplexities with which the Wealth of Nations abounds' (no, it isn't!); and is it 'merely pedantic or simply wrong to elevate the "dark" side of Smith' over his bright side, particularly because Smith never recognised the final paradox of his argument (yes, it is!).[7] The remote probability that the surface of the Earth may resemble that of Mars at some time in the future is not of much operational significance for policy making today, and nor is Smith's theoretical stagnation outcome of relevance for a society that evolved into something he had no means of anticipating or imagining when he was writing his model.

It is possible, as Professor Sir Alan Peacock has shown,[8] using a modern presentation of Smith's model of economic growth, that his treatment of technological change has been underplayed by economists and that once technological change is re-emphasised as an endogenous variable (i.e., one that changes from inside the changing variables of the model) the dire predictions of stagnation dissolve into irrelevance. Specifically, changes in capital per worker and output per worker (from market driven divisions of labour) for a given technology counteract the tendency for diminishing returns to capital over a limited range of output, because the curve relating capital per worker to output per worker for that level of technology shifts upwards from changes in technology, provided there is 'stable and wise government' and pervasive competition to discipline tendencies to monopoly (market failure) and to inhibit 'big' government (state failure), and restraints on high taxation (which would lower the savings rate needed for private investment).

Professor Irma Adelman presents a similar appreciation of Smith's growth model. Productivity arises from the division of labour and is restricted by the size of the market, the amount of capital, the degree of institutional freedom (natural liberty) and imposed inhibitions (monopoly) operating in the economy. The institutional framework of the economy is an important condition for deriving predictions of the 'time path' of Smith's model.[9] This last is absolutely crucial for understanding Smith's approach. Peacock spells it out forcefully in his presentation. Professor Walter Eltis provides an algebraic treatment of Smith's classical growth model, which is well worth reading, supported by his lucid explanation, if you wish to understand it for the context in which it was written.[10] Eltis also makes the point that the termination of growth within his model is 'not relevant to the main work of Smith … which was to provide and account of the working of the econom[y] in which [he] lived.'[11]

The supply of labour is influenced by the growth of income and capital; populations grow in expanding economies, in declining economies population declines and in stationary economies, population remains constant. This becomes a treadmill: each successive period must enjoy a rise in demand, otherwise wages will fall towards subsistence because wages above subsistence (inherited from the previous periods) promote population growth and in stationary or declining periods this provokes competition among labourers for work. Output expands because of positive net investment and expanding capital promotes greater divisions of labour and, hence, greater labour productivity. However, exogenous shocks to the system, mainly from existing institutional barriers or retrogressive changes in socio-cultural forces decrease growth rates, interrupting the treadmill, even reversing it into decline.

In its pure theoretical form, the logic of the stationary phase arises inexorably from within the mathematics of the smithian growth model. Growing income levels increase capital accumulation; larger capital stocks depress the rate of profit, whereas falling interest rates increase the rate of capital expansion, producing larger and larger increments in investment. Increased capital raises labour productivity and results in ever-greater increases in output. At some point the rate of interest falls to the minimum risk level lenders will tolerate, at which point 'the economy will have attained "its full complement of riches" and the stationary state sets in'.[12]

Adelman's focuses on exogenous influences on the institutional environment – 'the degree of regulation of commerce, the degree of monopoly or competition, and the control of international trade',[13] highlighting Smith's point that the interests of the co-operators in production and the receivers of profit do not always coincide with those of society. She could have added other forces in society to her list of those acting against the interests of society on occasion, such as the socio-political policies pursued by the government and dominant religious leaders, the customs and practices of classes, sects and ethnic groups, the proclivities for communal violence, war, terrorism and disorder, and the general state of justice and law and order.

Quite a lot is buried in the words 'institutional environment' and it is important to dig them out and *Wealth of Nations* is a classic example of such an integration of economics within the context of the institutional environment by a premier authority on how it should be done.

51
Of Grandchildren and Grandparents

The smithian stagnation problem lies in the meaning we place on 'full complement of riches'. Predicting the content of the 'full complement of riches' for future societies is notoriously difficult and probably impossible more than a few years, certainly decades, ahead. Each generation changes the definition of 'riches'. Few grandchildren, and adults unhappy with growing economies, would wish to return to the living standards and perceptions of 'riches' of their grandparents.

In 1930, John Maynard Keynes published *Economic Possibilities for Our Grandchildren*, in which he drew attention to the law of compound interest and asserted that at a modest 2 per cent growth in capital would increase national income by seven and a half times by 2030 (on current trends it is going to do much better than that!). He urged his readers to think what this would mean in material things – houses, transport, and the like – and suggested that this material prosperity would solve the economic problem of scarcity for the majority of people.[1] Wisely, he avoided specifying the economic resources people would spend their incomes on in 2030 (he didn't try to predict them even for 1940).

Only thirty years later in 1960, many new unanticipated products were commonplace in households in Europe and North America; thirty more years on in 1990, the plethora of material products increased yet again, with few of them imagined or imaginable in 1930. The same is true today: predictions of future tastes and 'riches' are usually fanciful; worse are current judgements on what will constitute 'enough' for future generations. It is a triumph for comfortable smugness over prudence to attempt to pronounce on what is 'enough' for others.

Keynes' opening paragraph captured the pessimism of the times (the shock of the 1929 Wall Street crash, with the depression years to follow) from extrapolating forward converging crises amidst disappointing events.

> We are suffering just now from a bad attack of economic pessimism. It is common to hear people say that the epoch of enormous economic

progress which characterised the nineteenth century is over; that the rapid improvement in the standard of life is now going to slow down – at any rate in Britain; that decline in prosperity is more likely than an improvement in the decade that lies ahead of us.[2]

To the pessimists of 1930, who believed society couldn't grow to higher levels of prosperity (for much of the 1930s, for many people it got worse, not better), new doomsayers now insist that even if we could get richer, we mustn't. This is not the forum to debate this, but we know for certain that wherever the 'full complement of riches' in Smith's time was located on a scale of 18th-century opulence, it was well short of where it is in the 21st century (let alone where it was in the 19th century).

The stagnation implications of Smith's model were not an immediate problem for his time, nor were they experienced in the two hundred years that followed. Nothing like stagnation came to pass. This must have been obvious to people living in New York in the mid-20th century. It was obvious to Adolph Lowe,[3] a colleague in the same university building upon whom Heilbroner based his analysis,[4] that the stationary state in Smith's analysis might 'tend' to 'occur only in the distant future', and that for all intents and purposes the smithian growth economy 'is never truly stationary'.[5]

When Smith made predictions of the growth path of commercial societies he alluded to the situation 'during the course of the present century' (i.e., 1676–1776), in which the 'real recompense of labour' had 'increased in still greater proportion than its money price.'[6] After a hundred years of rising real wages, there were no signs in 1776 of the dismal immiserisation of the labourers (a prediction revived by Karl Marx – a hundred years later).[7] Smith observes, in passing, 'that the labouring poor will not now be contented with the same food, cloathing and lodging which satisfied them in former times.'[8]

The so-called 'dark side' of *Wealth of Nations* has yet to cast its shadow in the real world, suggesting something sensible is missing in literal interpretations of the model's closure. I suggest that what is missing is the simple acceptance that no mathematical model (or its verbal equivalent) can capture enough of reality in its arguments to be a reliable predictor of long term outcomes of a real economy. The perils of extrapolation of a past trend should become a compulsory subject in every first year economics course, and perhaps a revision subject at the start of every subsequent course in their degrees, and regularly when they are working.

Heilbroner remarks that Smith 'passes over without comment the enormous social strains that might be expected to ensure from a descent from one state to the other'.[9] What would it have achieved in the reality of Georgian Britain in 1776 for Smith to publish a prediction of the 'enormous social strains' that would arise from reducing the real wages of labourers if the termination to growth were to occur at some unspecified 'distant' time in the future when Britain had 'acquired its full complement of riches'? As America was on the verge of a violent and bloody war with Georgian Britain at the time, under what kind of political regime do his critics think Smith was living? Smith's *en passant* remark was about as close as he could get without risking the accusation (and the dreadful punishments) if he was charged with encouraging disorders by predicting them?

Smith identified two countervailing tendencies to a declining rate of profit: the acquisition of new territories (i.e., colonies, like the Americas) and 'new branches of trade'. Predicting the incidence of either of these was not easy. One depended on international politics, the other on technological innovations and the division of labour. Smith wrote *Wealth of Nations* before the harnessing of steam power to drive large assemblies of machines in factories – and before electricity! His was a world dominated by agriculture, animal power, hand tools, small independent workshops and local markets, with a relatively small complement of potential 'riches' to match.

Smith described China as being in a stationary state through it acquiring its 'full complement of riches *which the nature of its laws and institutions permits it to acquire*' (emphasis added).[10] The italicised qualification is important. A country could slide into a stationary state, like China, because its 'laws and institutions' choked off natural growth long before it reached a state of opulence occasioned by natural liberty and justice. This puts a different slant on Heilbroner's dismal interpretation, because societies could experience the defects of stagnation not just from the imperatives of the endogenous arguments in the model in the distant future, but also from misguided exogenous interferences in its natural mechanisms by human folly. Even here, however, Smith notes that China was not going 'backwards', evidenced by the towns not being deserted and the labourers still toiling on the land, compared with Bengal where the demand for labour was falling year-by-year, reducing the 'miserable and scanty subsistence of the labourer'. This would continue until it 'had escaped either the tyranny or the calamity which had destroyed the rest'.[11]

Smith did leave a vague clue, upon which he did not elaborate, that is relevant for considering the practical validity of the stationary state implied in his growth model:

> The desire for food is limited in every man by the narrow capacity of the human stomach; but the desire of the conveniences and ornaments of building, dress, equipage, and household furniture, seems to have no limit or certain boundary. Those, therefore, who have the command of more food than they themselves can consume, are always willing to exchange the surplus, or, what is the same thing, the price of it, for gratifications of the other kind. What is over and above satisfying the limited desire, is given for the amusement of those desires which cannot

be satisfied, but seem to be altogether endless. ...Hence arise a demand for every sort of material which human invention can employ, either usefully or ornamentally, in building, dress, equipage, or household furniture; for the fossils and minerals contained in the bowels of the earth; the precious metals, and the precious stones.[12]

Smith's growth model was strictly limited to the known products and circumstances, including the technology, of his day. He was writing before the industrial revolution and when small-scale manufacturing was at the frontier of its technology, and when full-scale industrialisation was in the offing but not anticipated.[13]

The unknowable products of the future were beyond his and his contemporaries' imaginations and like him they were comfortably ignorant of what was to come. They had absolutely no idea of what was ahead, such as (even) the manufacture of cotton,[14] let alone that of electricity, petroleum, oils, plastics, metals, silicon, radio, air travel, motor vehicles, steam ships and air conditioning, etc.

Because their horizons were confined to a few relatively primitive products engaging 'desires which cannot be satisfied', what would they make of the vastly enhanced products of the modern commercial society and the enormous expansion of desires they would generate, which also 'cannot be satisfied' in mass consumer societies today? In this context, is it realistic to talk, except theoretically, of a society having 'acquired its full complement of riches' and ever having to experience the alleged 'dark side' of smithian political economy? Do economies ever reach the boundaries of their ever changing Samuelson production possibility frontiers'?

Was Smith's so called 'dark side' anything more than a literary device acknowledging that the future was unknowable. Is the reason why the 'paradox' was 'never recognised by Smith himself' explained simply by the fact that he never anticipated anybody proposing that it was a real issue? Presumably, Smith assumed that successive generations of readers would realise this and fill in the details for themselves from their knowledge of what followed after 1790.

Smith asks whether improving the circumstances of the lower ranks of the people is to be regarded 'as an advantage or as an inconveniency to society.'[15] That the question is posed strikes an unbiased reader as rather odd. How could it be inconvenient for the poorest labourers and their families to improve their circumstances? Smith answers his own question:

The answer seems at first sight abundantly plain. Servants, labourers and workmen of different kinds, make up the far greater part of every great political society. But what improves the circumstances of the greater part can never be regarded as an inconveniency to the whole. No society can surely be flourishing and happy, of which the far greater part of its members are poor and miserable. It is but equity, besides, that they who feed, cloath and lodge the whole body of the people, should have such a share of the produce of their own labour as to be themselves tolerably well fed, cloathed and lodged.[16]

Could there be a greater contrast between 20th century doom and gloom and Smith's 18th century optimism?

52
A 'Night Watchman' State?

An oft-quoted reference in a 1755 'paper' of Smith's, quoted in 1793 by Dugald Stewart (see Appendix), is a possible source for the mistaken myths and confusions that became popular in the 19th century of Smith's alleged preference for a 'night watchman state':

> Little else is requisite to carry a state to the highest degree of opulence from the lowest barbarism, but peace, easy taxes, and a tolerable administration of justice; all the rest being brought about by the natural course of things. All governments which thwart this natural course, which force things into another channel, or which endeavour to arrest the progress of society at a particular point, are unnatural, and to support themselves are obliged to be oppressive and tyrannical.[1]

In Smith's day, and before, oppressive and tyrannical regimes governed most of the world (and mostly still do). Countries that reach the higher degrees of opulence after millennia breaching most, if not all, of Smith's prescriptions, are seldom carried to opulence by 'the natural course of things', and those that are oppressive and tyrannical seem to get so far but no farther on the road to sustained growth.

From Smith's perspective, if the state had little to do beyond that which was, or became, necessary, its burdens could not be onerous upon the taxpayer. For example, if it kept out of foreign wars, its expenses would reduce accordingly; if it administered its laws effectively and justly, and eradicated all monopolies, then peace and prosperity would follow.

Those who seized on Stewart's quotation from a paper only he had seen, and which nobody knows what else Smith said from it, because apparently Stewart's son burned it (he suffered from serious mental illness),[2] ignore the far longer exposition on the role of the State in *Wealth of Nations*. Because Smith was cautious about the interpretation of the exact duties to be undertaken by the sovereign, his passage can be misread to proclaim him as the author of the minimal state, caricatured in the 19th century by the simile of the 'night watchman state' (Ferdinand Lassalle) or the phrase 'anarchy plus the constable' (Carlyle).[3] Rumour being the mother of belief, these misleading labels stuck and by the 20th century many believed erroneously that they originated from the author of *Wealth of Nations*.

The image of the night watchman – a lonely, elderly, figure, neither too inactive nor too alert – looking for persons intent on public harm while his employers slept soundly in their beds, appealed to those who believed in minimising presumptuous interference by the State in matters conducive to their private interests (for example, paying lower taxation to fund, say, minimal education for all children, not just their own, or interference in their freedom to send women and children down coalmines, etc.). By restricting the role of government to as few cases as possible, 19th-century proponents of laissez faire and the night watchman state, strove for a society a long way short of Natural Liberty and justice, as envisaged by Smith, without it troubling their consciences if they spread the untrue belief that they expressed his views.

What did Smith envisage as the appropriate boundary to State interventions? It was a far larger agenda than is generally thought and certainly beyond the imagery of Lassalle's night watchman.

First duty of the sovereign

> The first duty of the sovereign, that of protecting the society from the violence and invasion of other independent societies, can be performed only by means of a military force.[4]

The expenses for defence against the violence and invasion of neighbours were not minimal expenditures in 18th-century Britain, and they were destined to increase dramatically within a few years of his death.[5]

That Smith sanctioned defence expenditures and the raising of revenue for this purpose as the proper and first duty of the State above all others is well known. That this duty had important consequences in 18th-century Britain is less well known (its consequences in subsequent centuries are barely researched too). Britain was at war for seventy years of the period between the 'glorious revolution' (1688), leading to the Hanoverian succession, and the Battle of Waterloo (1816), a long enough period to test the impact of defence expenditures in an economy experiencing sustained periods of growth and increases in income per head.

Were these factors (defence expenditure and economic growth) related in some way, either negatively or positively? War involves retarding effects: '(1) physical destruction of real capital; (2) diversion of scarce labour, capital and raw material resources from productive to unproductive uses; and (3) an increase in the risks and uncertainties of mercantile and manufacturing enterprise.' War also promotes growth to the extent that its demand inducing effects: '(1) draw into productive use under-employed factors; (2) stimulate output in industries whose expansion reduces costs or creates opportunities for other branches of industry; and (3) precipitate fiscal or financial or organisational developments which redistribute incomes or opportunities in favour of innovating enterprise.'[6] The appropriate balance between these effects is an empirical question,[7] when taken in context with whatever other events affect the data.

Phyllis Deane cites Professor John's findings[8] that for 1700–63 defence expenditures were positively associated with growth, but less so during the American War (1776–83), when economic activity contracted following the disruptive loss of a major trading partner,[9] suggesting that losing wars that disrupt trade negatively affects growth.

Defence expenditures grew during the 18th century from £5–£6 million a year in the early part of the century to £40 million by its end. Allowing for inflation, this still amounted to a five-fold increase and, on a percentage basis, was about 5 per cent of national income at the close of Marlborough's wars and 15 per cent by 1801.[10] Such proportions were significant and their economic impacts require to be fully investigated by those who continue to deny a legitimate role for defence spending in economic development.[11]

It is not the total of defence expenditures that has an impact because between 40 and 50 per cent – the remuneration of the soldiers and seamen – makes no more difference to the economy than the pay of any other persons, because civilian and military household expenditures are identical and markets do not differentiate from whence consumers receive their incomes. But the impact of specific military expenditures on industrial technologies does impact way beyond their money amounts, and may have contributed qualitatively to the initial 'take-off' stages of the industrial revolution.

The connections between manufacturing, especially in shipbuilding and engineering, and war technologies, were particularly close in the initiation of industrial and commercial development[12] and in the development of military technologies.[13] The Carron Iron works (identified by Ashton as the progenitor of the industrial revolution)[14] was sustained by large government expenditures on naval gunnery (e.g., the infamous, because unreliable, though devastating, 'Carronades') for the end of century sea wars with France.

Government expenditures on defence goods are largely spent on the products of privately owned manufacturers. These add to aggregate demand in certain industries, inciting manufacturers to increase capacity to supply the government's orders. Inevitably, some suppliers tended to specialise in defence goods (ordnance, shipping, victuals, armour, carriages and field goods), while others treated it like any other market for their goods. A steady flow of procurement expenditures into local economies close to garrisons and ports had economic effects beyond the original outlays through what today we call 'multiplier' effects. The cumulative effect of these expenditures over many decades, and their increase from time to time, had beneficial effects over and above what the same amounts expended upon the 'dignity of the sovereign' and his associates would have achieved.

Britain had a busy 18th century fighting wars. The rise in its defence expenditures, both proportionately and absolutely, and expensive improvements in military technologies, necessitated concurrent improvements in manufacturing technologies. This boosted the technologies of the unanticipated industrial revolution.

Smith, however, did not raise these questions; his premise was that 'defence is more important than opulence'. If expenditures on defence led to capitals being directed into less productive enterprises than their natural commercial destinations, this for him was a necessary sacrifice of growth for reasons of state. He was neither unaware of the history of warfare through the four ages of man (from hunters to commerce), nor unaware of the growing expense of warfare in modern times.[15]

> In modern war the great expense of fire-arms gives an evident advantage to the nation which can best afford that expence; and consequently, to an opulent and civilised, over a poor and barbarous nation. In antient times the opulent and civilised found it difficult to defend themselves against the poor and barbarous nations. In modern times the poor and barbarous find it difficult to defend themselves against the opulent and civilised. The invention of fire-arms, an invention which at first sight appears to be so pernicious, is certainly favourable both to the permanency and to the extension of civilisation.[16]

The neglect of the economics of defence in the following two centuries reflects a non-realisation of just how important the defence sector, and its mainly State dependent private sector supplier industries, have been for the growth of British national income and, more recently, for the diffusion of modernity into developing societies.[17]

Of significance for Adam Smith's legacy, however, is that within the first duty provision there was a great deal of scope for governments to make substantial injections into the economy for defence purposes that went beyond the assumed paltry role assigned to the State by the mythical 'night-watchman' state.

53
Smith's Immodest Proposals for Public Expenditures

Justice is an essential pillar of society. Its expense has to be provided for either by the litigants or by the state from taxation. Where the officers of justice raise revenue for their recompense it leads to corruption (whoever has the largest 'present' for the judge had the best chance of wining the case)[1] and where it is dispensed free of charge, differential payments to lawyers and advisors necessarily imbalances the chances of success in favour of the hirers of the most talented (i.e., expensive) adversarial advocacy. Justice was the State's second duty.

Smith covered much of what is summarized in *Wealth of Nations* in *Jurisprudence*. His main conclusion was in favour of the separation of powers because:

> upon the impartial administration of justice depends the liberty of every individual, the sense which he has of his own security. In order to make every individual feel perfectly secure in his possession of every right which belongs to him, it is not only necessary that the judicial should be separated from the executive power, but that it should be rendered as much as possible independent of that power. The judge should not be liable to be removed from his office according to the caprice of that power. The regular payment of his salary should not depend upon the good-will, or even upon the good œconomy of that power.[2]

Once again, Smith makes clear that the objective he has in mind is not constrained by considerations of budgetary frugality. The issues at stake in justice and in defence supersede considerations of their expense.

A peculiarity of British history linked justice, or rather its aftermath, to the first duty of the sovereign and illustrates the law of unintended consequences. The problem was not so much the expenses associated with the administration of justice as the expenses after justice had been dispensed. What to do with convicted persons once the gaols were full? The number of crimes meriting capital punishment increased throughout the 18th century from about 54 in 1688 to 241 by 1819.[3] From a general reluctance of juries to convict people, except in seriously grisly cases, sentences of execution were sparingly imposed and transportation substituted instead. The war of independence ended transportation to America. It was replaced by the 'temporary' expedient, lasting 82 years, of housing those sentenced to transportation in privately owned ships' hulks. Meanwhile, government ministers and advisors discussed alternative destinations located in Africa, the Caribbean and Botany Bay,[4] but various obstacles stood in the way of parliamentary approval. Until, that is, the argument was advanced that far away Botany Bay – too far to make escape feasible – was an ideal location for a penal colony. It was also believed (erroneously) that New Zealand or Norfolk Island could become a new sources of supplies of Royal Navy masts, believed at that time (1786) to be at risk in Britain's forests denuded by war.[5]

Once the defence argument joined the penal argument the case for Botany Bay proved irresistible, even against claims that a penal colony violated the Charter of the East India Company. In 1787 the 'First Fleet' set out with 652 prisoners and arrived at Botany Bay in 1788 (moved shortly afterwards a few miles up the coast to what became known as Sydney Harbour). The First Fleet was followed by many more.[6]

The defence argument (naval supplies) did not produce many masts but it helped found a viable penal colony (justice) and, later, a major commercial partner; an example of the proper smithian role for government?

Third duty of the sovereign

Smith divided the sovereign's third duty into three: public works facilitating commerce, which were too expensive for private interests to erect or maintain; the education of youth at school (but not university); and the education of people of all ages (religion).

A highway, a bridge, or a navigable canal benefited commerce generally and he suggests these should be maintained out of revenue from small tolls on users to defray the costs of management and repairs. The State also provided coinage profitably when its face value exceeds its bullion content, to which approved State business he added the running of the post-office.[7] These projects were characterised by their suitability for generating revenue to defray necessary expenses and reducing the tax burden. Where revenue is not possible from beneficiaries a local or provincial administration may provide these expenses. Management and revenue collection could be farmed out to private persons, the test being utility not principle.[8]

Public works of benefit to commerce in a locality, for which their expense or maintenance could not be recovered by revenues, formed a special category of public finance. Smith concluded that they were best maintained by local or provincial administration, and thus opened a second tier of public expenditures, today known as local government, in addition to the first tier of the national State. He gave the example of the streets of London, the pavements and lighting of which were funded by local street, parish or district taxation. He preferred this system to funding from national revenue upon the general inhabitants of Britain, 'the greater part [of whom] derive no sort of benefit from the lighting and paving of the streets of London'.[9] He commented too that the 'abuses which sometimes creep into the local and provincial administration of a local and provincial revenue' are always 'trifling' compared to the abuses common in the 'revenue of a great empire', and they are 'more easily corrected.'[10]

Where projects are required for particular branches of commerce, the costs should fall on the trading beneficiaries who can be relied upon to pass these costs to their customers, the ultimate beneficiaries. This produced his extensive analysis of the great trading companies, including those in India, China and Africa, and his long disquisition on the dubious governance of various monopolies, including the 'execrable' East India Company, and the questionable efficacy of joint stock companies in general, particularly when the founders sought monopoly privileges. What began in India and Africa as small forts and garrisons to protect its traders drew the British State into empire building (imperialism) in the next century.

However, the principle of the application of state revenue to civil projects beyond the wealth of a private individual, and their management by public officials or private persons, opened the door to State intervention in aspects of the economy considered important for commerce. As with most doors to opportunity that open, people try to widen the original remit into areas not intended by crowding through them under the banner that the exception is the rule! If plausible, weak legislators concur. All projects falling within these duties of the sovereign breached laissez faire and the minimal state.

If the State did nothing about the absence of certain large projects in the economy nothing would be done by anybody, despite the great boost to commerce that good roads, navigable canals, deep ports and securely defended trading posts could provide. However, once the State entered onto this road, the end destination was not obvious, and Smith's name cannot be invoked with any justice in support or opposition to particular consequences because he confined his vision, and thereby his legacy, to the limitations of his horizons in the third quarter of the 18th century.

The implications of Smith's advocacy of State intervention to build roads in Britain have been downplayed as of little significance relative to the economy. One such example is the following from Paul Frankel:

> Adam Smith advocated a truncated state, limited in its functions to defending its citizens against foreign and internal aggression, and creating and maintaining certain necessary public works and institutions

'which it can never be in the interest of any small number of individuals to maintain' because the profit would not repay the expense. Of course, the inclusion of this 'public works' category of permissible state intrusions nullifies the claim that Smith was a laissez-faire purist, or a consistent advocate of natural harmony of interests. But its inclusion was a harbinger of things to come, and that is its greatest significance. If the 'system of natural liberty' broke down in certain cases, says Smith, and then we must be pragmatic instrumentalists in applying governmental remedies, why does it not break down in even more cases, inquired Smith's successors? Admittedly, Smith's own departures from non-interventionism were modest ones by contemporary standards – e.g. the state might intervene to provide such public works as roads, bridges, canals, lighthouses; to protect by tariffs industries necessary to defense and to retaliate against foreign tariffs; to grant temporary monopolies to joint-stock companies in unexplored areas; to regulate the banking industry; to prohibit usury; and to provide state funded education to children of the indigent; and to collect taxes – but they set a striking precedent for advocating interventions in future cases where markets were seen to operate inexpeditiously.[11]

Far from being 'modest ones by contemporary standards', if his programme had been carried out with any degree of diligence it would have amounted to a cost of many millions of pounds over many years, a major expenditure of public funds by any standards, just to build a national network of adequate roads between the major cities of the country.

The condition of what passed for road links between even major towns and cities was deplorable and unimaginable two centuries later. Samuel Smiles (1812–1904) published *The Life of Thomas Telford* in 1863. It took Telford 20 years to build 1,000 miles of roads in Scotland (an average of 50 miles a year), and many more thousands of miles were needed in England and Wales. Smiles' description of the condition of Scottish roads paints the scale of the problem:

In 1743 an attempt was made by the Town Council of Glasgow to set up a stage-coach or 'lando.' It was to be drawn by six horses, carry six passengers, and run between Glasgow and Edinburgh, a distance of forty-four miles, once a week in winter, and twice a week in summer. The project, however, seems to have been thought too bold for the time, for the 'lando' was never started. It was not until the year 1749 that the first public conveyance, called 'The Glasgow and Edinburgh Caravan,' was started between the two cities, and it made the journey between the one place and the other in two days. Ten years later another vehicle was started, named 'The Fly' because of its unusual speed, and it contrived to make the journey in rather less than a day and a half.

About the same time, a coach with four horses was started between Haddington and Edinburgh, and it took a full winter's day to perform the journey of sixteen miles: the effort being to reach Musselburgh in time for dinner, and go into town in the evening. As late as 1763 there was as only one stage-coach in all Scotland in communication with London, and that set out from Edinburgh only once a month. The journey to London occupied from ten to fifteen days, according to the state of the weather; and those who undertook so dangerous a journey usually took the precaution of making their wills before starting.

When carriers' carts were established, the time occupied by them on the road will now appear almost incredible. Thus the common carrier between Selkirk and Edinburgh, a distance of only thirty-eight miles, took about a fortnight to perform the double journey. Part of the road lay along Gala Water, and in summer time, when the river-bed was dry, the carrier used it as a road. The townsmen of this adventurous individual, on the morning of his way-going, were accustomed to turn out and take leave of him, wishing him a safe return from his perilous journey. In winter the route was simply impracticable, and the communication was suspended until the return of dry weather.

While such was the state of the communications in the immediate neighbourhood of the metropolis of Scotland, matters were, if possible, still worse in the remoter parts of the country.[12]

Scarcely any passable roads existed in mid-18th century Scotland and there were few across the whole of England. Laughable tales (at least in retrospect to us) were not uncommon of luckless retainers working walking beside the carriages of those rich enough to own them, and digging out the wheels from ruts and mud, so that the sorry passengers could travel at less than walking pace from one place to the next.[13]

Smith frequently took the 44-mile journey from Glasgow to Edinburgh to meet his friends and he wrote with feeling about the need for public expenditure on roads. When you suffer from their absence you are easily persuaded that 'something should be done' and you are less likely to consider prudence and frugality to be virtues. To conceive, therefore, of these potential expenditures as 'modest' reflects an ignorance of just how badly the roads needed major investment. Significantly, the immodesty of Smith's advocacy was disguised by the absence of estimates on what his 'modest' plans would cost (a tactic practised by all those proposing to spend public funds since States had any funds to spend).

54

Education and Health Expenditures

The expense of educating youth should be met either from the general revenue of society or from the beneficiaries (more correctly, their parents and guardians). Smith found himself in a bind here as he believed that services offered in return for a salary, paid by taxation, private endowments, charities or legacies, would deteriorate to the point of indifference in their quality:

> In every profession, the exertion of the great part of those who exercise it, is always in proportion to the necessity they are under of making that exertion. ... Where competition is free, the rivalship of competitors, who are all endeavouring the jostle one another out of employment, obliges every man to endeavour to execute his work with a certain degree of exactness.[1]

Salaries and their emoluments, the larger part of expenditure on education, when paid for fully (from whichever source) lead to their teachers' commitments to educating the young to decline to whatever standards they can get away with, it being 'in the interests of every man to live as much at his ease as he can'.[2] Not much has changed in this respect in public education, and large swathes of public service, in the intervening two hundred years. Today we call them 'sink schools.'

It remains a major problem in the economics of bureaucracy that the objectives of the administrators often conflict with the interests of the putative beneficiaries of their services and that the costs of administration of indifferently supplied public services are borne by taxpayers, many of whom are not even the beneficiaries. Professor Sir Alan Peacock has written extensively on this problem from a classical smithian perspective and I refer you to his work.[3]

Smith asserted that 'Publick services are never better performed than when their reward comes only in consequence of their being performed, and is proportioned to the diligence employed in performing them.'[4] But stating the problem did not solve it. Has it been solved even today? Current resistance to performance pay schemes, bitterly opposed by public sector unions, suggest it has not.

Might we extract some comfort at least from a notion that the education of youth is everywhere carried out indifferently but something of educational value 'sticks' for the majority of students, even at costs greater than is probably necessary? I raise this not to answer the question, but only to draw attention to Smith's 'failing' to solve the problems he raised in *Wealth of Nations* was of no more significance than the same failings of everybody in this controversial field since. Educational design, which usually means reform, is a deeply divisive subject, and the bias is towards criticism of the current system, with scarcely any agreement on the appropriate remedies for the perceived defects in either activity.

Smith, while unsure of how education should be paid for, had firm ideas on what could be achieved, particularly for the lower orders, beset, as we have discussed, in adulthood with problems arising from the division of labour into ever narrower tasks:

> But though the common people cannot, in any civilised society, be so well instructed as people of some rank and fortune, the most essential parts of education, however, to read, write, and account, can be acquired at so early a period of life, that the greater part even of those who are to be bred to the lowest occupations, have time to acquire them before they can be employed in those occupations. For a very small expense the publick can facilitate, can encourage, and can even impose upon almost the whole body of the people, the necessity of acquiring those most essential parts of education.
>
> The publick can facilitate this acquisition by establishing in every parish or district a little school, where children may be taught for a reward so moderate, that even a common labourer may afford it; the master being partly paid, but not wholly paid by the publick; because if he was wholly, or principally paid by it, he would soon learn to neglect his business. In Scotland the establishment of such parish schools has taught almost the whole common people to read, and a very great proportion of them to write and account. In England the establishment of charity schools has had an effect of the same kind, though not so universally, because the establishment is not so universal. If in those little schools the books, by which the children are taught to read, were a little more instructive that they commonly are: and if, instead of a little smattering of Latin; which the children of the common people are sometimes taught there, and which can scarce ever be of any use to them: they were instructed in the elementary parts of geometry and mechanicks, the literary education of this rank of people would perhaps be a complete as it could be. There is scarce a common trade which does not

afford some opportunities of applying to it the common principles of geometry and mechanicks, and which would not therefore gradually exercise and improve the common people in those principles, the necessary introduction to the most sublime as well as the most useful sciences. The Publick can encourage the acquisition of those most essential parts of education by giving small premiums, and little badges of distinction, to the children of the common people who excel in them.[5]

Examined dispassionately, Smith's proposals, modest as they are and well short of the universal compulsory education of over 100 years later, represented a substantial intervention by the State in the economic model of his narrative of perfect liberty and he recognized that intervention on the scale he proposed was not just financial but extended to curriculum design by the State too. He could not but have recognised that these consequences would temper the willingness of the government to undertake what could be, and undoubtedly was to become, a major financial and administrative burden. It is from these considerations that he exaggerated the debilitating effect of the division of labour in his rhetoric.[6] He made an overly strong case for his modest reforms so that they would be noticed and acted upon.

And if the qualms of conscience provoked by his rhetorical exaggerations about near brain dead labourers suffering from the alleged effects of the division of labour were insufficient to persuade legislators of the need to fund the education of the children of the common people, he made a no less strong appeal to the misgivings that 18[th-] century legislators felt about unrest among the lower orders, to prompt them to provide education:

The state, however, derives no inconsiderable advantage from their instruction. The more they are instructed, the less liable they are to the delusions of enthusiasm and superstition, which, among ignorant nations, frequently occasion dreadful disorders. An instructed and intelligent people besides are always more decent and orderly than an ignorant and stupid one. They feel themselves, each individually, more respectable, and more likely to obtain the respect of their lawful superiors, and they are therefore more disposed to examine, and more capable of seeing through, the interested complaints of faction and sedition. And they are, upon that account, less apt to be misled into any wanton or unnecessary opposition to the measures of government. In free countries, where the safety of government depends very much upon the favourable judgement which the people may form of its conduct, it must surely be of the highest importance that they should not be disposed to judge rashly or capriciously concerning it.[7]

Education did not fit into the pure system of his narrative because in such a world only the, mostly male, children of well-off parents were properly educated; the education of the children of the poor waited on opulence spreading down to their households (though the education of the poor in Scotland was better provided for than in England).[8] Neither would it fit completely into the real world unless the legislators took political action to direct public funds for this purpose. To advocate that they did so caused Smith to favour another major breach in laissez faire.

Smith's recognition that the expense of education cannot be left to natural liberty alone is of far greater significance than the modesty of his proposals. In much the same way, ingenious modern attempts to re-cast public funding of education into a quasi-market mode, via education vouchers, are truly smithian in scope. Like his modest education proposals, the voucher reformers have so far not overcome the political opposition of vested interests (mainly public sector trades unions), which oppose the use of taxation for any purpose unless the public sector not only funds, but also provides, monopolistically, its services through public sector employees at locations dictated by State employed bureaucrats. A more blatant form of restricting public funds for local monopoly suppliers cannot be imagined, nor one so at variance from Smith's radical recommendations.

In a little noticed paragraph in *Wealth of Nations*, Smith went much further in his advocacy of State intervention than the funding and provision of education. He proposed a small step from disease being the accepted lot of those unlucky to suffer its effects, to the State making modest funding available to ameliorate the consequences of certain diseases. And, interestingly, he did so without seeing a direct commercial advantage in doing it. If adopted, it was inevitable that the range of interventions in State health provision would, in time, expand (as they have).

At the end of a discussion on martial prowess, Smith compares the ancient institutions of Greece and Rome with the militias of the 18th century. His comparison did not favour the militias of 'modern times' and not just because the ancient militias 'required little or no attention from government to maintain them in the most perfect vigour', while any modern militia ('except, perhaps, that of Switzerland') 'requires the continual and painful attention of government, without which they are constantly falling into total neglect and disuse.'[9]

He approaches his subject via a discussion of the attributes of a 'coward', a man incapable of defending or revenging himself.' He first proposes a remedy for the spirit of cowardice:

> Even though the martial spirit of the people were of no use towards the defence of society, yet to prevent that sort of mental mutilation, deformity and wretchedness, which cowardice necessarily involves in it, from spreading themselves through the great body of the people, would still deserve the most serious attention of government; ...[10]

He is unspecific as to what should be the outcome of the 'most serious attention of government.' From his discussion of the ancient militias of Greece and Rome I discern a preference for regular and compulsory 'military and gymnastic' exercises. Instituting such a system in Britain required funds and resources (e.g., instructors and public fields under the supervision of the local magistrate).[11] Interesting, but not by as much as the rest of the sentence:

> ... In the same manner as it would deserve its most serious attention to prevent a leprosy or any other loathsome and offensive disease, though neither mortal nor dangerous, from spreading itself among them; though, perhaps, no other publick good might result from such attention besides the prevention of so great a publick evil.[12]

To the list of public works for the commercial good they do, we may add the 'prevention of so great a public evil' as disease 'to prevent that sort of mental mutilation, deformity and wretchedness' as found in cowardice, attitude of mind.

To start with public expenditures on the treatment of the foulest of diseases opens the door to wider funding for public health, physical and mental, for lesser, debilitating diseases. Adam Smith, a patron of a National Health Service? Perhaps not! However, that Smith included the treatment of disease as well as education in his discussion of public expenditures, suggests a more flexible mind than his false image as an exponent of laissez faire.

55
Public Revenues

Whatever amount is spent by the State on carrying out its three main duties it has to be raised by one means or another with 'the people contributing a part of their own private revenue in order to make up a publick revenue to the sovereign or commonwealth'.[1] In the absence of an independently wealthy sovereign, a feature of monarchy long since absent in Britain, taxation from the private revenues of the people was the main source of government revenue. Smith did not think much of the commercial prowess of sovereigns – and thought even less of the prowess of merchants, instancing those of the East India Company for particular contempt as they were 'bad traders' and 'bad sovereigns'.[2]

Smith outlined the 'maxims' (*not* 'canons'!) for a just taxation system: equality, certainty, convenience and economy.[3] Briefly, subjects should contribute taxes 'as nearly as possible, in proportion to their respective abilities, that is, in proportion to the revenue they respectively enjoy under the protection of the state';

the amount of tax to be paid should be certain not arbitrary:

inequality 'is not near so great an evil as a very small degree of uncertainty';

taxes should be levied at the most convenient time

when he buys the goods attracting a tax, or when he receives the rent, or imports the produce;

taxes should be 'so contrived as both to take out and to keep out of the pockets of the people as little as possible, over and above what it brings into the publick treasury of the state.'[4]

Smith laid no claim to the originality of the maxims (though often incorrectly labelled by modern economists as 'his' maxims or, worse, 'his' 'canons'), reporting that they had already been brought 'to the attention of all nations' by unnamed others.[5]

Professor Stigler, formerly of the University of Chicago and a distinguished Nobel Prize winner, applied the alleged smithian principle of 'self-interest' to the politics of public finance.[6] He found a puzzle in the abundant examples Smith provides of a failure of self-interest to account for the political behaviours of legislators. The 'canons of taxation'(!), if adopted by a Chancellor of the Exchequer, writes Stigler, 'would obtain for him at least the temporary admiration of the professors of moral philosophy but this is a slender and notably fickle constituency on which to build a party.'[7] Stigler may have missed Smith's point. The maxims were ideal guides to taxation policy, not iron bound prescriptions for, and certainly not descriptions of, past or current legislation on taxation.

Today's taxation regimes are the product of many parliaments consisting of the 'elected' interest groups, affiliated individuals and men of party that have crowded the benches of the British and foreign parliaments and legislatures since the 18th century. Stigler's substitution of 'two canons' for 'Smith's maxims' have an air of political modernity about them: 'The revenue system must not imperil the political support for the regime' and 'The revenue system must yield revenue.'[8]

In Smith's day, once a government achieved the necessary Parliamentary votes (most of whom were MPs with agricultural interests) it was unlikely to face the electoral wrath of the (few) enfranchised electors who might be imposed upon by what they voted for. The circumstances of electoral politics in 18th-century Britain produced confusing legislative programmes for the beneficiary interest groups listed by Stigler[9] and the necessity, alluded to by Smith, to apply the maxims to the collection of the revenues as closely as practicable in the circumstances, bearing in mind that of the 26 examples listed by Stigler, 19 of them were not taxation measures at all and therefore beyond the remit of taxation maxims.

Professor Peacock's criticism of Stigler's assertions should be unchallengeable:

> it is one thing to be employing one's commercial or political talents to promote self-interest in a society which has accepted the necessity for competition as a way for channelling self-interest towards the goals of society and another to do so under conditions where entrenched monopoly privileges abound.[10]

Perhaps the view from Kirkcaldy, Edinburgh and London, while Smith wrote *Wealth of Nations*, was closer to the reality of monopoly privileges distorting both commercial and political initiatives and self-interest in the 18th century than the view from Chicago two hundred years later. Strangely, Stigler critiques Smith's preference for moral suasion: 'at best this is an extraordinarily slow and uncertain method of changing policy; at worst it may lead to policies which endanger society.'[11] If persuasion is not likely to work, what exactly was Professor Stigler suggesting?

Stigler may have underplayed the significance of the qualifier in the passage he quotes from Smith to open his essay: 'The natural effort of every individual to better his own condition, *when suffered to exert itself with freedom and security*...'[12] When self-interest is not exerted in ' freedom and security', or in conditions of 'natural liberty and justice', because of monopolistic tendencies or attempts to introduce them, self-interest is not capable of carrying society to 'wealth and prosperity'.

Monopolistic self-interest becomes part of the 'hundred impertinent obstructions with which the folly of human laws too often encumbers its operations.' Stigler's errs in reporting Smith's wording. The 'folly of human laws' begins with self-interest attempting to alter the rules of anonymous competition. Legitimising the freedom of individuals or groups to do whatever they want, including narrowing competition to create monopoly, was never part of Smith's narrative of natural liberty and justice, which is why he was never happy with the open licence to do so embedded at the heart of laissez faire.

56
Government Failure

It is in the nature of modern debates about the role (and extent) of government intervention that the contending extremes (laissez faire *versus* socialist – though in unhelpful confusion we now have laissez faire socialists and anarchists from the left and laissez faire libertarian neo-conservatives from the right!) treat any leaning to one side or the other as an endorsement or vilification of their ideas. Therefore it is not sensible to leave aside Smith's recognition of the manifest failures of government and its agencies to perform the roles they assumed in the 18th century.

It was from concepts of market failure that he saw a role for government and its was from government failure that he took a cautionary stance when considering extending to government any role that could be left to competitive markets. As usual with Smith it is not safe to attribute to him clear-cut and dogmatic views relevant to the perennial 'markets versus governments' debates of subsequent centuries.

There are two considerations in judging the efficacy of a large public works project which, though it 'may be in the highest degree advantageous to a great society', it could 'never repay the expence to any individual, or small number of individuals' to 'erect or maintain'.[1] The cost of erecting a public works project was to be considered separate from the cost of maintaining them in proper working order.

If private individuals cannot erect or maintain advantageous public works (good roads, bridges, navigable canals, and harbours – though individual exceptions are well documented) to facilitate the commerce of any country, who can? Government is the only option, though this unqualified conclusion does not solve the real problems of government failure in important areas like efficiency, corruption, and the diversion of scarce capital into unproductive usage to the detriment of national economic growth. These considerations of finance take us to the heart of the concept of government failure and Smith had plenty to say about the reality of such failures.

Temporarily setting aside the costs of erecting public works, Smith considers how they are to be maintained. Roads and bridges need repairs,

canals and harbours need dredged to be kept navigable, and the beneficiaries of such works should be charged small tolls for the use of them.
Carriages using toll roads and bridges can be charged by their weight[2]
(though he also proposes charging according to the value of their contents
to make the rich contribute 'in a very easy manner to the relief of the
poor'),[3] navigable canals by the number and tonnage of the lighters, and
harbours by the tonnage loaded onto, and unloaded from, ships sheltering
in them.[4]

To these public works Smith adds the coinage which 'defrays its own
expence' and the post-office which 'over and above defraying its own
expence, affords in almost all countries a very considerable revenue to the
sovereign.'[5] In all these cases the beneficiaries identify themselves by their
use of the facilities and moderate charges would defray their expenses. It
seems, he notes, 'scarce possible to invent a more equitable way of maintain such works.'[6] Final consumers, the ultimate beneficiaries, pay the tolls
in the prices they pay and this too is equitable. Because of the direct connection between the need for a road, bridge, canal or harbour and the trade
carried on them, they will only be built where they are required and 'their
grandeur and magnificence' will be determined by what 'commerce can
afford to pay', hence capital diverted to their construction will not be
wasted on roads serving little commercial purpose and bridges 'where
nobody passes'. This is not the case where public works are funded by
'other revenue than that which they themselves are capable of affording.'[7]

Private persons may be driven by personal profit to keep the road or
canal properly repaired and maintained, otherwise their profit falls and
may disappear. Public commissioners may neglect that which is not theirs,
depending on their sense of public duty. It could go either way. Public
commissioners could dissipate tolls in 'ornamental and unnecessary
expenses' while letting the 'essential parts of the work ... go to ruin'.[8]
Private proprietors of a high road 'might neglect altogether the repair of a
road, and yet continue to levy very nearly the same tolls' necessitating that
the road 'should be put under the management of commissioners or
trustees'.[9] One gets the impression that Smith was not dogmatic about
these issues. Utility, not principle, was decisive, here as elsewhere.

A different problem arises from the latter arrangement: the diversion of
their surplus revenues over costs to meet the 'exigencies of the state.' Few
governments can resist the temptation to invent new ways of augmenting
their revenues and living off them. Road tolls suffer from private owners
and government commissioners raising them for general revenue, with
both agencies inadequately repairing the roads and both acting as a 'very
great incumbrance upon' the inland commerce of a country.[10]

The difference between incompetent private operators of road turnpikes
and incompetent government operators (both of which divert revenues for
purposes other than the repair and maintenance of deteriorating roads) is

that it is more difficult to compel government to spend the toll revenues appropriately, and the greater the revenues raised by the government appointed 'trustees' the greater the difficulty of altering their behaviours.[11]

Smith's tirades against monopolies in any form implied a need for vigilance, which implied intervention by agencies of the state, to observe, evaluate and decide what, if anything, had to be done to prevent them operating or from being established and, even in a system of natural liberty, to prevent them occurring by default or carelessness. Interventions were to be preventative not initiating; nobody would be told how to invest his stock or labour, only that he could not act non-competitively.

There is no doubt that competitors seek ways to reduce competition and, unless their conduct is monitored, they inevitably turn to thoughts of how to eliminate or deter competitive rivalry. To police a country's political economy requires the availability of instruments of intervention (legislation, inspection, policing, law courts and justice) as well as the political will and intention to intervene.

In addition, the duties of the sovereign introduced into his narrative specific and deliberate purposes for which state funding is preferred to reliance on natural liberty, largely on grounds that without defence against invasion and depredation precious little liberty would survive in an independent society. The defence sector was not a mere plaything of the sovereign – 'all the king's horses and all the king's men' romping around to the delight of little children – because war was a serious and expensive business, and was getting more so each decade (as Smith noticed).

Justice provided publicly funded employment for the courts and their officers (clerks, messengers, judges, sheriffs, police, jailers and executioners) and private funding for hundreds of lawyers, solicitors, barristers, advocates, legal scribes and clerks. The expenses of justice were no mean sum and with the rapid increase in Acts of Parliament towards the end of the century, including a leap in the number of capital crimes, the sums required to operate justice were bound to grow yet larger.

If Smith's modest educational reforms were put into effect the annual educational budget would have grown significantly. 'Little schools' across the land meant a large increase in expenditure on buildings (Smith's own 'Kirkcaldy High School' was a splendid little building with two tiny rooms – later a small storeroom for its larger replacement built in the 19th century) and on at least one, sometimes more, teachers on small annual salaries, for every 'little' school. On the Scot's principle that 'mony a mickle maks a muckle'[12] this could amount to a tidy annual sum too. It was, of course, a century or more before national elementary schooling commenced.[13]

57

Reclaiming Smith's Legacy

Those who misappropriate Adam Smith's legacy legitimise their errors by the sheer weight of repetition. Falsehood strides round the world in seven leagued boots (so we are told) while truth is still tying its laces, so recovering Smith's lost legacy awaits an almighty effort to make it succeed. Is it worth it? I believe it is, because the purloining of Smith's message on natural liberty and justice to replace it with irresponsible policies of laissez faire is an injustice to the memory of a moral philosopher. Let the proponents of laissez faire put their own names to their philosophy and leave Adam Smith's out of it.

Scott Gordon, searching through Victorian literature for the source of laissez faire policy making, confessed to being stumped by the paucity of sources for the popular myth that its ideology dominated the Victorian era, that it was expounded interminably in the debates of the House of Commons, that it guided governments and their civil servants in policy making and was reported daily in the press. He found unqualified support for laissez faire in the *Economist* under the editorship of its founder, James Wilson, from 1843, linked to the paper's free trade philosophy. But he found it nowhere else! Surprisingly, the *Economist* appears to have been a lone popular exponent of laissez faire in the Victorian Age in the UK.[1]

Gordon quotes Samuel Smiles, the archetypical Victorian individualist whose devastating dismissal of laissez faire captured all that is wrong, impractical and socially irresponsible with a reckless and unthinking advocacy of it:

When typhus or cholera breaks out, they tell us that nobody is to blame. That terrible Nobody! How much he has to answer for! More mischief is done by Nobody than by all the world besides. Nobody adulterates our food. Nobody poisons us with bad drink. Nobody supplies us with foul water. Nobody spreads fever in blind alleys and unswept lanes. Nobody leaves towns undrained. Nobody fills jails, penitentiaries and convict stations. Nobody makes poachers, thieves and drunkards.

Nobody has a theory too, a dreadful theory. It is embodied in two words: laissez-faire – Let alone. When people are poisoned by plaster of Paris mixed with flour, 'Let alone' is the remedy. When *Cocculus Indicus* is used instead of hops, and men die prematurely, it is easy to say, 'Nobody did it'. Let those who can, find out when they were cheated: *Caveat emptor*. When people live in foul dwellings, let them alone. Let wretchedness do its work; do not interfere with death.[2]

Anybody knowingly associating Smith's name with these implications of laissez faire – typical of the implications we can be sure he commented upon when he debated with those few French Physiocrats who promoted the flawed concept – should not claim his authority for speaking in his name.

Reclaiming Smith's legacy involves a modicum of research (starting with the reading of his books) and the dissemination of the conclusions to as wide an audience as possible. This is directed at public debates as well as scholars. Almost every week I read or hear references to what Adam Smith is alleged to have said, or supported, drip fed to the public by journalists, politicians and populist academics. Where possible, readers, who have realised the truth about him and his work, could help to recover what has been purloined by challenging the public image in any prudent and responsible manner they can devise.

It is also incumbent on the universities to redress the balance by re-introducing the study of the history of economic ideas into their courses, including research degrees. In most economics courses I know of, the history of economic ideas has all but disappeared as a subject that is regularly taught. This condemns new generations of economists to repeat the mistakes of past generations.

In the discipline of finance, each generation re-learns all the old cyclical lessons and treats them as new problems of the moment. It is not much different in the numerous sub-fields of economics, evidenced by the seasonal re-appearance of the old, unresolved, debates about the balance of private and public enterprise, the appropriate levels of national and local taxation, the amount of necessary and tolerable interference in markets, the extent to which labour costs should be loaded with 'red tape' for ends outwith those of the enterprise, the limits to the social obligations of entrepreneurs, problems and remedies for market failure, and government failure when substituting for markets, and the perennial problems of the political and ideological influences, when refusing to comply with and service the longer term benefits of international trade and relations.

Treating these and many other issues in political economy as if they were new to the each generation, and ignoring how they made their appearance in the past, indicates an alarming lack of knowledge of the history of political economy. In any such history, the work of Adam Smith is worthy of close attention, provided of course, that we start with what he said and wrote and not what others have messed about with for ends that were no part of his legacy.

Edinburgh in Smith's time and ours

Viewing Edinburgh today from the nearby Braid hills, its modern boundaries uncomfortably close to the open spaces occupied by its University's observatory and by four golf courses, it takes a leap in the imagination to see Smith's Edinburgh as he knew it, its then town limits now far to the north of the middle-class southern suburbs seen from a vantage point on the Braids, and its northern limits further north now well beyond the town limits as they then stood, before the New Town, and what became Waverley Bridge, were under construction. Smith lived in Panmure House, just off the High Street, for the last years of his life with his mother and maiden cousin.

Mary Cosh captures the rugged essence of Smith's Edinburgh, the outlines of which you can just discern in fleeting glimpses amidst its modern layout, before its architects, builders, and road and bridge engineers were let loose on it in the past two hundred years:

> The small capital city ... was confined to the top of a narrow ridge of rock, sloping downwards from the castle's high peak on the west, past the Kirk of St Giles and the Tolbooth, to the Canongate, a separate burgh with its own Kirk and Tolbooth. At the eastern limit was the old Palace of Holyroodhouse. The extent from end to end was one mile. From the central High Street, centipede legs bestrode the hill in the form of wynds and closes, few broad enough to accommodate even a horse, let alone cart or carriage. On the north, below the sheer rock, a stagnant loch defended the town, on the south a wall and town gates. So constricted was the area that its inhabitants had had to build high, in tenements or lands whose narrow, winding common stairs climbed ten or a dozen storeys – or even more – with seven or eight families to a stair: 'perpendicular streets', Benjamin Franklin called them. The families on a single stair were often unknown to one another, and living was neither convenient nor clean.[3]

His hometown, Kirkcaldy, a small port on the north shore of the Firth of Forth, consisted of little more than a long single High Street (locals called it the 'lang toon'). He could see the jagged skyline of Edinburgh a few miles across the Firth from his mother's garden. Travelling to and from Edinburgh took time, and a roundabout route, via ferry and a 25-mile walk or horse ride along poor roads. The ferry has gone and two large bridges (with talk of a third) take people in cars, buses and trains in their thousands across to the south shore and back each day. Smith travelled far beyond Edinburgh, but he always came back, eventually settling in the city until he died.

The physical geography of Edinburgh and its environs have changed dramatically since the 18th century, as has the economy and the society he analysed in painstaking detail. Scotland, a largely rural country in the early 18th century was backward compared to the south of England. Rural poverty was mean on those who lived in squalid housing, and appallingly so for those who lived on its margins. Money, in the form of coinage, was scarce to near non-existent, and exceedingly low real wages left the uneducated mass of near starving labouring people hardly better off than the lawless vagabonds prowling around looking for opportunities to create mischief. Indentured labour, treated no better than slaves, except for the mask of an agreed valuation, was so common in Scotland that it was exported to the Caribbean, until African slavery undercut it financially. The treatment of women and girls in this world can safely be described as despicable.

It was into this world that Adam Smith, from a frugal but privileged family, made his way, without ostentation and without menace, and without, it must be said, the pretensions and pathetic airs that are so evident in some of his contemporaries, such as the unpleasant trio of Alexander Carlyle, Adam Ferguson, and William Robertson (but not, of course, in David Hume, a saintly, modest man in comparison, with much less reason to be modest than all three of them together).

Smith's vision was formed from his research and observations, not from pre-set sentiments and precepts (*Wealth of Nations*, in essence, was a one-man Royal Commission into a pertinent question of what caused growing opulence). He saw in the promising because growing, re-birth of the age of commerce an opportunity to find solutions to the failings of society, less because these failings were endemic, more because they could be solved without an earthly version of fire and brimstone.

By taking the grand view of processes evident in society, he analysed the nature of the long run trends, using the gradual decline of the feudal interregnum over its centuries, not particular flashes of the instant, to track the cumulative consequences of individual actions. A theme from a single paragraph reveals Smith getting to grips with the big picture of social change at his analytical best:

All for ourselves, and nothing for other people, seems, in every age of the world to have been, the vile maxim of the masters of mankind. As soon, therefore, as they [the feudal lords] could find a method of consuming the whole value of their rents themselves, they had no disposition to share them with any other persons. For a pair of diamond buckles perhaps, or for something as frivolous and useless, they exchanged the maintenance, or what is the same thing, the price of the maintenance of a thousand men for a year, and with it the whole weight and authority which it could give them. The buckles, however, were to be all their own, and no other human creature was to have any share of them; whereas in the more antient (sic) method of expense they must have shared with at least a thousand people. With the judges that were to determine the preference, this difference was perfectly decisive; and thus for the gratification of the most childish, the meanest and the most sordid of all vanities, they gradually bartered their whole power and authority.[4]

He was not concerned with momentary title-tattle, or the accidents of personalities, neither of feudal lords, nor with those of landowners, merchants and manufacturers. It is not the first drop of water that counts; it is the myriad drops that find their way into the ship that sinks it or stay under the ship and float it. Standing back to widen his perspective was Smith's way of integrating the great laboratory of empirical history into his philosophy, jurisprudence and political economy, while looking for the determining trends that mark his attention to the essential details in *Moral Sentiments* and *Wealth of Nations*.

Smith perceived the fourth age of commerce to be an enlightened, and enlightening, world of gradually rising opulence, making the rich even richer, which he considered a small price to pay if it mitigated the parlous conditions of those living in real poverty, providing that it made the lives of the labouring poor and their families more bearable and, in due course, more opulent. His optimism that this happy state would emerge from the spread of agricultural improvement to raise nourishing food supplies – diets of fish and meat to supplement plain and monotonous Scottish diets of vegetables and oats – and from the deepening of markets and the division of labour to raise the comfortable consumption of personal and household manufactures, shines through *Wealth of Nations* at every stage of his argument, and it should shame those who find his book 'distracting' or 'difficult'. They must have hearts of stone.

Smith was not naïve about a new age of commerce embedded in a predominantly agricultural society, and ruled by a political elite reaping from taxation the early fruits of what would become a source of funds for their seriously disabling adventures in war and conquest and inefficient administration. He understood their institutional softness on the removal of impediments to economic growth and the wealth of nations, and their hardness on the perceived dangers of liberty and democracy for their extravagances. He detailed their woeful inadequacies as providers of education, health and welfare for the majority of children of the poor and disadvantaged.

I often wonder whether Smith, not long after the publication of *Wealth of Nations*, suspected that his vision of the extension of the harmonious resolution of inter-personal conflict, aided by the impartial spectator, and the resolution of dyadic conflict through truck, barter and exchange, would join his sombre assessment of the probability of freedom of trade being restored in Britain. His reasons for pessimism are instructive: the 'prejudices of the publick, but what is more unconquerable, the private interests of many individuals, irresistibly oppose it.'[5]

If he genuinely believed that the opponents of his idyll were as 'unconquerable' and 'irresistible' as his pessimism implies, it might go someway to explaining why he gave up serious work to promote the wider agenda in *Wealth of Nations* after 1776. If he had realised that versions of his Work too would be joined to the 'unconquerable' and 'irresistible' opposition of private interests to modest, but necessary, reforms of commerce, as it was transformed into capitalism in the 19th century and beyond, he could have reflected on his assessment of the fate of a member of parliament who attempts to thwart the monopolists. In the MP's case:

> neither the most acknowledged probity, nor the highest rank, nor the greatest publick services can protect him from the most infamous abuse and detraction, from personal insults, nor sometimes from real danger, arising from the insolent outrage of furious and disappointed monopolists.[6]

What would Smith have made of the manner in which his fierce opposition to monopolists and their anti-competitive practices was to be turned on its head and re-branded to portray him as being in favour of leaving them alone, under the ascribed maxim of laissez faire, to behave as they saw fit? All monopolists start as competitors. Left alone, successful competitors become monopolists.

It was not necessary, however, for the monopolists to vent their fury and hound Smith as they would hound members of parliament who opposed them. All they had to do was misappropriate his legacy and, with the aid of some lazy, or mischievous, scribblers, buy their respectability to assure the uninformed that Adam Smith, the 'high priest of capitalism' (or similar nonsense), said what he didn't say and wrote the opposite of what they claimed.

In this context, the recent announcement that a statue of Adam Smith is to be commissioned, and erected in the High Street, Edinburgh, near to where he worked as a Commissioner of Customs and a short walk from where he lived in Panmure Close, raises an interesting issue: which Adam Smith is the statue to celebrate: the mythical Adam Smith, high priest of capitalism and promoter of laissez faire, or the real Adam Smith, restored to his legitimate legacy as a moral philosopher and political economist?

We cannot know what Adam Smith would have said about the depredations of his legacy in the two centuries since his death. But, what is of more importance for you, is what you will say about his lost legacy and what has been done with it the next time you have an opportunity to comment.

Appendix: Smith's '1755 Paper'

Introduction

Adam Smith's 1755 paper allegedly arose from his apprehension that others were about to claim precedence for his ideas on political economy[1] but his 'indignant warmth' has been misinterpreted. Stewart read his eulogy on Smith over two meetings (21 January and 18 March 1793) of the literary section of the Royal Society of Edinburgh (RSE). No further meetings of RSE were held in 1793, except one on 11 December, followed by only one (14 December) in 1794.[2] In contrast to these intermittent meetings forty years later, intellectual life in Edinburgh and Glasgow in the 1750s was well served by Clubs to which the brightest of the generations mixed and mingled, ate and argued and, seemingly never tiring of each other's company, met several times a week in both cities, primarily for dining and discoursing. Smith was an avid 'clubber' and enjoyed the intellectual and social life of his many clubs.[3]

Reasons for the 1755 paper

Stewart says that Smith's 1755 paper contained:

> a pretty long enumeration ... of certain leading principles, both political and literary, to which he was anxious to establish his exclusive right; in order to prevent the possibility of some rival claims which he thought he had reason to apprehend, and to which his situation as a Professor, added to his unreserved communications in private companies, rendered him peculiarly liable.[4]

The conventional version interprets Smith as trying to prevent somebody plagiarising *his* 'exclusive right' to his 'leading principles'.

Stewart reports on the tone of the 1755 paper:

> It is expressed with a great deal of that honest and indignant warmth, which is perhaps unavoidable by a man who is conscious of the purity of his own intentions, when he suspects that advantages have been taken of the frankness of his temper.[5]

Yet, Smith was relaxed about others using his ideas, with or without acknowledgement, for example, Blair (1783)[6] and Robertson, (1769).[7] Rousseau's *Discourse on Inequality*, reviewed by Smith in the *Edinburgh Review*, without signs of apprehension, had 'stages' from 'rude' to 'civilised' society similar to Smith's, who said it was 'almost entirely of rhetoric and description' and from 'an author more capable of feeling strongly than analysing accurately'.[8]

Stewart, however, slips in what amounts to a different explanation of Smith's 'indignant warmth':

> After all, perhaps the merit of such a work as Mr Smith's is to be estimated less from the novelty of the principles it contains, than from the reasonings [sic] employed to support these principles, and from the scientific manner in which

they are unfolded in their proper order and connection. General assertions with respect to the advantages of free commerce may be collected from various writers of an early date. But in questions of so complicated a nature as occur in political economy, the credit of such opinions belongs of right to the author who first established their solidity, and followed them out to their remote consequences; not to him who, by a fortunate accident, first stumbled on the truth.[9]

The inference is that Smith was under attack for 'borrowing', even plagiarising, from others. Professor Rashid has documented Smith's 'borrowings' recently.[10]

Rumours to this effect would be exceedingly damaging personally. Foes in Glasgow University, jealous of his (too) rapid progress from student to Professor (1746 to 1751), may have fanned the rumours.[11] Smith's assertion of his priority was not just a dispassionate discourse on his rights. He was passionate in his outrage, and driven by more than apprehension that anybody might believe the charges of borrowing, amounting to plagiarism, when he had hundreds of witnesses to the contrary.

I conclude that the reason for the 1755 paper was a threat to Smith's reputation and that the paper was a warning to spreaders of offensive rumours that he was 'calling out' the rumourmongers. Nothing else but the rumour of being a serial borrower could have excited Smith so much, no other charge cut to his very core as a moral philosopher, and nothing was more likely to drive him to present his paper in public.

The 1755 paper asserts his originality in the leading principles of his political economy. The rumours cut Smith to the quick, causing a continuing rankle in his demeanour throughout his life.

> A great part of the opinions (he [Smith] observes) enumerated in this paper is treated of at length in some lectures which I have still by me, and which were written in the hand of a clerk who left my service six years ago. [1749] They have all of them been the constant subjects of my lectures since I first taught Mr Craigie's class, the first winter I spent in Glasgow [1751] down to this day [1755] without any considerable variations. They had all of them been the subjects of lectures which I read at Edinburgh the winter before I left it, [1750] and I can adduce innumerable witness, both from that place and from this, who will ascertain them sufficiently to be mine.[12]

His words 'from that place and from this' refer to Edinburgh (where he first stated his ideas) and Glasgow (where Stewart says he read the 1755 paper). He claimed unchallengeable precedence for the contents of the lectures that he delivered in both cities. (1748–55). But what was he claiming? That he was the first to make a coherent synthesis of disparate insights and ideas in numerous contemporary sources, or the first to discover the very ideas that he linked together into a coherent political economy?

While authors before Smith might have accidentally 'stumbled on the truth', it did not follow that they were the inventors of the analysis explaining how the newly discovered principles worked through to their remote consequences.[13] Addressing those in the RSE audience who believed that Smith was guilty as charged, Stewart said that Smith most definitely was the inventor of the solid theory of free commerce, albeit implied by the earlier insights of others. A masterly drafting, intended to mollify the frayed sensitivities of both sides?

Smith's rebuttal of plagiarism (or lack of originality) with the dates when he first delivered his concepts in public did not dispel the rumours. While you cannot plagiarise if you made the leading principles public first, you can still be accused of excessive unaccredited 'borrowings'. The latter are the gist of Rashid's assertions.[14] This interpretation shows that the disagreeable tensions were not about plagiarisms of Smith's ideas, but were about Smith's claims to ideas from writers who had noted before him the advantages of 'free commerce', and others, like Montesquieu, who preceded him on jurisprudence. Having dated Smith's claims to have lectured on free commerce during 1748–51, Stewart concluded that only Smith had explained how they worked in 'so complicated a nature as occur in political economy.' Both sides of the still fractious dispute could consider their 1755 opinions confirmed.

Adam Ferguson and the rumours

Adam Ferguson (born in June 1723) was the same age as Smith. He graduated from St. Andrews University in 1742, becoming Chaplain to the Black Watch Regiment and served in Flanders, notably at the bloody Battle of Fontenoy in May 1745. He returned home in 1755, the year Smith wrote his angry paper. He was a Highlander and a Gaelic speaker and empathised with the moral virtues of the old Highland Clans, though not a Jacobite.

Like Smith before him, Ferguson sought a professor's chair. He gained the Chair in Natural Philosophy in 1759, for which he was singularly unsuited, and then transferred in 1764 to the more congenial Chair in Moral Philosophy. He was a scholar familiar with literature and ambitious for a professorship. He required introductions to Scottish society and the best route was to become a 'Clubber'. It was natural for him to contact Adam Smith.[15]

The two men had a turbulent relationship over the years, alternatively effusively warm and bitter cold. Few details have survived, but the quarrel kept erupting on matters related to the originality of their ideas. There are a number of confusing distractions in the story of their grievances, so first let me clear them away.

James Bonar[16] speculated that the person who had plagiarised Smith 'may possibly have been' Adam Ferguson (1723–1816). Though Ferguson was in Edinburgh 1755, he did not publish his *History of Civil Society* until 1767. The misleading confusion arose because Stewart wrongly interpreted the source of Smith's 'apprehensions'. Finding Ferguson not guilty of plagiarism in 1767 does not relive him of responsibility for the 1755 rumours.

Alexander Carlyle, a life-long carping critic of Smith's social 'awkwardness', added to the confusion:

> Smith had been weak enough to accuse [Ferguson] of having borrowed some of his inventions without owning them. This Ferguson denied, but owned he had derived many notions from a French author, and that Smith had been there before him.[17]

This is claimed to be evidence that Smith accused Ferguson of plagiarising *Moral Sentiments*. But, for one thing, that would not be relevant to the 1755 charges, and for another, Ferguson's riposte is unsupported by the contents of *TMS*. It is also inconsistent with Smith's attitude to users of his ideas (Blair, Robertson, Kames and Dalrymple).[18] Smith's ill-tempered remark to Ferguson was more from his lingering annoyance about the events in 1755 than anything to do with 1767.

The French author was Montesquieu.[19] And Smith acknowledged Montesquieu six times in his jurisprudence lectures.[20] The editors of LJ cite a further 20 unacknowledged

244 *Appendix: Smith's '1755 Paper'*

references from Montesquieu, but these omissions may be due to the students' incomplete note taking and the awkwardness of constant source referencing in speech.

John Millar, Smith's former student and later Professor of Law at Glasgow, makes reference to the debt of Smith to Montesquieu in his civil law but not in his moral philosophy lectures and places it in the context of a continuation of the development by Smith of Montesquieu's original but incomplete ideas:

> I am happy to acknowledge the obligations I feel myself under to this illustrious philosopher [Adam Smith], by having, at an early period of life, had the benefit of hearing his lectures on the History of Civil Society, and of enjoying his unreserved conversation on the same subject. The great Montesquieu pointed out the road. He was the Lord Bacon in this branch of philosophy. Dr. Smith is the Newton.[21]

Plausible suspicions of Smith's originality in 1755, based on reports from persons mildly acquainted with his lectures on 'The History of Civil Society' and re-told to others gave credence to the rumours. Ferguson had read Montesquieu and there is no doubt that Montesquieu influenced Smith. There were many other connections showing the influence of Montesquieu on the Scottish Enlightenment. 'It is entirely possible', suggests Ian Ross, 'that interest in Montesquieu's "philosophical history" was reflected in Smith's Edinburgh lectures on "civil law"'.[22]

In 1755, there were many people, perhaps amounting to several hundred persons, who had heard Smith's lectures, any of whom Ferguson was likely to have met and from whom he heard reports of the lectures they had attended, or read surviving fragments of their notes of them. That he had access to versions of Smith's lectures on his 'leading principles' might constitute circumstantial evidence that he had spread rumours, thereby starting off, or adding to, the gossip that eventually found its way to Smith's ears.

Ferguson, in his 1773 edition of *History of Civil Society*, conscious of his debts to Montesquieu, makes a bizarre apology:

> In his [Montesquieu's] writings will be found, not only the original if what I am now, for the sake of order, to copy from him, but likewise probably the source of many observations, which in different places, I may, under the belief of invention, have repeated, without quoting the author.[23]

In effect, he confesses to his own 'previous offences' of plagiarism when, 'under the belief of invention' he repeated Montesquieu's ideas as if they were his own. It was the same rumour affecting Smith's reputation.

Hutcheson's political economy

If the authors of the rumours read Hutcheson's posthumously published *System of Moral Philosophy* (1755) and used it to question claims by Smith to originality in political economy, we can see why he responded with a barrage of warm invective. Hutcheson's ideas on political economy were part of his lectures when Smith was his student, 1737–40.[24]

A case could be made merely by comparing some topics in Smith's Lectures on Jurisprudence, given in Glasgow from 1751 to 1755, with Books II and III of Hutcheson's book. A list of topics from Hutcheson includes: 'That opulence arises from the division of labour'; That the division of labour multiplies the product'; 'What gives occasion to the division of labour'; 'That the division of labour must be proportioned to the extent of commerce'; 'Natural price'; 'Market price'; Relations between market price and natural price'; 'Money as a measure of value'; Money as a medium of exchange'; national opulence does not consist of money'; 'Theory and the rate of interest'; 'Explanation of rent'; 'Education'; 'National and international trade'; 'Arms'; 'Maxims of taxation'.[25]

Stewart reported that 'many of the most important opinions' in the *Wealth of Nations* were detailed in the 1755 paper, suggesting that his principles were in circulation. Allegations of Smith's borrowing were fed by rumours of Hutcheson's 1755 book, some of them emanating from within Glasgow University.

Was James Wodrow, Library Keeper at the University, the source of the rumours? In 1752 he wrote: 'I hear [Smith] has thrown out some contemptuous Expressions of Mr Hutchinson. [sic] Let the young man take care to guard his Censures ... For there are some of Mr H[utcheso]ns scholars still about the Coll[ege] who perhaps will try to turn the mouths of the Cannon against himself.'[26] Hutcheson's son published his father's book in 1755. Did he fire the 'Cannon's mouth' at Smith's reputation, stirred by Wodrow? As Wodrow became a minister in Ayr in 1755, did Smith's rebuttal force him out?

A case against Ferguson

The authors of the gossip circulating in Edinburgh and Glasgow in 1755 cannot be identified. Gossip is not stored in libraries. It is in the nature of rumour that its sources dissolve in the re-telling, and that the certainties of the alleged details increase in specificity: what begins innocently with 'he was not the first' becomes 'his claims can be challenged' and may end with 'he is a plagiarist.'

Smith's leading principles, expressed orally, were in circulation, and were almost certainly accompanied by informal student notes. Ferguson, a well-read man, knew of 'similar' ideas in circulation authored by others (including Professor Hutcheson as reported in his 1755 book), though he was not a political economist able to distinguish between early insightful generalisations and more precise formulations. He admitted candidly, during a period in which he and Smith were getting on well, to Smith being a 'superior authority' in political economy.[27] He added one sentence and a footnote to the 1773 edition of his *History of Civil Society*, in which he 'willingly quit a subject [industry and trade] in which I am not conversant':

> Speculations on commerce and wealth have been delivered by the ablest writers, and the public will probably soon be furnished with a theory of national economy, equal to what has ever appeared on any subject of science whatever*.
> '*By Mr Smith, author of the *Theory of Moral Sentiments*'.[28]

Now, recall how Ferguson had denied that he had plagiarised Smith, but admitted he 'had derived many notions from a French author [Montesquieu], and that *Smith had been there before him*'. Ferguson's book was published in 1767, long before Smith published *Wealth of Nations* in 1776. Therefore, how did Ferguson know that 'Smith had been there before him'? In which of Smith's works was there evidence that Smith had plagiarised Montesquieu? In 1767 Smith's only published book was *Moral Sentiments* (1759), yet it hardly mentions subjects found in Montesquieu's *Esprit des*

Lois (1748) and certainly not enough to justify Ferguson's sarcastic riposte. If Smith's 'borrowings' were not in TMS, then where were they?

The only other source for rumours of Smith's plagiarisms of Montesquieu (or Hutcheson) were his (unpublished) lectures in jurisprudence and political economy, which he had been giving since before 1750. These certainly included references to Montesquieu (indeed, John Millar believed that in the civil law lectures Smith 'followed a plan that seems to be suggested by Montesquieu'). For Ferguson to justify his putdown reported by Carlyle, he had to be familiar with Smith's lectures and he could only have been familiar with them from discussions with people who had heard them – plus discourses with Smith himself – during which Ferguson thought he recognised the ideas of other people. Because Ferguson was never a student of Smith's and he had not been in Edinburgh during the 1748–51 lectures, and nor was he in Glasgow during 1752–4, there were no other sources for his information that Smith 'had been there before him'.

If Ferguson was a source of academic gossip about Smith, we have two proud men, basking in their own indignant innocence; one claiming others misquoted his innocent remarks about Montesquieu's originality; the other intimately knowledgeable of how extensively he had re-worked Montesquieu's and Hutcheson's contributions – an author knows the progeny of his ideas like a mother knows her children – and damning the gossip as an infamous calumny.

Perhaps Ferguson's acknowledgement of Smith's superiority in political economy was his way of apologising for speculating wrongly on the originality of Smith's leading principles 18 years earlier? The quid pro quo for agreeing to a published public apology might have been Smith's attempts on Ferguson's behalf to secure for him the tutorship of a ward of the Earl Stanhope in September 1773 and a general warming of their relationship for a short while.[29]

Smith was smart enough to realise the implication, as reported by Carlyle, of Ferguson's intemperate counter-charge. Ferguson confirmed that he knew of the contents of Smith's lectures when he accused Smith of having plagiarised Montesquieu in them twelve years earlier. If Ferguson still felt so strongly about it after 1767, Smith must have realised that Ferguson's incriminating self-denunciation made him a prime suspect for the rumours that had so enraged him in 1755.

This might explain why Smith's relations with Ferguson blew cold over his later years. Relations were still 'a little awkward' up to Smith's final illness in 1790, as Ferguson acknowledged in a letter to Sir John Macpherson reporting on Smith's death:

> We knew he was dying for some months, and though matters, as you know, were a little awkward when he was in health, upon that appearance I turned my face that way and went to him without further consideration, and continued my attentions to the last.[30]

Smith reacted negatively to Ferguson's the self-incrimination as a source for the 1755 allegations but, too ill to carry on an old fight on his deathbed, he accepted Ferguson's attempts to make amends with good grace.

The RSE meeting

We can return now to the 1793 meetings of the Royal Society of Edinburgh. There is a paucity of detail but no lack of curiosity into hinted discord among the Fellows, apart from the troublesome attention accorded to Dugald Stewart and others among Smith's friends by the authorities and the awesome shadow of the Edinburgh Sedition Trials over what should have been a solemn occasion in tribute to one of Scotland's praiseworthy luminaries.

John Rae concluded, most curiously of all, in his comments on the internal discord that 'had Ferguson been the cause of offence, Stewart would have probably avoided the subject altogether in a paper to the Royal Society, of which Ferguson was still an active member'.[31]

Because no attendance lists appear to have been taken or kept of the Fellows present at the RSE meetings of 21 January and 18 March 1793, we do not know if Adam Ferguson was present; we only know he was an 'active member'. Stewart's wording of certain of his remarks suggests that Ferguson was present. For example, Stewart included an enigmatic sentence in his address:

> For reasons known to some members of this society, it would be improper, by the publication of this manuscript, to revive the memory of private differences; and I should not have alluded to it, if I did not think it a valuable document of the progress of Mr Smith's political ideas at a very early period.[32]

Some of the Fellows knew full well to what and to whom Stewart referred, for Smith we can be sure had told many people in the years after 1755 his opinions of the spreaders of the rumours against him.

Publication of the 1755 manuscript would indeed revive the memory of 'private differences' in the RSE and, in deference to Smith's wishes, Stewart justified his partial 'publication' by asserting that the document had historical value and established 'the progress of Mr Smith's political ideas at a very early period.' However, if publication was to be avoided it is difficult to see how a mere assertion without proof could achieve the intention of establishing what was claimed for it. Was the evidence sufficient for us to rely solely on Stewart's assertions of the contents of the paper? Ian Ross hints at his scepticism about the 1755 'paper' (e.g., 'Stewart would have us believe').[33]

Stewart quoted from a paper to which nobody else had access; nobody else confirmed his selections from it or his descriptions of its tone and content; and no copies of it appear to have survived. Stewart's own copy 'disappeared': 'His son, Colonel Stewart, gave some documents of a mathematical nature to the United Service Club and burned the rest; It is to be feared that this manuscript was included in the fire.'[34]

We rely, therefore, on a second-hand report of an alleged primary source. Stewart's actions did not stifle the controversy, either about the dispute 'known to some members of this society', or about the validity of Smith's claims to his leading principles of political economy.

In an age when citation was haphazard, widespread disorder in the attribution of original work was common. It was Newton who averred, in an outburst of unnecessary modesty, that he had 'stood on the shoulders of giants'. Smith, in another context, commented on the modest indifference of great mathematicians (among them his contemporaries, 'Drs Matthew Stewart [Dugald's father and former student friend of Smith's] and Robert Simson') to public recognition of their discoveries.[35] Donald Winch notes that 'Smith was not, of course, alone in dealing with the commerce and liberty theme', and he cites both Montesquieu and Hume among it progenitors, supported by various other major contributors to the Scottish

Enlightenment (Lord Kames, Adam Ferguson, William Robertson and John Millar).[36] Smith's originality, Winch suggests, consisted of 'giving more prominence to the subject', of introducing 'a number of significant changes of emphasis which entail a shift towards a more complex and qualified story than the one to be found in the pages of Montesquieu and Hume'. Together Smith's contribution 'constitutes a major modification to the older portrait' of these other writers.[37]

Notes

Preface and Acknowledgements

1 Stewart, 1793; Rae, 1895
2 Ross, 1995: 133
3 Denis, 2003
4 see: Loasby, 2002
5 Woodrow, 1751

General Introduction

1 LJ(B) 331–2: 540–1
2 WN IV.vii.b.11: 570
3 TMS VI.ii.2.17
4 TMS VI.ii.2.15
5 TMS VI.ii.2.16

Part I   The Man

Introduction

1 EPS Stewart, 1793
2 Rae, J. 1895
3 Ross, I. 1995
4 Carlyle, A. 1860; Clayden, P. W. 1887
5 Scott, W. R. 1937; Rothschild, 2001

1   Smith's Family Background

1 EPS Stewart, I.2
2 Ross, I. 1995: 246
3 EPS Stewart, Note K, 349–50
4 Ross, I. 210, 213, 214
5 Ross, I. 214
6 EPS Stewart, V.3
7 Hirst, 1904
8 Corr. no. 237

2   Disease of the Learned

1 WN V.i.f.8
2 EPS Stewart, II.46
3 TMS VII.ii.1.27
4 Corr. no. 3

5   Corr. no. 1
6   Mossner, 1980: 67
7   Scott, 1937: 42; cf. Ross, 1995: 77–8
8   Corr. no. 6
9   Rae, 1895: 25
10   Berkeley, 1744
11   Ross, 1995: 76, quoting Barfoot, 1991
12   Berkeley, 1744
13   Rae, 1895: 25; Mossner, 1980: 67–80
14   Mossner, 1980: 70, citing Hume, 1932
15   Corr. no. 10 and Notes 2, 3 and 4
16   Corr. no. 156
17   Corr. no. 137
18   Corr. no. 157
19   Corr. no. 165
20   Corr. no. 166
21   Corr. no. 168
22   Corr. no. 170
23   Corr. no. 171
24   Ross, 1995: 304
25   Corr. no. 172
26   Corr. no. 208; Reeder, 1977: 99–102

3   His 'Juvenile Work'

1   EPS 31–105
2   Corr. no. 137
3   EPS Intro: 6–7; II.12, n.12; IV.75 n.16, 17
4   EPS II.12
5   EPS III.1
6   Ellingson, 2001
7   EPS Intro 1
8   EPS II.12
9   EPS II.9
10   Dawkins, 1998
11   EPS II.10
12   EPS II.10
13   EPS II.12
14   Buchan, 2003: 125
15   EPS III.2
16   EPS III.2
17   EPS III.2
18   Frazer, 1890
19   Campbell, 1971: 69
20   Mossner, 1954: 74
21   Hume, 1739–40
22   *Optiks*, 1721, cited in Mossner, 1954: 73–4
23   Bonar, 1932: 122
24   TMS VII.iii.3; cf. Montes, 2004: 130–64
25   EPS IV.76

26 Campbell, 1975: 70
27 EPS II.12

4 Bad Days at Balliol

1 McCulloch, 1855; 1862: ii; Scott, 1937: 42; Ross, 1995: 77, cites: J. Strang, 1857: 28
2 TMS VII.ii.1.25
3 TMS VII.ii.1.26
4 Ross, 1995: 79
5 Corr. no. 1
6 EPS Stewart, I.11
7 Scott, 1937: 43
8 EPS Stewart, I.11
9 Rae, 1895: 22
10 Scott, 1937: 44
11 Rae, 1895: 25–26
12 Ross, 1995: 78
13 Ross, 1995: 79, citing Addison, 1901: 19–22

5 A Game of Great Skill

1 Beaglehole, 1974; Kennedy, 1989
2 Corr. no. 238
3 Corr. no. 66
4 Corr. no. 224
5 Corr. no. 236
6 TMS. VII.ii.1.24
7 Corr. no. 6
8 Heilbroner, 1961
9 Ross, 1995: 142, 152, 226, 237, 245, 310, 316, 317
10 Cosh, 2003: 23
11 Carlyle, 1860
12 Scott, 1937: 62–3
13 Scott, 1937: 77–8

6 His Strategic Allegiance

1 Shaw, 1999: 72
2 Shaw, 1999: 66
3 Shaw, 1999: 67
4 Carlyle, 1860: 382
5 Ross, 1995: 68, citing Balliol MS, 11 March 1740
6 Rae, 1895: 20
7 Ross, 1995: 151, citing GU Archives 26645
8 Rae, 1895: 31–32
9 LRBL: 8, quoting Tyler, 1807: I, 190
10 Rae, 1895: 31–32; Ross, 1995: 86
11 Corr. no. 25

7 Professor Smith!

1 Ross, 1995: 84
2 Emerson, 1995: 21–39
3 Corr. no. 304
4 Ross, 1995: 109
5 Scott, 1937: 137–8
6 Corr. no. 8
7 Rae, 1895: 42; Ross, 1995: 109
8 Corr. no. 8
9 Lenman, 1981: 31
10 EPS Stewart, I.17
11 Corr. no. 9
12 Corr. no. 9
13 Corr. no. 10; Hirst, 1904: 27
14 Scott, 1937: 140
15 TMS Introduction: 36; Corr. no. 33

Part II   Impartial Spectators

Introduction

1 Berkeley, 1744

8 The Religious Climate

1 Hirschman, 1977: 15
2 Matthew, 19.24
3 Matthew, 6.19, 6.24
4 Matthew, 19.24
5 Mark, 8.36
6 I. Timothy, 3.2–3, 6.10
7 Muller, 1993: 41–44; Parry & Bloch, 1989
8 Gibbon, 1776–88
9 Hirschman, 1977; Muller, 1993
10 Braudel, 1979: 171–2
11 Minowitz, 1993

9 On Benevolence

1 Corr. no. 31
2 TMS VII.ii.3.2
3 TMS VII.ii.3.3; cf. Montes, 2004, note 14
4 TMS VII.ii.3.2
5 TMS VII.ii.3.2
6 TMS VII.ii.3.3
7 TMS VII.ii.3.4
8 TMS VII.ii.3.4
9 TMS VII.ii.3.5

10 TMS VII.ii.3.6
11 TMS VII.ii.3.6
12 TMS VII.ii.3.6
13 TMS VII.ii.3.7
14 TMS VII.ii.3.7
15 TMS VII.ii.3.12
16 TMS VII.ii.3.14
17 TMS VII.ii.3.16
18 TMS VII.ii.3.16
19 TMS VII.ii.3.16
20 TMS VII.ii.3.18
21 John, 14.2
22 TMS VII.ii.18
23 TMS VII.ii.3.1–3.21
24 cf. Montes, 2004: 15–56

10 A Poem about a Louse

1 Burns, 2001: 130–2: *To a Louse: On Seeing One on a Lady's Bonnet at Church* (1786)
2 Rae, 402
3 Macfie, 1967: 66; Raphael, 1975: 89, n.18
4 TMS III.4.6
5 Noble and Hogg, 133
6 TMS II.2.1
7 TMS II.2.1
8 Hobbes, (1651) 1946: 82–83
9 TMS II.ii.2.1
10 TMS II.ii.2.2
11 TMS II.ii.2.1
12 TMS II.ii.3
13 TMS II.ii.3 n.1

11 The Impartial Spectator

1 TMS I.i.1.1
2 TMS I.i.1.2
3 TMS I.i.1.3
4 *As You Like It*, Act II, Scene VII
5 Griswold, 1999: 63–70
6 TMS I.i.1.5
7 TMS I.i.1.5 n.1
8 TMS I.ii.2.1
9 TMS I.i.2.2
10 TMS I.i.2.4
11 TMS I.i.3.1
12 TMS I.i.3.8
13 TMS I.i.4.6
14 TMS I.i.4.9
15 Montes, 2004: 40–41; Nieli, 1986; Otteson, 2000
16 TMS I.i.4.7

17   TMS I.i.4.10
18   TMS I.i.5.4
19   TMS I.i.5.5

12   The Looking Glass

1   TMS III.1.2
2   TMS III.1.3
3   TMS III.1.3
4   TMS III.I.3
5   TMS III.1.4
6   TMS I.1.5
7   TMS I.1.5
8   TMS I.1.6
9   TMS III.1.7
10   TMS III.2.1
11   TMS III.2.3
12   TMS III.2.4
13   TMS III.2.4

13   Social Cohesion

1   Matthew, 4.4
2   TMS VI.ii.1.1
3   TMS VI.ii.1.3
4   TMS VI.ii.1.7
5   TMS VI.ii.1.11
6   TMS VI.ii.1.16
7   TMS VI.ii.1.17
8   TMS VI.ii.1.19
9   TMS VI.ii.1.20
10   Millar, (1771) 1806
11   TMS VI.ii.1.20
12   TMS VI.ii.1.20
13   TMS II.ii.3.1
14   TMS II.ii.3.1
15   TMS II.ii.3.2
16   TMS II.ii.3.3
17   TMS II.ii.3.4
18   Otteson, 2002: 170–98
19   Kropotkin, 1939; Otteson, 2000: 51–74
20   TMS II.ii.3.4
21   Montesquieu, 1949: xiv

14   The Ends of Nature

1   Cropsey, 2001: 1
2   TMS II.i.5.10
3   TMS II.i.5.9

4 TMS II.i.5.10
5 TMS II.ii.5.10
6 TMS II.ii.3.6
7 TMS II.ii.3.6
8 TMS II.ii.3.7
9 TMS II.ii.3.9
10 TMS II.iii.3.1
11 TMS II.iii.3.2
12 TMS II.iii.3.3
13 Cropsey, 1
14 Montes, 2004: 41, n.48

Part III Impartial Jurists

Introduction

1 Corr. no. 248; Ross, 1995: 101, 405, 413
2 EPS Stewart, II.53
3 TMS VII.iv.37
4 TMS advertisement
5 *Lectures in Jurisprudence (Report of 1762–3; Report dated 1766)*, hitherto LJ(A) and LJ(B)

15 Justice as a Negative Virtue

1 TMS II.ii.1.4
2 Shaw, 1978: 25
3 Hume, 1985 (1740): 549
4 Haakonsson, 1981: 89
5 TMS VII.iv.36
6 TMS VII.iv.36
7 TMS II.ii.2.2; cf. Fleischacker, 2004
8 TMS II.ii.2.2
9 TMS III.6.10–11
10 LJ(B) 11
11 LJ(B) 13; cf. TMS I.iii.2.1–2.3; I.iii.3.2; VI.ii.1.20–1.21
12 LJ(B) 13–14
13 Ross, 1972; Herman, 2001: 89-90
14 LJ(A) 101–148; LJ(A) 438-458; Sutherland, 1995: 97–121; cf. Dwyer, 1998; Buchan, 2003

16 Constitutional Monarchy

1 LJ(B) 14
2 LJ(B) 15
3 LJ(B) 15
4 Forbes, 1975: 179–201; Winch, 1978: 46–69
5 LJ(A) v.5
6 LJ(A) v.1

17   Foundations of Liberty

1   LJ(A) v.5–6
2   LJ(A) v.15
3   LJ(A) v.7–8
4   LJ(A)x LJ(A) v.31; v.35; v.37; v.40, n.90
5   LJ(A) v.6–7
6   LJ(A) v.8
7   LJ(A) v.10–12
8   GUA 26645; S 187, in Ross, 1995: 151

18   History as Imagination

1   Charlevoix, (1722) 1761; Lafitau, 1974 (1735); Cook (1774, 1784)
2   Olson, 2002: 205
3   Locke, 1690: 343; Meek, 1976: 22, 40–1
4   Hobbes, 1946 [1651]: 82
5   Rousseau, 1984 [1755]
6   Hobbes, 1946 [1651]: 82
7   Hobbes, 1946 [1651]: 83
8   Hobbes, 1946 [1651]: 83
9   Hobbes, 1946 [1651]: 83, (emphasis added)
10   LJ(A) i.28
11   Meek, 1976: 14; Grotius, 1964 [1625]: 186–90
12   Genesis, 3.17–19
13   WN V.1.a., note 2
14   Cavalli-Sforza and Cavalli-Sforza, 1995; Olson, 2002
15   Boyd and Silk, 1997; Deacon, 1997
16   WN I.ii.1

19   The Four Stages

1   Stordalen, 2000
2   Genesis, 3.1–19; and 4.2–16
3   Genesis, 4.16
4   Genesis, 4.17
5   LJ(A) i.27
6   Meek, 1976: 29; Pescarelli, 1986: 84
7   Muller, 1993: 117; Lehmann, 1971: chapters 12–13; Meek, 1971: 3–27; 1976: 110
8   Meek, 1976; Dalrymple, 1757; Kames, 1758
9   Rousseau, J-J. 1984 [1755]: intro: 29; Meek, 1976: 76–94; Darwin, 1859; Kohn, 1999
10   Charlevoix, 1744; LJ (A) i.47 note 21; LJ(A) iv.5, note 43
11   LJ(B) 19
12   LJ(A) i.28
13   Kennedy, 1989; Mackaness, G. 1931
14   LJ (A) i.28
15   LJ(B) 20–22
16   Genesis, 11.27–25.8
17   LJ(A) i.29

18 cf. Tudge, 1998
19 LJ(A) i.30
20 Matthew 13.3–8
21 LJ(A) 15
22 LJ(A) 15–16; my emphasis
23 LJ(A) 16

20 Was He Aware of a Fifth Stage?

1 Ginzberg, 2002: 68–69
2 Cropsey, 2001: 67–8
3 Reid, 1989: 59–70
4 Malthus, 1798
5 Reid, 1989: 3–29

Part IV Impartial Competition

Introduction

1 Hutcheson, 1755; Pesciarelli, 1986
2 Bonar, 1932: Montesquieu, 118–9; Cantillon, 40; Quesnay, 152–4; Mirabeau, 117; and Turgot, 188.
3 Eltis, 1984: chapter 9: 310–38
4 WN IV.ix.38
5 EPS Stewart, III.12

21 A Linguistic Osmosis

1 Samuelson, 9th ed. 1973: 840
2 Stigler, 1975: 237
3 Rosenberg, 1975: 377
4 West, 1975: 543
5 Teichgraeber, 1986: 5 and 7; Preface, xiii
6 Winch, 1978: 1
7 Rashid, 1998: 47
8 Williams, 2000: 8
9 Cropsey, 2001: Introduction
10 Otteson, 2002: 175 (See also footnote 5, p. 175)
11 Tribe, 1995: 41
12 Griswold, 1999: 8–9
13 MacGregor, 1949; Brown, 1994; Robbins, 1998; Peacock, 1997; Rothschild, 2001; Ginzberg, 2002; Montes, 2004
14 Viner, 1928: 154–55, in Clark, 1928
15 Brown, 1994: 220

22 Insufficiency of Self-love

1 WN I.ii.2
2 WN I.ii.1
3 WN I.ii.2

4   LRBL 201–226
5   Kohn, 1999; Schick & Toth, 1993
6   WN I.ii.2
7   LJ(A) v.45

23   Self-love and Conditionality

1   LJ(B) 219–20
2   WN I.ii.2
3   WN I.ii.2
4   WN I.ii.2
5   WN I.ii.2
6   WN I.ii.2
7   LJ(A) vi.45
8   LJ(B) 219
9   WN I.ii.2
10   WN I.ii.2
11   WN I.ii.2
12   Nash, 1950; 1953
13   Browne and Taylor, 1994: 19
14   Wicksteed, 1910: 174–80, cited in Robbins, 1933: i.174; 1998: 132–3; cf. Wilson, 1976: 81, n.9
15   Wilson, 1976: 82

24   Of the Process of Negotiation

1   TMS II.ii.3.2
2   Kennedy, 1998: 5
3   Douglas, 1962; Walton & McKersie, 1965
4   Kennedy et al, 1980; Rackham & Carlisle, 1978
5   TMS I.i.4.9
6   TMS I.i.4.10
7   TMS I.i.3.2
8   TMS I.i.4.5
9   Zeuthen, 1930; Pen, 1952; Shackle, 1964; Cross, 1965; Coddington, 1968
10   TMS I.i.4.7
11   TMS I.i.4.8
12   TMS I.i.4.9
13   TMS I.i.4.10

25   Of Distracting and Dismal Confusions

1   WN I.ii.2
2   LJ(A) vi.46
3   LJ(B) 219
4   Macpherson, 1899: 75–6
5   Macpherson, 1899: 78
6   Rae, 1895
7   West, 1975: 548–9

8 Zeuthen, 1930; Hicks, 1931
9 Cross, 1965; Young, 1975

26 Of Pins and Things

1 Robbins, 1998: 129
2 Pesciarelli, 1986
3 WN I.iii.1
4 Plato, 1987 *The Republic*
5 Petty, 1683
6 WN I.i.3
7 Rashid, 1998: 14–29; 1997
8 Rogers, 1909: 26–7
9 Rogers, 1909: vii
10 WN I.i.3
11 WN I.i.6
12 Petty, 1683: 36–7; cited in WN: n.13
13 WN I.i.5
14 WN I.i.8
15 Rashid, 1998: 23
16 WN I.i.9
17 WN V.i.f.50; West, 1975: 547–8
18 WN I.i.9
19 WN I.i.9
20 WN I.i.9
21 WN I.i.10

27 Of Common Coats and Opulence

1 WN I.i.10
2 Mandeville, (1724) in Kaye, ed.
3 WN I.i.11
4 WN I.i.11
5 Robbins, 1998: 131
6 LJ(A) vi.26
7 LJ(A) vi.28

28 Alienation: Rhetoric or Substance?

1 WN V.i.f.50
2 Ferguson, (1767) ed. Forbes, 1966: 182–3
3 Marx, 1867: 123, n.1; 354; 361–2
4 WN 143–4
5 Hirschman, 1977: 105
6 WN V.i.f.50
7 Ferguson, ed. Forbes: 232–3; 270–1
8 WN V.I.f.54
9 McCulloch, 1863, ed. 58, n.1
10 McCulloch, 1863, ed. 550, n.1; West, 1975: 550, n.10

29   What Industrial Revolution?

1 Rae, 1895: 71; Hirst: 1904: 83; 96–7
2 Rostow, 1971: 38
3 Ashton, 1948: 65
4 Corr. no. 147
5 Hollander, 1973: 222, 237 and 241
6 Koebner, 1959: 389; Blaug, 1968: 39; Hollander, 1973, n.43, 89; Rashid, 1998
7 Kindleberger: 6
8 Hartwell, 1967: 1–52; 1971; 1976: 33–41
9 Hartwell, 1976: 34
10 Hartwell, 1976: 38
11 Rae, 1895: 169
12 Bonar, 1932
13 Hartwell, 1976: 38
14 Corr. no. 121
15 Corr. no. 145
16 Corr. no. 85
17 Corr. no. 132
18 Corr. no. 147

30   Significance of Smith's 'Unawareness'?

1 Cunningham, 1912: 612–4
2 Uglow, 2002: 21
3 WN I: x.1.42; I.x.c.9; III.iii.20
4 Silver, 1995
5 Talbot, 2002; Gupta, ed., 2002
6 WN I.viii.24; cf. Wood, 1996
7 WN IV.vii.c.79

31   Why Smith 'Retired'

1 Corr. no. 208
2 WN IV.vii.c.78
3 WN IV.vii.c.77
4 WN IV.vii.c.79
5 Rothschild, 2001: 55–6
6 Corr. no. 208
7 Corr. no. 208
8 Corr. no. 208
9 EPS Stewart, IV.7
10 EPS Stewart, IV.2
11 EPS Stewart, Note (G): 339
12 Osborne, B. D. 1997; Logue, 1979
13 Stewart, 1858: vol. 10
14 Howell, 1817; Cockburn, 1856, 1888; Stewart, 1858; Rothschild, 2001, 56–61; Logue, 1979

Chapter 32   On Laissez Faire

1   Jones, 1963: 263
2   EPS 322, emphasis added
3   LRBL i.1
4   WN IV.v.b.1–53; cf. Rashid, 1998: 115–34
5   WN IV.v.b.43
6   WN IV.ix.2
7   WN IV.ix.50
8   WN IV.ix.51
9   Corr. nos. 89, 91, 105, 126, 130, 194, 199, 213, 218, 277; EPS, 217–225; Clayden, 1887: 166–7; Bonar, (1894), 1932; Ross, 1995: 364–70
10 MacGregor, 1949: 54–55
11 MacGregor, 1949: 54–89
12 MacGregor, 1949: 57
13 MacGregor, 1949; cf. EPS Stewart, IV.23
14 MacGregor, 1949: 65
15 Quesnay, 1767
16 MacGregor, 1949: 66
17 MacGregor, 1949: 56
18 Samuelson, 9th ed. 1973: 840

33   The Wonderful World of Adam Smith?

1   Heilbroner, 1961
2   cf. Carroll, 1998
3   Heilbroner, 2000
4   Heilbroner, 1997
5   Heilbroner, 1961: 43
6   Heilbroner, 1961: 42
7   Heilbroner, 1961: 44
8   Heilbroner, 1961: 51
9   Heilbroner, 1961: 52–3
10 Ross, 1995: 214–17
11 Heilbroner, 1961: 54

34   In the Absence of Perfect Liberty

1   TMS VI.ii.2.17
2   WN I.viii.12
3   WN I.viii.13
4   WN I.viii.13
5   WN I.viii.13
6   WN I.viii.13
7   Logue, 1979: 155–60

35   Monopolists in Product Markets

1   WN I.vii.27
2   WN I.ix

3   Ross, 1995: 146–7; Rae, 1895: 71; Scott, 1937: n.149
4   WN IV.ii 43
5   WN I.vii.24
6   WN I.x.c.6
7   WN I.x.c.18
8   WN I.x.c.21
9   WN I.x.c.25
10 WN I.x.c.27
11 WN I.x.c.31

36   Against the Public Interest

1   WN I.xi.p.10
2   WN I.xi.p.10
3   Robbins, 1952; Blaug, 1971 (1958), Coats, 1971b

37   The Impartial Competitor

1   WN I.x.10
2   Rosenberg, 1975: 381
3   Rosenberg, 1975: 380
4   WN I.viii.44
5   Young, A. 1771
6   Temple, 1758, quoted in Rosenberg, 1975: 379
7   WN II.iii.31
8   WN II.iii.28
9   WN I.viii.43
10 Hollander, 1973: 97
11 WN I.xi.p.8
12 WN I.xi.p.9
13 WN I.xi.p.10
14 WN I.xi.p.10
15 WN I.xi.p.10

38   The Mercantile System

1   WN Book IV
2   WN IV. introduction
3   Gray and Thompson, 1980: 53–82
4   WN IV.i.10
5   WN IV.i.17
6   WN IV.i.11
7   WN IV.ii.1

39   The 'Invisible Hand'

1   WN IV.ii.2
2   EPS III.2; TMS IV.1.10; WN IV.ii.9
3   WN IV.ii.4–12
4   TMS IV.1.10

5 TMS IV.1.10
6 Denis, 2003
7 Rothschild, 2001: 119
8 Macbeth, Act III.2
9 WN IV.ii.4–6
10 WN IV.ii.9

40 The Ends of Monopoly?

1 WN IV.ii.11
2 WN IV.ii.12
3 WN IV.ii.15

41 Smithian Markets

1 Braudel, 1985: 28–9
2 Braudel, 1985: 42
3 Braudel, 1985: 44–47
4 Braudel, 1985: 36

42 Commercial Revival

1 Devine, 1995: 17–36
2 Devine, 1995: 25
3 Devine, 1995: 19
4 Devine, 1995: 23
5 Devine, 1995: 24
6 Devine, 1995: 27
7 Devine, 1995: 30
8 Devine, 1995: 27
9 Devine, 1995: 34, n.31
10 Uglow, 2002: 17; citing *Sketchley's Birmingham Directory*, 1767
11 Uglow, 2002: 23
12 WN I.x.b.42
13 WM III.iii.20
14 Walsh & Gram, 1980
15 Walsh and Gram, 1980: 26
16 Rude, 1974: 84, cited in Walsh & Gram, 1980: 27
17 O'Farrell, 2004: 21

43 Of the Virtues of Frugality

1 WN II.iii.6
2 WN II.iii.14
3 WN II.iii.7
4 WN II.iii.20
5 WN II.iii.25
6 WN II.iii.26
7 Eltis, 1984: 64–105; Walsh & Gram, 1980: 61–70; Ginzberg, 2002
8 WN III.iv.24

9 WN III.iv.24
10 Dwyer, 1998
11 WN III.iv.19

44 On Market Interference

1 WN I.x.c.7
2 WN I.x.c.12
3 WN I.x.c.13
4 WN I.x.c.16
5 WN I.x.c.16
6 WN I.x.c.61
7 WN I.x.c.61
8 WN I.x.c.45
9 WN I.x.c. n.50

45 Famous Exceptions to Free Trade

1 Viner, 1928; Gordon, 1971; Lubasz, 1975
2 WN IV.ii.30
3 WN IV.ii.26
4 WN IV.ii.30
5 WN I.ii.31
6 WN I.ii.35
7 WN I.ii.38
8 WN I.ii.40

46 Of Strawberries and Buttons

1 Viner, 1928: 118
2 Viner, 1928: 126
3 Millar, 1806
4 Cropsey, 2001: 89–90; Pownall, 1776: 13–15; Rashid, 1998: 30–51
5 Cairnes, 1874; Hutchison, 1953
6 Reid, 1989
7 Clayden, 1887
8 WN I.vii.4
9 Corr. no. 150
10 WN I.vii.9
11 WN I.vii.13
12 WN I.vii.14
13 WN I.vii.30
14 WN I.vii.15
15 Steuart, 1966 (1767)

47 Cheerful and Hearty Economics

1 WN I.viii.6
2 WN I.viii.7–8
3 WN I.xi.a.5

4   WN I.Viii.11
5   WN I.viii.15
6   WN I.viii.17
7   WN I.viii.19
8   WN I.viii.21 – emphasis added
9   WN I.viii.22
10   WN I.viii.43
11   WN I.ix.2
12   WN I.x.b.1

48   Accumulation and Employment of Stock

1   WN II.3
2   WN II.i.4–5
3   WN II.i.8
4   WN II.i.12
5   WN II.i.13–17
6   WN II.i.18–22
7   WN II.i.30

49   On Doing More Harm than Good

1   Walsh & Gram, 1980: 67; Ginzberg, 2002
2   Eltis & Bacon, 1976
3   WN II.iii.14
4   WN II.iii.16
5   Haddon, 1981
6   WN V.i.e.7
7   WN V.i.e.10
8   WN V.i.e.10
9   WN V.i.e.3.18
10   WN V.i.e.3.18
11   WN V.i.e.30
12   WN V.i.e.32
13   WN V.i.e.40
14   WN V.i.e.40
15   WN V.i.e.21
16   Porter, 1990: 87
17   WN V.i.e.29

50   Doom and Gloom?

1   Heilbroner, 1975: 524–39
2   Heilbroner, 1975: 528–9
3   Lowe, 1975: 415–25; Heilbroner, 1975: 526
4   WN I.ix.14
5   WN I.ix.14–15 n.32
6   Lomberg, 2001; Malthus, 1798; Meadows, D. et al, 1972
7   Heilbroner, 1975: 536
8   Peacock, 1997: 48–55; also Eltis, 1984: 100–05

9 Adelman, 1961: 25–42
10 Eltis, 1984: 91–100; 1975: 426–54
11 Eltis, 1984: 105
12 Adelman, 35
13 WN I.ix.14–15; Adelman, 1961: 37

51 Of Grandchildren and Grandparents

1 Keynes, J. M. (1930) 1952: 364–5
2 Keynes, 1930: 358
3 Lowe, 1975: 415–25
4 Heilbroner, 1975: 526
5 Lowe, 1975: 421
6 WN I.viii.35
7 Eltis, 1984: 303–9
8 WN I.viii.35
9 Heilbroner, 1975: 536
10 WN I.viii.24; I.ix.15
11 WN I.viii.26
12 WN I.xi.c.7
13 Lowe, 1975: 420
14 Hollander, 1973: 240–1
15 WN I.viii.36
16 WN I.viii.36

52 A 'Night Watchman' State?

1 EPS Stewart, IV.25
2 Macintyre, 2003
3 Robbins, 1952: 34
4 WN V.i.a.1
5 Kennedy, 1975: 23–39
6 Deane, 1975: 91
7 Benoit, 1973: 17–24
8 John, 1954: 344
9 Deane, 1975: 92
10 Mathias, 1975: 73
11 cf. Benoit: 1973; Kennedy, 1974; Winter, 1975
12 Winter, 1975
13 Kennedy, 1974
14 Ashton, 1948: 65
15 WN V.i.a.1–44
16 WN V.i.a.44
17 Kennedy, 1974

53 Smith's Immodest Proposals for Public Expenditures

1 WN V.i.b.14
2 WN V.i.b.25

3 Shaw, 1978: 25
4 Johnson, 1978: 43
5 Shaw, 1978: 48; Martin, 1978
6 Shaw, 1978: 363
7 WN V.i.d.3
8 WN V.i.d.7
9 WN V.i.d.18
10 WN V.i.d.19
11 Frankel, 1980
12 Smiles, 1863, Chapter iv; cf. Pike, R., 1974: 142–53
13 Smiles, 1863

54 Education and Health Expenditures

1 WN V.i.f.4
2 WN V.i.f.7
3 Peacock, 1992: 57–83; 1978: 117–28
4 WN V.i.b.20
5 WN V.i.f.54–56
6 WN V.i.f.50
7 WN V.i.f.61
8 WN V.i.f.55
9 WN V.i.f.60
10 WN V.i.f.60
11 WN V.i.a.12; WN V.i.f.58
12 WN V.i.f.60

55 Public Revenues

1 WN V.ii.a.21
2 WN V.ii.a.7
3 Peacock, 1975: 561
4 WN V.ii.b.3–6
5 WN V.ii.b.7
6 Stigler, 1975
7 Stigler, 1975: 243
8 Stigler, 1975: 243
9 Stigler, 1975: 238–9
10 Peacock, 1975: 566
11 Stigler, 1975: 244
12 WN IV.v.b.43; emphasis added

56 Government Failure

1 WN V.i.c.1
2 WN V.i.d.3
3 WN V.i.d.5
4 WN V.i.d.1
5 WN V.i.d.3

6   WN V.i.d.4
7   WN V.i.d.6
8   WN V.i.d.7
9   WN V.i.d.8
10   WN V.i.d.12
11   WN V.i.d.14
12   Robinson, 1985: 427
13   Blaug, 1975: 568–99

57   Reclaiming Smith's Legacy

1   Gordon, 1971: 202; 1955
2   Smiles, 1889: 358–9; cited in Gordon, 1971: 184; cf. Cairnes, 1965: 247–252
3   Cosh, 2003: 1–2
4   WN III.iv.10
5   WN IV.ii.43
6   WN IV.ii.43

Appendix   Smith's '1755 Paper'

1   EPS Stewart, 1793: IV.25
2   RSE, 1793: 79
3   Rae, 1895: 101–40; Ross, 1995: 140
4   Stewart, 1793: IV.25
5   EPS Stewart, 1793: IV.25
6   Ross, 1995: 95–96; Rae, 1895: 33
7   Robertson, 1769; Ross, 1995: 105–6; Callander, EUL; Scott, 1937: 55
8   Rousseau, 1755; Smith, 1755; Lindgreen, 1967: 25, 162; Meek, 1976: 116
9   EPS Stewart, 1793: IV.26
10   Rashid, 1998; cf. Gray, 1948: 18–19; cf. Meek, 1973
11   Woodrow, 1751; Ross, 1995: 111
12   EPS Stewart, IV.25
13   EPS Stewart, IV.26
14   Rashid, 1998
15   Corr. no. 17; no. 18
16   Bonar, 1932 [1894]: 68–9
17   Carlyle, 1860
18   Kames, 1758; Dalrymple, 1757
19   Montesquieu, 1748
20   LJ: index
21   J. Millar, 1803; Ross, 1995: 120
22   Ross, 1995: 107
23   Forbes, ed., 1966: 65
24   Scott, 1937: 112
25   Pesciarelli, 1986, Table 3, p. 77; cf. LJ, passim; Hutcheson, 1755: Books II and III
26   Ross, 1995: 111
27   Ross, 1995: 230
28   Forbes ed., 1966: 144–5; 287
29   Corr. no. 138; no. 139; no. 141; no. 142; no. 154; no. 155; Ross, 1995: 253–4
30   Ross, 1995: 404

31 Rae, 1895: 65
32 EPS Stewart, IV. 25
33 Ross, 1995: 107
34 Scott, 1937: 120
35 TMS 124
36 Winch, 1978, p. 70
37 Winch, 1978, p. 71

Select Bibliography

Addison, W. L. 1901. *The Snell Exhibitions from the University of Glasgow to Balliol College, 1728–1858*, J. Maclehose, Glasgow

Adelman, I. 1961. *Theories of Economic Growth and Development*, Stanford University Press, Stanford

Annas, J. 1981. *An Introduction to Plato's Republic*, Oxford University Press, Oxford

Ashton, T. S. 1948. *The Industrial Revolution: 1760–1830*, Oxford University Press, Oxford

Barfoot, M. 1991. 'Dr. William Cullen and Mr Adam Smith: a case of hypochondriasis?' *Proceedings of the Royal College of Physicians of Edinburgh*, 1991, vol. 21, pp. 204–21

Beaglehole, J. C. 1974. *The Life of Captain James Cook*, London

Benoit, E. 1973. *Defense and Economic Growth in Developing Countries*, D. C. Heath, Lexington, Mass.

Berkeley, G. 1744. 'SIRIS: a chain of Philosophical Reflexions and Inquiries Concerning the Virtues of Tar-Water', Innys and Hitch, London

Blaug, M. 1968. *Economic Theory in Retrospect*, 1968, 2nd Ed., London

Blaug, M. 1971 (1958). 'The Classical economists and the Factory Acts – a re-examination,' in Coats, 1971: 104–122

Blaug, M. 1975. 'The Economics of Education in English Classical Political Economy: a re-examination,' in Skinner and Wilson, 1975: 568–99

Bonar, J. 1932 (1894). *A Catalogue of the Library of Adam Smith*, 1894 (2nd edition 1932)

Boyd, R. and Silk, J. 1997. *How Humans Evolved*, Norton, New York

Braudel, F. [1979], 1985. *The Wheels of Commerce*, vol. II, *Civilisation and Capitalism 15th–18th Century*, trans S. Reynolds, Collins, London

Brown, V. 1994. *Adam Smith's Discourse: canonicity, commerce and conscience*, Routledge, London

Brown, K. and Taylor, W. B. 1994. *The Horner Papers, selections from the Letters and Miscellaneous writings of Francis Horner, MP, 1795–1817*, Edinburgh University Press, Edinburgh

Buchan, J. 2003. *Capital of the Mind: how Edinburgh changed the world*, John Murray, London

Cairnes, J. E. 1965 [1873]. *Essays in Political Economy*, Augustas Kelly, New York

Cairnes, J. E. 1874. *Leading Principles of Political Economy, Newly Expounded*, Macmillan, London

Callander, J. Edinburgh University Library, MSS. La II, pp. 451/2

Campbell, T. D. 1971. *Adam Smith's Science of Morals*, George Allen & Unwin, London

Campbell, T. D. 1975. 'Scientific Explanation and Ethical Justification in the *Theory of Moral Sentiments*', in A. S. Skinner and T. Wilson, 1975: 68–82

Cannan, E. ed. 1928. *Adam Smith Lectures Commemorating the Sequicentennial of the Publication of the Wealth of Nations*, University of Chicago Press, Chicago

Cantillon, R. 1971 (1755). *Essai sue la Nature du Commerce en General*, edited and translated, Henry Higgs, A. M. Kelly, New York

Carlyle, A. (1860, 2nd ed.), *Autobiography of the Rev. Dr Alexander Carlyle, Minister of Inveresk, containing memorials of the men and events of his time*, Blackwood, Edinburgh

Carroll, M. C. 1998. *A Future of Capitalism: the economic vision of Robert Heilbroner*, St Martins Press, New York

Cavalli-Sforza, L. L. and Cavalli-Sforza, F. C. 1995. *The Great Human Diasporas: the history of diversity and evolution*, Addison-Wesley, Reading, Mass.

Charlevoix, Pierre-Francois-Xavier de, [1722] 1761. *Journal of a Voyage to North-America, Undertaken by Order of the French King*, London

Charlevoix, 1744, *Histoire et description de la Nouvelle France, avec le Journal Historique d'un Voyage dans l'Amérique Septentrionale*, 6 vols. Paris (Bonar, p. 44)

Clark, J. M., et al, [1928] 1989. *Adam Smith, 1776–1926. Lectures to commemorate the sesquicentennial of the publication of the 'Wealth of Nations'*, University of Chicago Press, 1928; Augustus Kelly Reprints of Economic Classics, Chicago

Clayden, P. W. 1887. *The Early Life of Samuel Rogers*, Smith Elder & Co. London

Coats, A. W. ed. 1971a. *The Classical Economists and Economic Policy*, Debates in Economic History series, Methuen & Co, London

Coats, A. W. 1971b. 'The Classical Economists and the Labourer', in Coats A., 144–179

Cockburn, 1856. *Memorials of His Time*, A & C Black, Edinburgh

Cockburn, 1888. *An Examination of the Trials for Sedition which have hitherto occurred in Scotland*, D. Douglas, Edinburgh

Coddington, A. 1968. *Theories of the Bargaining Process*, Allen & Unwin, London

Cook, J. 1777. *A Voyage towards the South Pole*, London

Cook, J. and King, J. 1784. *A Voyage Towards the Pacific Ocean*, London

Copley, S. and Sutherland, K. eds 1995. *Adam Smith's Wealth of Nations: new interdisciplinary essays*, Manchester University Press, Manchester

Cosh, M. 2003. *Edinburgh: the golden age*, John Donald, Edinburgh

Cropsey, J. [1951] 2001. *Polity and Economy, with Further Thoughts on the Principles of Adam Smith*, St Augustine's Press, Indiana

Cross, J. G. 1965. 'A Theory of the Bargaining Process', *American Economic Review*, LV: 67–94

Cunningham, W. 1912. *The Growth of English Industry and Commerce in Modern Times*, 2 vols. Cambridge University Press, Cambridge

Currie, J. 1831. *Memoirs*, 2 vols. Longman, London

Dalrymple, J. (1759). *Essay Towards a General History of Feudal Property in Great Britain*, Dublin

Darwin, C. 1859. *On the Origin of Species by Means of Natural Selection*, John Murray, London

Dawkins, R. 1998. *Unweaving the Rainbow, science, delusion and the appetite for wonder*, Allen Lane, London

Deacon, T. 1997. *The Symbolic Species: the co-evolution of language and the human brain*, Allen Lane, London

Deane, P. 1975. 'War and industrialisation, in Winter, ed. 1975: 91–102

Denis, A. 2003. 'The Invisible Hand of God in Adam Smith', unpublished PhD thesis, Chapter 4, City University, London

Devine, T. W. 1995. 'The Merchant Class of the Larger Scottish Towns in the 17th and 18th Century', *Exploring the Scottish Past: themes in the history of Scottish Society*, Tuckwell Press, East Linton

Douglas, A. 1962. *Industrial Peacemaking*, Columbia University Press, New York

Dwyer, J. 1998. *The Age of Passions: an interpretation of Adam Smith and Scottish Enlightenment Culture*, Tuckwell, East Lothian

Ellingson, T. 2001. *The Myth of the Noble Savage*, University of California Press, Berkeley

Eltis, W. 1975. 'Adam Smith's Theory of Economic Growth', in Skinner & Wilson, 1975: 426–54

Eltis, W. 1984. *The Classical Theory of Economic Growth*, Macmillan, London

Eltis, W. & Bacon, R. 1976. *Britain's Economic Problem: too few producers*, Macmillan, London

Emerson, R. L. 1995. *Politics and the Glasgow Professors, 1690–1800*, in Hook and Sher, eds 1995: 21–39

Evensky, J. 2001. 'Adam Smith's lost legacy', *Southern Economics Journal*, vol. 67

Fetter, F. W. ed. 1957. *The Economic Writings of Francis Horner in the Edinburgh Review, 1802–6*, Series of reprints of Scarce Works in Political Economy, no. 13, London School of Economics and Political Science, London

Fleischacker, S. 2004. *A Short History of Distributive Justice*, Harvard University Press, Cambridge, Mass.

Foley, V. 1974. 'The division of labour in Plato and Smith.' *History of Political Economy*, vol. 6, pp. 220–42

Forbes, D. ed. 1966, Ferguson, A. [1767, 1773, 1814]. *An Essay on the History of Civil Society*, Edinburgh University Press, Edinburgh

Forbes, D. 1975. 'Sceptical Whiggism, Commerce and Liberty,' in Skinner and Wilson, eds 1975: 179–201

Frankel, P. E. 1980. 'Laissez Faire in Nineteenth Century Britain: fact or myth?' *Literature of Liberty*, vol. III, no. 4, Winter

Frazer, J. G. (1890) 1993. *Golden Bough: a study of magic and religion* (Macmillan, London) Wordsworth Edition, Ware, Hertsfordshire

Fitzgibbons, A. 1995. *Adam Smith's System of Liberty, Wealth, and Virtue: the moral foundations of the Wealth of Nations*, Clarendon Press, Oxford

Gibbon, E. 1776–88. *The History of the Decline and Fall of the Roman Empire*, 6 vols, W. Strahan & T. Cadell, London

Ginzberg, E. 2002 [1934]. *Adam Smith and the Founding of Market Economics, with a new introduction by the author*, Transaction Publishers, New Jersey

Gordon, H. S. 1955. 'The London *Economist* and the High Tide of *Laissez-faire*, *Journal of Political Economy*, vol. 63, December: 461–88

Gordon, H. S. 1971. 'The Ideology of Laissez-faire' in Coats, ed. 1971: 180–205

Gray, A. 1948. *Adam Smith*, Historical Association, George Philip, London

Gray, A. and Thompson, A. E. 1980 [1931]. 2nd ed., *The Development of Economic Doctrine, an introductory survey*, Longmans, London

Griswold, C. L. 1999. *Adam Smith and the Virtues of Enlightenment*, Cambridge University Press, Cambridge

Grotius, H. [1625] 1964. *The Law of War and Peace*, Trans. F. W. Kelsey, Carnegie Endowment for International Peace, Washington (reprint: Oceana Publications, New York

Gupta, U. D. ed. 2002. *The World of the Indian Ocean Merchant, 1500–1800*, Oxford University Press, Oxford

Haakonsson, K. 1981. *The Science of a Legislator: the natural jurisprudence of David Hume and Adam Smith*, Cambridge University Press, Cambridge

Haddon, T. 1981. *Company Law and Capitalism*, Law in Context Series, Wiedenfield & Nicolson, London

Haldane, R. B. 1887. *Life of Adam Smith*, Walter Scott, London

Hartwell, R. M. ed. 1967. *The Causes of the Industrial Revolution in Europe*, Debates in Economic History, Methuen, London

Hartwell, R. M. 1971. *The Industrial Revolution and Economic Growth*, Methuen & Co., London

Hartwell, R. M. 1976. 'Comments' in Wilson and Skinner, 1976: 33–41

Heilbroner, R. L. 1961 [1953, 2000]. The Worldly Philosophers: the lives, times and ideas of the great economic thinkers, Revised Edition, Simon & Schuster, New York, 2000, 7th Edition, Penguin

Heilbroner, R. L. 1975. 'The Paradox of progress: decline and decay in The Wealth of Nations', in Skinner and Wilson, 1975: 524–39

Heilbroner, R. 1997. *Teachings for the Worldly Philosophers*, Norton, New York

Herman, A. 2001. *How The Scots Invented the Modern World*, Crown Publishing, New York

Hicks, J. 1931. *The Theory of Wages*, Macmillan, London

Hirschman, A. O. 1977. *The Passions and the Interests: political arguments for capitalism before its triumph*, Princeton University Press, Princeton, N.J.

Hirst, F. W. 1904. *Adam Smith*, Macmillan & Co., London

Hobbes, T. 1946 [1651]. *Leviathan or the matter, forme and power of a Commonwealth ecclesiasticall and civil*, London, ed. M. Oakeshott, Blackwell, Oxford

Hook, A. and Sher, R. S. eds 1995. *The Glasgow Enlightenment*, Tuckwell Press, East Linton

Howell, T. B. and Howell, T. J., eds 1817. *A Complete Collection of State Trials*, T. C. Hansard, London

Hollander, S. 1973. *The Economics of Adam Smith*, Heinemann, London

Hume, D. 1985 [1739–40], *A Treatise of Human Nature*, London; edited, E. C. Mossner, Penguin Books, London

Hume, D. 1768. *An enquiry concerning human understanding*, London

Hume, D. 1997 (1777). *My Own Life*, Mermaid Turbulence, Dublin

Hume, D. 1932. *The Letters of David Hume*, ed J. Y. T. Greig, Oxford, 2 vols

Hutcheson, F. 1725. *An Inquiry into the Original of our ideas of Beauty and Virtue*, p. 195, cited in R. F. Teichgraeber, III, 1986, p. 42

Hutcheson, F. 1755. *A System of Moral Philosophy*, 3 vols. A. Millar, London

Hutcheson, F. 1969 [1755]. *Collected Works*, facsimile edition, George Holms, Hildesheim

Hutchison, T. W. 1953. *A Review of Economic Doctrines 1870–1929*, Clarendon Press, Oxford

John, A. H. 1954. 'War and the English Economy, 1700–63,' *Economic History Review*, 2nd ser., vii

Johnson, W. B. 1978. *The English Prison Hulks*, Phillimore, London

Jones, H. P. ed. 1963. *Dictionary of Foreign Phrases and Classical Quotations*, John Grant, Edinburgh

Kames, Lord [Henry Home], (1758) 1976. *Essays on the Principles of Morality and Natural Religion* (2nd edition), Reprint, Hildersheim

Kames, Lord, 1758. *Historical Law Tracts*, Edinburgh

Kennedy, G. 1974. *The Military in the Third World*, Duckworth, London

Kennedy, G. 1975. *The Economics of Defence*, Faber & Faber, London

Kennedy, G., Benson, J. B. and Macmillan, J. 1980. *Managing Negotiations*, Business Books, London

Kennedy, G. 1989. *Captain Bligh: the man and his mutinies*, Duckworth, London

Kennedy, G. 1998. *Kennedy On Negotiation*, Gower, Aldershot

Keynes, J. M. (1930) 1952. 'The economic possibilities for our grandchildren' in *Essays in Persuasion*, pp. 358–73, Rupert Hart-Davis, London

Kindleberger, C. P. 1976. 'The Historical Background: Adam Smith and the Industrial Revolution', in Wilson & Skinner, eds, 1976: 7–25

Koebner, R. 1959. 'Adam Smith and the industrial revolution,' *Economic History Review*, vol. XI

Kohn, M. 1999. *As We Know It: coming to terms with an evolved mind*, Granta, London

Kropotkin, P. 1939 [1901]. *Mutual Aid: a factor of evolution*, Pelican, Harmondsworth

Kuhn, T. S. 1962. *The Structure of Scientific Revolutions*, University of Chicago Press, Chicago

Lafitau, J-F. *Customs of the North American Indians Compared with the Customs of Primitive Times*, ed. and translated, W. N. Fenton and E. L. Moore, Chaplain Society, Toronto, 1974. 'In Smith's library, following Bonar, p. 99: *Histoires des Découverts et Conquestes des Portugais dans le Nouveau Monde*, 2 vols, Paris, 1735

Lehman, W. C. 1971. *Henry Home and the Scottish Enlightenment: a study in national character and the history of ideas*, The Hague

Lenman, B. 1981. *Integration, Enlightenment, and Industrialisation, Scotland 1746–1832*, New History of Scotland Series, no. 6, Edward Arnold, London

Lindgreen, J. R. ed. 1967. 'A Letter to the Authors of the Edinburgh Review', [1755] *The Early Writings of Adam Smith*, Augustus M. Kelly Reprint, [New Jersey]

Loasby, B. J. 2002. 'Content and Method: an epistemic perspective on some historical episodes', *The European Journal of the History of Economic Thought*, vol. 9, no. 1, Spring: 72–95

Locke, J. (1690) 1988. *Two Treatises on Government*, ed. Peter Haslett, Cambridge University Press, Cambridge

Logue, K. J. 1979. *Popular Disturbances in Scotland: 1780–1815*, John Donald, Edinburgh

Lomberg, B. 2001. *The Skeptical Environmentalist: measuring the real state of the world*, Cambridge University Press, Cambridge

Lowe, A. 1975. 'Adam Smith's System of Equilibrium Growth,' in Skinner and Wilson, 1975: 415–25

Lubasz, H. 1975. 'Adam Smith and the "Free Market",' in Copley and Sutherland, 1975: 45–69

McCulloch, J. R. 1855. *Sketch of the Life and Writings of Adam Smith, LL.D*, Murray and Gibb, Edinburgh

McCulloch, J. R. ed. (1828) 1863. *Smith's Wealth of Nations, with a life of the Author, an introductory discourse, notes and supplemental dissertations*, New Edition Adam and Charles Black, Edinburgh

Macfie, A. L. 1967. *The Individual in Society: papers on Adam Smith*, George Allen & Unwin, London

MacGregor, D. H. 1949. *Economic Thought and Policy*, Oxford University Press, London

Macintyre, G. 2003. *Dugald Stewart: the pride and ornament of Scotland*, Sussex Academic Press, Brighton

Mackaness, G. 1931. *The Life of Vice-Admiral Bligh R.N., F.R.S*, 2 vols. Angus Robertson, Sydney

MacPherson, H. C. 1899. *Adam Smith*, Famous Scots Series, Oliphant Anderson & Ferrier, Edinburgh

Malthus, T. 1798. *An Essay on the Principle of Population as it Affects the Future Improvement of Society*, London

Mandeville, B. [1705–1732] 1924. *The Fable of the Bees, or, Private vices, publick benefits, with a commentary, critical, historical and explanatory*, by F. B. Kaye, 2 vols. Clarendon Press, Oxford

Martin, G. ed. 1978. *The Founding of Australia: the argument about Australia's origins*, Hale and Iremonger, Sydney

Marx, K (ed. Engels), 1961 (1867). *Capital: a critical analysis of capitalist production*, Moscow

Mathias, P. 1975. 'Swords and Ploughshares: the armed forces, medicine and public health in the late eighteenth century' in Winter, ed. 1975: 73–90

Meadows, D. and Meadows, D. Randers, J. Behrens, W. W. 1972. *The Limits to Growth: a report for the Club of Rome project on the predicament of mankind*, Pan Potomac Books, London

Meek, R. L. 1971. 'Smith, Turgot and the "four stages" theory', *History of Political Economy*, vol. 3, pp. 3–27

Meek, R. L. ed. 1973: *Precursors of Adam Smith, 1750–1775*, Readings in Economic History and Theory, Dent, London

Meek, R. L. 1976. *Social Science and the Ignoble Savage*, Cambridge University Press, Cambridge

Millar, J. 1990 [1806]. *The Origin of the Distinction of Ranks: or an inquiry into the circumstances which give rise to the influence and authority in the different members of society*, 4th edition, in which is prefixed an Account of the life and writings of the author, by John Craig, Blackwood and Longmans, Edinburgh and London, 1806; 1990, Introduced by J. V. Price, London, Thoemmes, Bristol

Millar, J. 1803. *An Historical View of English Government: from the settlement of the Saxons in Britain to the Revolution in 1688; to which are subjoined some dissertations connected with the history of government from the revolution to the present time*, ed. J. Craig and J. Milne, 3rd ed. 4 vols. Mawman, London

Minowitz, P. 1993. *Profits, Priests, and Princes: Adam Smith's emancipation of Economics from politics and religion*, Stanford University Press, Stanford, Ca.

Montesquieu, B. 1949 [1748]. *Esprit de Lois, The Spirit of the Laws*, Trans. T. Nugent, Intro. Neuman, F. Hafner Publishing, New York

Montes, L. 2004. *Adam Smith in Context: a critical reassessment of some central components of his thought*, Palgrave Macmillan, Basingstoke

Morrow, G. R., 1928. 'Adam Smith; moralist and philosopher', in Cannon, ed. 1928: 116–59

Mossner, E. C. 1980 (1954). *The Life of David Hume*, Clarendon Press, Oxford

Muller, J. 1993. *Adam Smith in His Time and Ours*, Princeton University Press, Princeton, New Jersey

Nash, J. 1950. 'The Bargaining Problem', *Econometrica*, 18: 155–62

Nash, 1953. 'Two Person Cooperative Games', *Econometrica*, 21: 128–40

Nieli, R. 1986. 'Spheres of Intimacy and the Adam Smith Problem', *Journal of the History of Ideas*, 47: 4: 611–24

Noble, A. and Hogg, P. S. eds 2001. *The Canongate Burns: the complete poems and songs of Robert Burns*, Canongate Classics, Edinburgh

O'Farrell, P. 2004. *Heriot-Watt University: an illustrated history*, Pearson Education, London

Olson, S. 2002. *Mapping Human History: unravelling the mystery of Adam and Eve*, Bloomsbury, London

Osborne, D. B. 1997. *Lord Braxfield: the hanging judge, The Life and Times of Lord Justice-Clerk, Robert MacQueen of Braxfield*, Argyll Publishing, Glendaruel, Argyll

Otteson, J. R. 2000. 'The Recurring "Adam Smith Problem"', *History of Philosophy Quarterly*, 17: 1: 51–74

Otteson, J. R. 2002. *Adam Smith's Market Place of Life*, Cambridge University Press, Cambridge

Parry, J. and Bloch, M. eds 1989. *Money and the Morality of Exchange*, Cambridge University Press, Cambridge

Peacock, A. and Wiseman, J. 1964. *Education for Democrats*, Institute of Economics Affairs, London

Peacock, A. 1975. 'The Treatment of the Principles of Public Finance in *The Wealth of Nations*', in Skinner and Wilson, ed. 1975: 553–67

Peacock, A. 1978. 'The Economics of Bureaucracy: an insider's view', in *The Economics of Politics*, Institute of Economics Affairs, London

Peacock, A. 1980. 'On the Anatomy of Government Failure', *Public Finance*, 32. 1: 33–3

Peacock, A. 1992. *Public Choice Analysis in Historical Perspective*, Cambridge University Press, Cambridge

Peacock, A. 1997. *The Political Economy of Economic Freedom*, Edward Edgar, Cheltenham

Pen, J. 1952. 'A General Theory of Bargaining,' *American Economic Review*, vol. 42, 24–42

Pesciarelli, E. 1986. 'On Adam Smith's Lectures on Jurisprudence', *Scottish Journal of Political Economy*, vol. 33, no. 1 February: 75–85

Petty, W. 1683. *Another Essay in Political Arithmetick, concerning the growth of the City of London*, London; reproduced in Hull, C. H. 1899; *The Economic Writings of Sir William Petty*, i. 260, Cambridge University Press, Cambridge

Pike, E. R. 1974. *Human Documents of Adam Smith's Time*, George Allen and Unwin, London

Plato, 1987. *The Republic*, Penguin, Harmondsworth

Porter, R. 1990. *English Society in the Eighteenth Century*. Penguin, Harmondsworth

Pownall, T. 1776. *Letter to Adam Smith, being and Examination of Several Points of Doctrine laid down in his Inquiry, into the Nature and causes of the Wealth of Nations*, London

Pufendorf, *The Law of Nature and Nations*, 1672

Quesnay, F. 1767. *Tableau Economique*, in Du Pont de Nemours edition

RSE, Literary Section, National Library of Scotland, Ms. Acc 10,000/3, p. 79

Rae, J. 1895. *Life of Adam Smith*, Macmillan, London; (1965) intro. Jacob Viner, Augustus Kelly, Hairfield, New Jersey

Rackham, N. and Carlise, J. 1978. 'The Effective Negotiator', *Journal of European Training*, vol. 2, no. 6: 162–5

Raphael, D. D. 1975. 'The Impartial Spectator,' in Skinner and Wilson, 1975: 83–99

Rashid, S. 1997. 'The Ambitious, Accommodative Adam Smith,' *Independent Review*, vol. II, no. 1, Summer, pp. 98–108

Rashid. S. 1998. *The Myth of Adam Smith*, Edward Edgar, Cheltebham

Reeder, J. 1977 ed. *On Moral Sentiments: contemporary responses to Adam Smith*, 1977, Thoemmes Press, Bristol

Reid, G. 1989. 'Adam Smith's Stadial Analysis of a Sequence of Societal Growth Trajectories', *Scottish Journal of Political Economy*, vol. 36, no. 1, pp. 59–70

Reisman, D. A.1976. *Adam Smith's Sociological Economics*, Croom Helm, London

Robertson, W. (1769). *Works*, 12 vols. Edinburgh, ref. in Ross, 1995, p. 469

Robbins, L. ed. 1933. *The Commonsense of Political Economy*, Routledge, London

Robbins, L. 1952. *The Theory of Economic Policy in English Classical Political Economy*, Macmillan, London

Robbins, L. 1998. *A History of Economic Thought: the LSE Lectures*, ed. S. G. Medema & W. J. Samuels, Oxford University Press, New Delhi.

Robinson, M. 1985. *The Concise Scots Dictionary*, Aberdeen University Press, Aberdeen

Rogers, J. E. T. 1909 [1891]. *The Industrial and Commercial History of England (lectures delivered to the University of Oxford)*, T. Fisher Unwin, London

Ross, I. S. 1972. *Lord Kames and the Scotland of his Day*, Oxford University Press,

Ross, I. S. 1995. *The Life of Adam Smith*, Clarendon Press, Oxford

Rosenberg, N. 1975. 'Adam Smith on Profits – Paradox Lost and Regained,' in Skinner and Wilson, 1975: 377–89

Rostow, W. 1971. *The Stages of Economic Growth*, Cambridge University Press, London

Rousseau, J. J. 1984, [1755]. *Discourse on the Origins and Foundations of Inequality Among Men*, Trans. Maurice Cranston, Penguin, London

Rothschild, E. 2001. *Economic Sentiments: Adam Smith, Condorcet, and the Enlightenment*, Harvard University Press, Cambridge

Rude, G. 1974. *Paris and London in the 18th Century*, Fontana/Collins, London

Samuelson, P. 1973. *Economics*, 9th ed. McGraw-Hill, Tokyo

Schumpeter, J. 1954. *History of Economic Analysis*, Oxford University Press, New York

Schick, K. D. and Toth, T. 1993. *Making Silent Stones Speak: human evolution and the dawn of technology*, Simon & Schuster, New York

Scott, W. R. 1937. *Adam Smith as Student and Professor, with unpublished documents, including parts of the 'Edinburgh Lectures', a draft of The Wealth of Nations, Extracts from the Muniments of the University of Glasgow and Correspondence*, Jackson and company, Glasgow

Shaw, A. G. L. 1978. *Convicts and Colonies: a study of penal transportation from Great Britain and Ireland to Australia and other parts of the British Empire*, Melbourne University Press, Melbourne

Shackle, G. L. S. 1964. 'The Nature of the Bargaining Process,' in Dunlop, J. T. (ed.) *The Theory of Wage Determination*, Macmillan, London

Shaw, J. S. 1999. *The Political History of Eighteenth Century Scotland*, Macmillan Press, Basingstoke, Hamps

Silver, M. 1995. *Economic Structures of Antiquity*, Greenwood Press, Conn.

Skarzynski, W. von. 1878. *Adam Smith als Moralphilosoph und Schoepfer de National-oekonomie*, Berlin

Skinner, A. S. and Wilson, T. 1975. *Essays on Adam Smith*, Clarendon Press, Oxford

Smiles, S. 1863. *The Life of Thomas Telford*, 'Roads and Travel in Scotland in the last century', *Lives of the Great Engineers*, John Murray, London

Smiles, S. 1889. *Thrift*, Belford Clark, Chicago

Smith, Adam: TMS, 1759. *The Theory of Moral Sentiments*, The Glasgow Edition of the Works and Correspondence of Adam Smith, 1976, Oxford University Press; Liberty Fund, edition, 1982

Smith, Adam 1761. 'Considerations Concerning the First Formation of Languages and the Different Genius of original and compounded Languages', *The Philological Miscellany*, May 1761, pp. 440–79; 3rd edition TMS, 1767, pp. 437–78; LRBL, Glasgow Edition, Oxford University Press, 1983 (Liberty 1987), pp. 203–226

WN, 1776, *An Inquiry into the Nature and Causes of the Wealth of Nations*, 2 vols. Edited by R. H. Campbell and A. S. Skinner, Textual editor, W. B. Todd, The Glasgow Edition of the Works and Correspondence of Adam Smith, 1976, Oxford University Press, Liberty Fund, edition, 1979

LJ, 1762–3 and 1766, *Lectures on Jurisprudence*, edited by R. L. Meek, D. D. Raphael, and P. G. Stein, The Glasgow Edition of the Works and Correspondence of Adam Smith, 1978, Oxford University Press, Liberty Fund edition, 1982

EPS, [1743–46?] 'The Principles which lead and Direct Philosophical Enquiries: illustrated by the History of Astronomy', *Essays on Philosophical Subjects*, The Glasgow Edition of the Works and Correspondence of Adam Smith, 1980, Oxford University Press, Liberty Fund edition, 1982

Corr., *Correspondence*, edited by E. C. Mossner and I. S. Ross, The Glasgow Edition of the Works and Correspondence of Adam Smith, 1977, revised 1987, Oxford University Press, Liberty Fund edition, 1987

LRBL, [1762]. *Lectures on Rhetoric and Belles Lettres*, edited by J. C. Bryce, The Glasgow Edition of the Works and Correspondence of Adam Smith, 1983, Oxford University Press, Liberty Fund edition, 1985

Smout, T. C. ed. 1986. *Scotland in Europe, 1250–1860*, John Donald, Edinburgh

Steuart, Sir J. 1966 (1767). *An Inquiry into the Principles of Political Economy*, 2 vols. Oliver and Boyd, London

Stewart, D. 1793. 'Account of the Life and Writings of Adam Smith LL.D,' *Transactions of the Royal Society of Edinburgh*, T. Cadell, London, 1794; Dickson and Balfour, Edinburgh

Stewart, D. 1982. 'Account of the Life and Writings of Adam Smith LL.D,' *Essays on Philosophical Subjects*, pp. 269–351, The Glasgow Edition of the Works and Correspondence of Adam Smith, Oxford University Press, Liberty Fund edition, 1982

Stewart, D. 1854–60. *Collected Works*, ed. Sir William Hamilton, Constable, Edinburgh

Stigler, G. J. 1975. 'Smith's Travels on the Ship of State,' in Skinner and Wilson, 1975: 237–246

Stones, L. 1984. 'The Life and Career of John Snell, c.1629–1679', *Stair Society Miscellany*, 2. pp. 148–85

Stordalen, T. 2000. *Echoes of Eden: Genesis 2–3 and symbolism of the Eden Garden in Biblical Hebrew literature*, Peeters, Leuven

Strang, J. 1857. *Glasgow and its Clubs*, 2nd ed., R. Griffin, London and Glasgow

Sutherland, K. 1995. 'Adam Smith's master narrative: women and the Wealth of Nations', in S. Copley and K. Sutherland, 1995

Talbot, C. 2002. *Precolonial India in Practice: society, religion and identity in medieval Andhra*, Oxford University Press, Oxford

Teichgraeber, III, R. F. 1986. *'Free Trade' and Moral Philosophy: rethinking the sources of Adam Smith's Wealth of Nations*, Duke University Press, Durham, NC

Tribe, K. 1995. 'Natural Liberty and *Laissez-faire*: how Adam Smith became a free trade ideologue,' in Copley and Sutherland, 1995: 23–44

Tudge, C. 1998. *Neanderthals, Bandits and Farmers: how agriculture really began*, Weidenfield & Nicolson, London

Tyler, A. F. 1807. *Memoirs of the Life and Writings of the Honourable Henry Home of Kames, containing sketches of the Progress of Literature and General Improvement in Scotland during the greater part of the eighteenth century* by Lord Kames, Edinburgh, 2 vols

Uglow, J. 2002. *The Lunar Men: the friends who made the future, 1730–1810*, Faber, London

Viner, J. 1928. *Adam Smith and Laissez-faire*, in Clark, et al, 1928

Viner, J. 1965. *Guide to John Rae's Life of Adam Smith*, Augustus M. Kelly, Fairfield, N.J.

Walsh, V. & Gram, H. 1980. *Classical and Neoclassical Theories of General Equilibrium: historical origins and mathematical structure*, Oxford, New York

Walton, R. E. & McKersie, R. B. 1965. *A Behavioural Theory of Labour Negotiations*: an analysis of a social interaction system, McGraw Hill, New York

West, E. G. 1975. 'Adam Smith and Alienation: wealth increases, men decay', in Skinner & Wilson, eds, 1975: 540–552

West, E. G. 1976. *Adam Smith: the man and his works*, Liberty Press, Indianapolis

Whatley, A. 1997. *The Industrial Revolution in Scotland*, Cambridge University Press, Cambridge

Williams, G. M. 2000. *Adam Smith: wealth without nations*, Athol Books, London

Wilson, T. and Skinner, A. 1976. *The Market and the State: essays in honour of Adam Smith*, Oxford University Clarendon Press, Oxford

Winch, D. 1978. *Adam Smith's Politics: an essay in historiographic revision*, Cambridge University Press, Cambridge

Winter, J. M. ed. 1975. *War and Economic Development: essays in memory of David Joslin*, Cambridge University Press, Cambridge

Woodrow, J. 1751. Glasgow University Library, Murray MS 506

Wood, F. 1996. *Did Marco Polo Go to China?*, Westview Press, Boulder, Col

Yanaihara, T. 1951. *A Full and Detailed Catalogue of Books which belonged to Adam Smith: now in the possession of the Faculty of Economics, University of Tokyo, with notes and explanations*, Augustus

Young, A. 1771. *The Farmer's Tour through the east of England, being the register of a journey through various counties in this kingdom, to enquire into the state of agriculture*, 4 vols. W. Strahan, London

Young, O. R. ed. 1975. *Bargaining: formal theories of negotiation*, University of Illinois Press, Chicago

Zeuthen, F. 1930. *Problems of Monopoly and Economic Warfare*, Routledge, London

Index